A Jo

AN INTROD

A Journey of Faith

An Introduction to Christianity

H. Wayne Ballard, Jr. (Old Testament)
Donald N. Penny (New Testament)
W. Glenn Jonas, Jr. (Church History)
Dean M. Martin (Christian Theology)

Mercer University Press • 2002

ISBN 0-86554-746-7   MUP/P221

A Journey of Faith: An Introduction to Christianity
Copyright ©2002
Mercer University Press
All rights reserved
Printed in the United States of America
First published August 2002

[Credits and acknowledgments appear on page 304 below.]

The paper used in this publication meets the minimum requirements
of American National Standard for Information Sciences—
Permanence of Paper for Printed Library Materials, ANSI Z39.48-1984.

Library of Congress Cataloging-in-Publication Data

A journey of faith : an introduction to Christianity /
H. Wayne Ballard, Jr. . . . [et al.].
    p. cm.
Includes bibliographical references and index.
ISBN 0-86554-746-7 (pbk.)
    1. Christianity.   I. Ballard, Harold Wayne, 1963–
BR121.3.J68 2002
230—dc21

2002009163

CONTENTS

PART TWO. THE NEW TESTAMENT

Part Three. Church History

PART FOUR. CHRISTIAN THEOLOGY

PREFACE

A Journey of Faith: An Introduction to Christianity represents the collaborative efforts of Wayne Ballard, Glenn Jonas, Dean M. Martin, and Donald Penny, members of the Department of Religion and Philosophy of Campbell University. It is designed specifically for use in our course entitled "An Introduction to Christianity." This course and its accompanying textbook provide college students with a general understanding of the Christian faith including its foundational documents, its history, and its traditions. In addition to its use in the classroom, the book also provides a general overview for those who are interested in or curious about the Christian faith. It is accessible for everyone from laypersons who attend church regularly to the individual who may never darken the door of a sanctuary.

The text is divided into four major units of study. The first unit, written by Wayne Ballard, provides a general introduction and overview of the contents of the Old Testament and its significance for understanding the world and culture that served as a background for the birth of Jesus Christ. This study of the Old Testament includes a brief summary of the Pentateuch, an overview of the "history of Israel," an introduction to the Poetic Literature of Israel, and a brief description of the role of the Prophets.

A brief survey of the New Testament, by Don Penny, is the second major unit. This unit provides the student with a general orientation to the New Testament. Furthermore, it presents an overview of the ministry and message of Jesus of Nazareth and the rise of the Christian church in response to Jesus, as a basis for understanding the historical origins of the Christian faith. This unit is subdivided into an introduction to the Gospels and the world of the New Testament, the ministry and message of Jesus, the rise and growth of the Christian church, and an overview of the New Testament letters and Revelation.

A survey of church history, by Glenn Jonas, comprises the third major unit. It presents the major movements and personalities in the history of Christianity. This unit investigates Early Christianity, Medieval Christianity, the Reformation of the sixteenth century, and Modern Christianity.

Christian Theology, by Dean Martin, is the final unit and has as its aim to present the fundamental elements of the Christian faith, pertaining specifically to the Protestant tradition. Subjects under discussion in this unit include preliminary topics relevant to theology; the nature and activities of God; the paradoxical nature of Christ as both divine and human; the role of the Holy Spirit; and the nature of the church.

The authors would like to thank those individuals who helped make this project a reality. We want to thank Marc Jolley and Edmon L. Rowell, Jr. of Mercer University Press, for supporting and overseeing this endeavor. A word of thanks is also due to Phebie Smith, our administrative assistant in the Department of Religion and Philosophy at Campbell University. Her commitment to excellence supports our mission and work as a department. Stephen J. Hamilton has provided hours of legwork in the final stages of manuscript preparation. Steven Harmon and Barry Jones of the Campbell University Divinity School provided proofreading and timely suggestions for the development of the text. Mel Hawkins of Carson Newman College also helped in the proofreading process.

Finally, let us thank you, the reader. We hope you find this text helpful in your understanding of the Christian faith.

Buies Creek, North Carolina   *H. Wayne Ballard, Jr.*
August 2002   *W. Glenn Jonas, Jr.*
                                                          Dean M. Martin
                                                         Donald N. Penny

BOOKS OF THE OLD TESTAMENT/HEBREW BIBLE[1]

Old Testament

(The Pentateuch/Law)
Genesis
Exodus
Leviticus
Numbers
Deuteronomy
(The Historical Books)
Joshua
Judges
Ruth
1, 2 Samuel
1, 2 Kings
1, 2 Chronicles
Ezra
Nehemiah
Esther
(The Poetical and Wisdom Books)
Job
Psalms
Proverbs
Ecclesiastes
Song of Songs/Solomon
(The Prophetic Books)

Isaiah	Hosea
Jeremiah	Joel
Lamentations	Amos
Ezekiel	Obadiah
Daniel	Jonah
	Micah
	Nahum
	Habakkuk
	Zephaniah
	Haggai
	Zechariah
	Malachi

Hebrew Bible

(Torah, The Five Books of Moses)
Genesis
Exodus
Leviticus
Numbers
Deuteronomy
(Nevi'im, The Prophets)
Joshua
Judges
Samuel
Kings
Isaiah
Jeremiah
Ezekiel
(Book of the Twelve)

Hosea	Nahum
Joel	Habakkuk
Amos	Zephaniah
Obadiah	Haggai
Jonah	Zechariah
Micah	Malachi

(Ketuvim, The Writings)
Psalms
Proverbs
Job
Song of Songs
Ruth
Lamentations
Ecclesiastes
Esther
Daniel
Ezra/Nehemiah
Chronicles

---

[1]The names of the individual books and their order follows that of Protestant Bibles for the Old Testament and that of *TaNaKh—The Holy Scriptures. The New JPS Translation according to the Traditional Hebrew Text* (1985). Section designations (Law, History, Prophets, etc.) of course are arbitrary and (may) differ from one tradition to another.

APOCRYPHA/DEUTEROCANONICALS[2]

NEW TESTAMENT

Tobit
Judith
Additions to Esther (Greek)
Wisdom of Solomon
Sirach (Ecclesiasticus)
Baruch
Letter of Jeremiah
Additions to Daniel
   Prayer of Azariah and the
      Song of the Three Jews
   Susanna
   Bel and the Dragon
1, 2 Maccabees
(In some Orthodox Bibles, not RCC)
1 Esdras
Prayer of Manasseh
Psalm 151
3 Maccabees
(In Slavonic Bibles and Vulgate appendix)
2 Esdras
(Appended to some Greek Bibles)
   4 Maccabees

(Gospels)
   Matthew
   Mark
   Luke
   John
(History)
   Acts of the Apostles
(Letters)
   (Pauline Letters)
      Romans
      1, 2 Corinthians
      Galatians
      Ephesians
      Philippians
      Colossians
      1, 2 Thessalonians
      1, 2 Timothy
      Titus
      Philemon
   (General Epistles)
      Hebrews
      James
      1, 2 Peter
      1, 2, 3 John
      Jude
(Apocalypse)
   Revelation

---

[2]The names and order of the apocryphal and/or deuterocanonical books follows that of the so-called "ecumenical" editions of Protestant Bibles, e.g., the expanded edition of the RSV and of the NRSV and CEV. Older Protestant Bibles— namely, KJV and ERV—have only fourteen or fifteen apocryphal books (depending on whether one counts Baruch and the Letter of Jeremiah as one book or two), and they appear in the more traditional order, beginning with 1, 2 Esdras.

Part One

THE OLD TESTAMENT/HEBREW BIBLE

Chapter 1

INTRODUCTION TO THE PENTATEUCH

Genesis, Exodus, Leviticus, Numbers, and Deuteronomy form the collection of books known as the Pentateuch or "five books." In the Hebrew Bible these books are referred to as the Torah, meaning "instruction, discipline, or law." In the Christian Old Testament they are often simply called "the Law." This term is adequate, but it does not express the diversity of literature found in these books. Along with "the Law," there are narratives, genealogies, blessings, curses, prayers, and many other types of literature found in the Pentateuch.

The Pentateuch is composed of three principle narratives or stories. The Primeval History or prehistorical narrative, found in Genesis 1–11, describes the creation of the world and the development of humanity and concludes with four stories regarding the fallen state of humanity. These "fall stories," as they are commonly known to the Christian community, include the "Fall of Man" in Genesis 3, the murder of Abel by his brother Cain found in Genesis 4, the beloved story of Noah and the Flood told in Genesis 6–9, and in Genesis 11, the story of the Tower of Babel and humanity's attempt to draw nearer to equality with God.

The Patriarchal Narratives in Genesis 12–50 comprise the second major narrative section in the Pentateuch. Abraham, Isaac, Jacob, and Joseph are the primary foci of these narratives. The text takes the careful reader on a journey beginning in Mesopotamia with Abraham to his migration to Palestine, and continues until the descendents of Abraham arrive in Egypt during the life of Joseph. These stories set the stage for what may be viewed as the most important event in the Old Testament— the Exodus.

The events of the Exodus are recorded in the books of Exodus, Leviticus, Numbers, and Deuteronomy. The Exodus begins with God's miraculous deliverance of the Israelite people from Egypt under the direction of Moses. The Exodus event continues as Moses leads the large band of people into the desert on their pilgrimage to the land of Canaan. God's faithfulness is made manifest throughout this great narrative. God defeats the armies of Pharaoh, delivers the Ten Commandments to Moses at Sinai, and provides for the daily needs of the Israelites. The children of Israel are in pursuit of the fulfillment of the promise God made to Abraham—they are to become a great nation and possess their own land.

PRIMEVAL HISTORY

In the beginning is one of the most recognizable introductions to any body of literature in the English language. It provides the introduction for the story of beginnings in Genesis and for the Bible as a composite. Genesis 1:1 also contains a powerful theological affirmation "In the beginning, God. . . . " From the outset of the Old Testament the existence of God who is Creator is assumed and sustained.

Two competing interpretive models traditionally dominate the way readers view the texts of Genesis 1–11. A literal approach is one method readers use when interpreting the stories about the creation and subsequent fall of humanity. This method usually entails viewing creation as occurring in seven twenty-four hour periods or literal "days," describing Adam and Eve as a literal couple from whom all humans are derived, and understanding the Garden of Eden as the literal "cradle" of civilization.

A theological approach is a second method readers employ in interpreting Genesis 1–11. This approach is less concerned with the literal questions that arise from a careful reading of the text. It assumes Genesis 1–11 to be exemplary of a typical worldview found throughout the ancient Middle East during the time of Israel's development and tenure as a nation in Palestine. In the theological approach, God is affirmed as Creator without regard to the specifics of how God accomplishes this activity. Coinciding with this truth is the understanding that as God created, humanity fell short of God's original design or purpose. In simple terms, a theological approach can be stated as "God did it, but man blew it." Therefore, a theological approach does not regard the events found in Genesis 1–11 as history or science, but as theological assessment. All that is good comes from God, and human sin is a blight on God's creative activity.

The Creation account of Genesis is actually a combination of two separate versions. The careful reader notices similarities *and* differences between Genesis 1:1–2:4a and Genesis 2:4b-25. Four major areas of difference are accentuated between these accounts. First, the order of Creation is different. In the first account (Genesis 1:1–2:4a), the order of creation is presented in the successive steps of light, firmament, land and vegetation, heavenly bodies (sun, moon, and stars), birds and fish, and animals and humanity. In the second account (Genesis 2:4b-25), God first creates a male human named Adam. The Garden of Eden is created next, followed by the creation of trees including the Tree of Life and the Tree of the Knowledge of Good and Evil. Animals are then created followed by the apex of the second account, a woman named Eve.

A second major difference focuses on the specific details of the creation of humankind. The first account states that man is created in the image of God, both male and female (Genesis 1:26-27). The second account begins with a description of the creation of one man named Adam, whose name means "humanity" in Hebrew. It concludes by describing how the first woman, Eve, whose name means "life" in Hebrew, is created from Adam's side to be a partner with him.

The third difference is found in the focus of each creation account. The first account describes in a sevenfold manner the creation of the entire universe: the sky, the stars, the land of the earth, and all that exists are formed. The Garden of Eden is the focus of the second account. It is limited in its scope. It focuses on a specified area with specific elements being created within its boundaries.

Two different words for the act of creation serve as the fourth difference between the two creation accounts. The Hebrew word *bara* "create" is used in the first account. It is a word reserved for the creative works of the God of Israel. God alone creates when the word *bara* is used. The Hebrew word `asah, "to do or make," is used in the second account. This word is used throughout the Old Testament applying to the works of God *and* of humanity. These differences have led many readers of Genesis 1 and 2 to believe that indeed two different creation stories have been placed side by side in a parallel fashion to introduce the story of Israel's beginnings.

The two creation stories also share two important similarities. In both accounts, the God of Israel is affirmed as the Creator who creates with absolute sovereignty. In addition, humanity is held in high esteem. This point is emphatically made by emphasizing humanity's special relationship with the Creator "in the image of God he created him; male and female he created them" (Genesis 1:27 RSV).

The Creation accounts of Genesis 1 and 2 are also similar in content and cosmology to creation accounts of the ancient Near and Middle Eastern world. The Gilgamesh Epic and the Enuma Elish, mythological stories from ancient Mesopotamia, share a similar description of how the world was created. All of these accounts presume a three-tiered universe. The first level is the area above the great dome in the sky, which is covered by a great canopy of water. In Genesis 1, the first level is also the dwelling place of God. The second level is the earth and all that is seen in the sky. It is descriptive of all one can see as one turns in a 360-degree fashion, examining all that is visible. The heavenly bodies, the clouds, the mountains, the bodies of water, and all the physical elements of earth are part of this second level. The third level is the area beneath the earth. Sheol, the shadowy underworld, is found here. Waters also exist in level three sometimes rising to the earth's surface in the form of dew or forming springs. It was also believed the land of the earth itself rests upon great pillars rising up from the third level. This worldview is evident in three passages in the Hebrew Bible: Psalm 148:4, Genesis 1:6-7, and Exodus 20:4.

A THREE-TIERED MODEL OF THE UNIVERSE

Level 1
The Dwelling Place of God
Waters above the earth

Level 2
Everything one can see or experience
on the sphere known as earth

Level 3
Sheol and the waters beneath the earth

You shall not make for yourself an idol, whether in the form of anything that is in *heaven above* or that is on the *earth beneath*, or that is in the *water under the earth*. (Exodus 20:4 NRSV, italics added)

In essence, the creation accounts of Genesis 1 and 2 are not unique in their description of the created order. They reflect the prevailing description of the structure of the world typical of the ancient Near and Middle East. Their uniqueness lies in their portrayal of God. While other ancient Near Eastern creation accounts describe numerous gods who are embodied in natural forces, Genesis 1 and 2 describe a single God who is separate from and sovereign over the created order.

PATRIARCHAL HISTORY

"Father Abraham had many sons / Many sons had father Abraham" are the first two lines to a popular ditty sung by children in churches today. This song encapsulates the content of the Patriarchal History recorded in Genesis 12–50. The events and times of the founding fathers of Israel are told and retold from the perspective of the redemptive activity of God intervening in human history. Indeed, this lengthy narrative can be said to primarily provide the backdrop for the beginning of God's redemptive activity with humanity. The years 2000 to 1500 BCE constitute the time frame for the narrative. The Patriarchal Narrative is said to be the true "beginning" of the history of Israel. God extends a call to a man named Abraham who is said to be living in Ur, in the heart of Mesopotamia. (See map below.) He is instructed to gather his family, leave his country, his people, and his father's household and proceed to a land God would show him. The resulting story in Genesis 12–25 details Abraham's response in faith, his journey, and God's reward for his obedience.

How does one interpret the Patriarchal Narratives? This question has been the focus of much study. Some scholars advocate reading the narratives as literal history. This approach, designated as the "traditional" approach, portrays the patriarchs as historical individuals whose lives are accurately reflected in the text of Genesis. A second approach views the Patriarchal Narratives as stories of Israelite clans told to explain their eponymous ancestry.[1] This approach views Abraham, Isaac, Jacob, and Joseph as representative of the major clans of Israel. A third approach considers these narratives as primarily literary creations. Form criticism provides the methodological framework for this approach.[2] Thus, the narratives are regarded as folktale sagas that combine historical remembrances with exciting folk legends resulting in the stories of the patriarchs, but the combination is thought to contain more legend than history.

---

[1]An eponym is a word describing a person for whom something is named. It can refer to the name of a person or a mythical character from which another name or term is derived. See "eponym" in, e.g., *Encarta. World English Dictionary* (New York: St. Martin's Press, 1999).

[2]Form Criticism is an approach used by many biblical scholars that focuses on the history and development of a given text. It asks questions of the context for the original writing, the "type" of writing used, and searches to understand the purpose(s) for a such a text.

There are many other ways of interpreting the narratives, but these three provide a fair sampling. For the purpose of this study, the traditional approach will provide the background for the forthcoming overview of the Patriarchal Narratives.

Abraham. Adventure, romance, and intrigue fill the texts surrounding Abraham, whose name in Hebrew means "father of many." Genesis 12–25 outlines Abram's call to continue the journey first started by his father Terah who journeyed with this family from Ur in Mesopotamia and settled in Haran. Genesis 12 and 15 recount the covenant God makes with Abram, a covenant that promises to make him the father of a great nation though his wife Sarai is barren and they are advanced in age. The writer of the narrative describes Sarai's response as more than mild amusement—she laughs out loud—as Abram receives the news of an impending birth. The barren-wife motif is an important motif serving as the backdrop for many stories in the Hebrew Bible.[3] Abram is commanded to be circumcised as a sign of his willingness to accept God's covenant. God's covenant with Abraham, found in Genesis 12 and 15, describes the agreement made between God and Abraham providing Abraham the promise that one day his descendants will become a vast nation. The act of circumcision becomes the confirmation of the covenant by Abram and his descendents. The narrative continues with the birth of Isaac, whose name means "laughter," and the changing of the names of Abram and Sarai to Abraham and Sarah.

The stories of Abraham's nephew, Lot, and the destruction of the cities of Sodom and Gomorrah give further insight into the actions of the God of Abraham. This story of Abraham's relative demonstrates God's seriousness towards sin and rebellion against God. The Abraham narrative reaches a crescendo in Genesis 22 with the call of Abraham to sacrifice his only son Isaac. Traditional Christian and Jewish interpretations differ concerning the description and/or title for this event. Christians often refer to this passage as the Sacrifice of Isaac while Jewish interpreters describe it as the Binding of Isaac. Regardless of one's approach, the text dramatically captures the journey of Abraham and Isaac to the place known later as Mount Moriah where Abraham prepares to sacrifice his

---

[3]God's blessing the infertile womb is a theme displayed prominently throughout the Old and New Testaments. In addition to the episode of Abraham and Sarah are the stories of Jacob and Rachel (Genesis 30:1-24), Elkanah and Hannah (1 Samuel 1:1-20), and Zechariah and Elizabeth (Luke 1:5-25).

only son. The angel of the Lord miraculously prevents the slaughter of Isaac when God instead provides a ram for the sacrifice. This is a disturbing text. What kind of God demands the sacrifice of children?

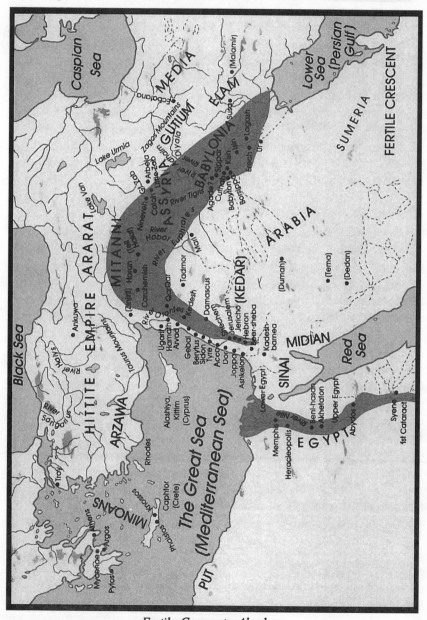

Artwork by Margaret Jordan Brown © Mercer University Press

Fertile Crescent—Abraham

What kind of father willingly agrees to place his child in such a precarious position? In the end there is resolution. But it remains a disquieting scene in the Patriarchal History.

Isaac. Isaac plays a supporting role in the Patriarchal History. His story is subsumed in the narrative treating his father Abraham and again by those describing Isaac's twin sons, Jacob and Esau. Genesis 26 is the only chapter in the narrative strictly devoted to the life of Isaac. It describes the renewing of God's covenant with Isaac along with Isaac's dealing with a certain king Abimelech of the Philistines. Genesis 24 tells a beautiful story of God's provision of a spouse for Isaac. Concerned over the suitability of a desirable mate for his son in the land of Canaan, Abraham sends a servant back to his homeland (described as Aram-Naharaim) to find a proper wife. The servant dutifully fulfills his obligation, returning to Canaan with Rebekah as Isaac's intended bride. Twin sons, Jacob and Esau are born from this union.

Jacob. Jacob is portrayed as a trickster in the patriarchal narratives. Jacob, the second of twin sons born to Isaac and Rebekah, aspires to the place of leadership over the descendants of Abraham. He achieves his purpose by scheming against his brother and deceiving his father. Jacob determines to have Esau's birthright. Esau, as the firstborn male, was due a blessing worthy of a double inheritance and the inherited position of patriarchal leadership for the clan. Jacob barters this birthright from his brother Esau by exchanging a bowl of soup for Esau's rightful position. One obstacle remained however for Jacob: Isaac had yet to bestow the blessing of the birthright to its rightful heir, Esau. With the aid of his mother Rebekah, Jacob intercepts the birthright-blessing by deceiving Jacob's aging father. Jacob assumes Esau's physical appearance and asks Isaac for the blessing. The blessing is secured before the deception is detected. This action leads to a period of estrangement between Jacob and Esau. The story also provides a foundational motif for later narratives in the Hebrew Bible. God does not always choose the firstborn, the strongest, or the obvious choice according to human qualities. God often uses those considered undesirable by society, or the less likely people, to accomplish divine purposes.

An ironic twist occurs in the Jacob narrative. Jacob, the trickster, is himself duped by one who proves more cunning. Jacob's encounter with Laban is recorded in Genesis 29–31. Jacob becomes infatuated with Laban's beautiful daughter Rachel. He agrees to work for Laban for seven years in order to marry Rachel. The wedding night comes, the wedding party is given, but the next morning the ironic plot is revealed. The trickster has been tricked. Jacob has not married Rachel, but her older and "less-attractive" sister Leah. Jacob protests, but ultimately reconciles himself to this woeful deception. Jacob agrees to work another seven years to earn the right to marry his true love, Rachel. Jacob succeeds and ultimately the narrator describes Jacob plotting and completing his revenge on Laban by manipulating herd production in his favor. Modern readers have little context for grasping the richness of this story. The idea of working fourteen years for the right to marry your spouse is hardly conceivable today.

Jacob's wrestling with God is an integral part of the Patriarchal History in Genesis 32. Jacob encounters one described by the text as "a man" beside the Jabbok stream. The wrestling match lasts throughout the night. Jacob demands that the man reveal his identity, but he refuses. He does, however, give Jacob a new name, "Israel." The name Israel is the contraction of two Hebrew words meaning, "contends with God." The match is a stalemate until the unidentified man strikes Jacob's hip and dislocates the hip from the socket. Jacob comes away with a new identity and a limp as a reminder of his encounter with God. Like many of the Patriarchal Narratives this story is filled with etiological material describing the origin of names. These names include Jacob's new name, Israel "Contends with God," the place of the event is Peniel "the face of God," and the text also relates to the Israelite practice of not eating meat taken from the hip socket of animals.

Jacob, or Israel, also serves as an important patriarch because of his progeny. Genesis 35:22-26 records the genealogy of Jacob. Leah, Rachel, and their two handmaidens, Bilhah (Rachel's maiden) and Zilpah (Leah's maiden), provide twelve sons for Jacob. Their names are Reuben (Jacob's firstborn), Simeon, Levi, Judah, Issachar, Zebulun, Dan, Naphtali, Gad, Asher, Joseph, and Benjamin. These twelve sons provide the nucleus for what later becomes known as the Twelve Tribes of Israel. The descendents of Levi, the priestly tribe, are not allowed to own land and therefore the name of Levi is not included as one of the twelve tribes. The name Joseph is also not included among the listing of the twelve tribes in later texts, but his two sons Ephraim and Manasseh are included thus bringing the number of tribes back to the renowned number of twelve.

Joseph. The final section of the Patriarchal History is dedicated to the Joseph novella in Genesis 37–50. This story is an isolatable subunit that is freestanding in the larger narrative. Unlike the previous saga cycles descriptive of Abraham, Isaac, and Jacob, the Joseph story is told in a protracted narrative with a thoughtful plot. It tells the story of how a young boy named Joseph, highly favored by his father Jacob, endured the jealousy of his older brothers, and overcame many obstacles along the way to become a leading figure in the affairs of Egypt. The Joseph story serves as a literary bridge between the patriarchal fathers and the beginning of the Exodus.

Children are often introduced to the Joseph cycle through the story of the coat of many colors in Genesis 37. Jacob fashions a coat for his teenage son to the dismay of his jealous brothers. Following a dream interpreted by Joseph's brothers as another instance of Joseph's narcissistic self-aggrandizement, they determine to do away with him. Joseph is seized and thrown into a cistern and left to die. Judah leads the brothers to sell Joseph to a passing Midianite caravan; thus he is taken to Egypt and sold to Potiphar, the captain of Pharaoh's guard.

Potiphar's wife becomes the focus of the next major event in the life of Joseph. Joseph is placed in charge of Potiphar's household. Potiphar's wife makes a series of advances toward the handsome young Joseph, but each time he denies her advances. One day she throws herself upon him only to be rejected once again. She screams, claiming that Joseph has accosted her. Joseph takes flight, leaving Potiphar's wife clinging to Joseph's outer garment in her hands. When Potiphar arrives home he is told of Joseph's indiscretions. He is outraged and immediately throws his Hebrew slave into prison.

The theme of unjust suffering recurs throughout the Joseph novella. Time after time Joseph continuously finds himself in peril, but he remains faithful to his belief system. The story offers hope to those who find themselves in less-than-pleasant circumstances. It issues a strong call to offer one's best regardless of the existing conditions. In spite of the insidious plans others devise for Joseph, Joseph's God continues to bless him, providing a watchful eye over this servant.

The culmination of the Joseph story coincides with the purpose of the narrative itself. Joseph is summoned by Pharaoh to interpret a dream. Joseph reveals to Pharaoh that his dream is a portent of seven years of prosperity to be followed by seven years of famine. He encourages Pharaoh to enact a plan to make preparations for the upcoming famine. Pharaoh concedes and proceeds to make Joseph the overseer of the task. Joseph has gone from being thrown into a cistern in Palestine by his brothers to a position of being second in command in Egypt! When the foretold famine ensues, the Egyptians are spared the brunt of the disaster because of their careful preparation. Peoples from neighboring lands flock to Egypt for relief, including the brothers of Joseph who are sent by Jacob to find help. The brothers are reunited with Joseph though they do not immediately recognize who he is. Eventually, Joseph persuades his brothers and their extended families to come to Egypt and survive the famine.

The Patriarchal Narrative is thus complete. Abraham sets out on a journey from his home country in Mesopotamia and settles in Canaan. His descendants multiply in Canaan and eventually move from Canaan into the land of Egypt under the leadership of Joseph. The stage is now in place for the apex of the drama involving the descendants of Abraham, the Exodus.

THE EXODUS

The Exodus is the central event in the history of Israel. This event is the main theme of the last four books of the Pentateuch: Exodus, Leviticus, Numbers, and Deuteronomy. The central character of the Exodus is Yahweh, the God of the Israelites, not Moses. Moses is the great lawgiver and shepherd who leads the children of Israel from the oppression of the Egyptian Pharaohs to the edge of the land of promise, Canaan. It is Yahweh who actively breaks into human history, directing Moses and the people of Israel, providing for them at every turn, turning them from a group of slaves into a chosen nation. The Exodus event is generally considered the beginning of the history of the *nation* of Israel. The children of Abraham are transformed from a ragged collection of tribal clans into a mighty people who seek fulfillment for the covenant made with Abraham. All that follows in the Old Testament is interpreted in light of the Exodus.

It is sometimes frustrating to the Western reader that ancient writing was not written with a concern for precise dating. For example, if the Exodus is indeed the single most important event in Israelite history, then why do we not have more detail given in regard to the dating of this event? Exodus 1:11 is often used as a marker for dating the Exodus.

Therefore they set taskmasters over them [the Israelites] to oppress them with forced labor. They built supply cities, Pithom and Rameses, for Pharaoh.   (NRSV)

Pithom and Rameses, two supply cities built during the reigns of Seti I (1308–1290 BCE) and Rameses II (1290–1224 BCE), serve as historical markers for dating the Exodus. Thus by taking a biblical reference and using Egyptian records the date of 1290–1250 becomes a likely date for the Exodus. First Kings 6:1 is another text sometimes used to date the Exodus.

> In the four hundred eightieth year after the Israelites came out of the land of Egypt, in the fourth year of Solomon's reign over Israel, in the month of Ziv, which is the second month, he began to build the house of the LORD. (NRSV)

A careful reading of this text gives the reader a second opinion on the precise dating for the Exodus. By counting backward 480 years from the time of the beginning of the building of the Temple (circa 960 BCE) one arrives at a tentative date of 1440 BCE for the Exodus. From our perspective today, does it really matter? To take into account both suggestions, it may be best to say the Exodus occurred sometime between 1450 and 1200 BCE.

Moses is introduced in the story of the Exodus as a young child who narrowly escapes an infanticide pogrom ordered by the Pharaoh. Exodus 2 records how Moses' mother and sister and the daughter of Pharaoh save the young Moses from pharaoh and the Nile River. Moses, born of Hebrew slaves, grows up in the home of pharaoh, privileged to the favors afforded a grandson of a king. Moses' world is shattered by the harsh atrocities imposed upon the Hebrew people by the Egyptian taskmasters. In a fit of outrage Moses slays an Egyptian taskmaster for his harsh treatment of a slave. When his misdeed is discovered, he flees to the desert of Midian. Jethro, a priest of Midian, takes in the refugee and offers his daughter, Zipporah, to Moses in marriage. The next several years Moses spends living in the desert caring for the flocks of his father-in-law Jethro until God once again breaks into human history.

Exodus 3 records the unusual story of Moses tending flocks somewhere in the desert when he sees a most unusual sight. On a mountain-side, he sees a bush that is burning with fire, yet neither the bush nor the fire is consumed. As Moses approaches the burning bush a voice calls out to him instructing him to remove his sandals from off his feet, for the place on which he is standing is "holy ground." God speaks to Moses from within the strange burning bush that does not burn up, calling upon Moses to be the agent of deliverance for his people, the Hebrew slaves who are in bondage in Egypt. Moses protests, decrying his unworthiness for such a task. Following a debate with God, Moses asks for a name with which to identify God. God responds to Moses' request with a veiled answer. Exodus 3:14 records that

> God said to Moses, "I AM WHO I AM." He said further, "Thus you shall say to the Israelites, 'I AM has sent me to you.' "   (NRSV)

The name usually translated as "Lord" or "Yahweh" in English Bibles is a shortened form of the Hebrew phrase given as a response from God to Moses. This word is known by the term *Tetragrammaton*, meaning "(having) four letters." The name is sacred to the Jewish people. Jewish readers never pronounce the divine name but instead will substitute descriptive phrases such as "the name" or "the Lord" when reading or referring to the divine name. Thus, Moses is now armed with the name of God, "I AM," to accompany him on his mission.

Moses continues to protest God's selection of him for this task. God supplies two further confirmations of his divine appointment. God turns Moses' staff into a serpent, then causes Moses' hand to become leprous. Moses reminds God that he is not eloquent in his speech. God responds by assuring Moses that Aaron, the brother of Moses, will act as his spokesperson. Moses finally capitulates and travels with Aaron to Egypt. Moses comes into the presence of Pharaoh and boldly proclaims, "Let my people go!" Pharaoh is undaunted by this sojourner's request, and casually responds, "Who is the LORD, that I should heed him and let Israel go?" (Exodus 5:2 NRSV). Pharaoh meets Moses' response with disdain, now ordering the Hebrew slaves to make bricks without straw, thus adding to their oppression.

God responds to the stubbornness of Pharaoh by unleashing ten plagues upon the nation of Egypt. This theophany[4] entails nine events related to natural phenomena in Egypt, and one event that moves beyond the natural. Plagues one through six all relate to activity associated with the annual rise of the Nile River. The first plague describes the Nile River "turning into blood." Red tides are a naturally occurring phenomenon caused by algae. Exodus 7:22 records the magicians of Pharaoh duplicating this feat. The appearance of frogs, the second plague, is a natural

---

[4]A theophany is the appearance of God in a form visible to humanity. The plagues are viewed by the Israelites as God's breaking into human history on their behalf.

outcome of receding floodwaters: as frogs begin to die and decompose, plagues three and four appear as lice/gnats and flies, respectively. Plagues five and six relate to the diseases spread by the insects, as there are now diseased cattle and then boils on people. Plagues seven through ten relate to meteorological events. The seventh plague describes a great storm complete with hail and lightning. The eighth plague tells of an invasion of locusts. Pestilence was a common recurrence in the ancient world. Darkness, the ninth plague, frequently results from the *Khamsin*, a desert sand storm. The final plague, the death of the firstborn, results not from naturally occurring phenomena, but through God's intervention in sending an angel of death throughout the land of Egypt. The Israelites are saved by placing the blood of a lamb over the frames of the doors of their homes. This final plague proves to be too much for Pharaoh to bear. At long last, he allows the Israelites to leave! The Passover celebration is the joyous festival day that commemorates this event.

There is a troubling question one may ask concerning the events of the plagues. The texts repeatedly describe God as hardening Pharaoh's heart in response to Moses' request. The question naturally arises, "Why does God make this task harder for Moses and the people of Israel?" Two responses are commonly given to this question. First, God is providing a justification for pouring out his fierce wrath upon the oppressors of Abraham's descendants. Second, this roadblock may be viewed as a means for strengthening the faith of the peasants who have been oppressed so long. They are witnessing the power of God before their very eyes. God's wrath against the Egyptians culminates in the defeat of Pharaoh's army in the Sea of Reeds described in Exodus 14 and 15.[5]

The journey to the land of promise begins with the Israelites camped at Mt. Sinai, somewhere in the Sinai Peninsula. A covenant is made between Yahweh, the God of Israel, and the descendants of Abraham. Exodus 19:4-6 records the framework for the covenant by listing the accomplishment of God in the Exodus event followed by the stipulations placed upon the people of Israel. At Sinai, the Ten Commandments are given to Moses to provide a basic guide for how the Israelites may demonstrate their faithfulness to the covenant. Therefore, the giving of the law to Moses is initially an instrument of grace. The people of Israel

---

[5]The Greek translation known as the Septuagint (LXX) names the body of water crossed as the "Red Sea." The Hebrew text literally reads *Yam Suph* or "Sea of Reeds."

know they have kept their part of the covenant when they have carried out the law in their lives.

The Ten Commandments represent the two directions of human relationships for the Israelites. A vertical relationship between the people of Israel and their God is reflected in the first four commandments. A horizontal relationship between the people of Israel and others is reflected in the final six commandments. When either the vertical or the horizontal relationship is violated the other is affected.

THE TEN COMMANDMENTS

I. You shall have no other gods before me
II. You shall not make for yourself an idol
III. You shall not make wrongful use of
the name of the LORD your God
IV. Remember the sabbath day, and keep it holy
V. Honor your father and your mother
VI. You shall not murder
VII. You shall not commit adultery
VIII. You shall not steal
IX. You shall not bear false witness against your neighbor
X. You shall not covet

(Exodus 20:1-17; Deuteronomy 5:6-21)

Exodus 22 begins a sizable section of legal material that extends largely uninterrupted until the end of Leviticus. The book of Leviticus is sometimes called the "Ritual Handbook" of Israel. It details the ritual practices prescribed for the Levites, Israel's priestly tribe. Christians often neglect Leviticus today because they see little value in understanding the ancient practice of Jewish law. Much can be learned from a careful reading of Leviticus. One example is the nature of atonement/absolution for the ancient Israelites. An understanding of the early Israelites' view of atonement may be attained through a careful reading of Leviticus 16, which describes the ancient celebration of the Day of Atonement.

The journey to the land of Canaan, sometimes called the "Wandering in the Wilderness," comprises the remainder of the Pentateuch. The Book of Numbers relates various challenges that confronted the leadership of

Moses and Aaron. The English title of the book is taken from the Latin title *Numeri*, "Numbers," but the Hebrew title *bemidbar*, "in the wilderness," more accurately reflects the contents of the book.

The first four chapters of Numbers describe Moses physically counting the number of Israelites with him in the desert, but the remainder of the book focuses upon events in the wilderness and various admonitions concerning ritual practices of the Israelites. Numbers 22 records the humorous story of Balaam and his donkey. The text is rich in Hebrew humor as the Moabite prophet, Balaam, proves less discerning than a jackass.

The final book of the Pentateuch, Deuteronomy, can be described as the "swan song" of Moses. As Deuteronomy begins, the Israelites are camped on the eastern shore of the Jordan River opposite of the city of Jericho. Moses has been told by God he will not be allowed to enter into the land of promise because of his outrage at Meribah (Numbers 20). In his final farewell, Moses urges the Israelites to remember they are only able to possess the land because of the mercies of God. The Hebrew word *zakar* "remember" is repeatedly used throughout Deuteronomy emphasizing the need for the Israelites to live in gratitude and dependency upon God. Moses' death is recorded in Deuteronomy 34 along with God's burial of God's servant. Deuteronomy 34:5,6 records:

> And Moses the servant of the LORD died there in Moab, as the LORD had said. He [the LORD] buried him in Moab, in the valley opposite Beth Peor, but to this day no one knows where his grave is.   (NIV)

CONCLUSION

The Pentateuch introduces the reader of the Bible to the God of Israel who is Creator. The Primeval History credits the God of Israel with the creation of all that is. God's creation includes all the elements in the universe, a garden with all the necessities of life, and humanity as represented by Adam and Eve. The Patriarchal History details God's covenant with Abraham and his descendants. The narrative shows the migration of this family from Mesopotamia to Canaan, and finally to Egypt. The narrative also introduces God's redemptive work for humanity through the family of Abraham. The Exodus event tells of the maturing of the descendants of Abraham who are now led by Moses, beginning as a large band of slaves but emerging as a people who are primed to gradually become a mighty nation. The law of God is also brought before the Israelites as a means for keeping the covenant they have made with God. The background for the founding of the nation of Israel is now established. Deuteronomy serves as a literary bridge between the developing history of Israel and the Conquest of the Promised Land which thrusts Israel into the role of a nation of collective tribes.

Chapter 2

THE HISTORY OF ISRAEL

The history of Israel is the story of God's great love for the children of Abraham. In our Protestant Bible, Joshua through Esther comprises the section of the Old Testament generally described as the Historical Books of the Old Testament. The historical timeline begins with the Conquest of Canaan and concludes with the Israelites in captivity under Persian control. The Hebrew Bible, however, classifies these books somewhat differently. In the Hebrew Bible, Joshua, Judges, 1-2 Samuel, and 1-2 Kings—Samuel and Kings are each only one book in the Hebrew Bible— are known by the title Former Prophets. Chronicles (1-2, also only one book in the Hebrew Bible), Ezra-Nehemiah (Ezra and Nehemiah are also placed together in one book in the Hebrew Bible), Ruth, and Esther are considered part of *Ketuvim*, "Writings," and are thus separate from the Former Prophets in order. The distinction between the Former Prophets and the accounts found in the Chronicles through Ezra and Nehemiah is significant because they trace much of the same story but from a some-times very different perspective.

In the following pages, we will look at the historical writings of Israel (represented in the Protestant canon in Joshua–Esther). We will recon-struct when possible a general overview of the historical timeline of Israel from its inception as a nation through the time of the Persian period when the exiles were allowed the freedom to return to their homeland.

Our task is threefold. First, the books known in the Hebrew Bible as the Former Prophets (Joshua, Judges, Samuel, and Kings) will be examined as a "history of Israel." Second, the books of Chronicles, Ezra, and Nehemiah will be examined as a record of an alternative view of the history of Israel. Finally, the books of Esther, Ruth, and Daniel will be discussed in light of their historical contributions to the larger understand-ing of Israel's history.

DEUTERONOMISTIC HISTORY

Joshua, Judges, Samuel, and Kings record the events of the Conquest led by Joshua through the destruction of Jerusalem and the beginning of the Exile following the subjugation of Zedekiah, the last king of Judah. Historically, this material spans from 1200 to 500 BCE. Martin Noth was one of the first Old Testament scholars to identify the uniqueness of the Former Prophets as having a distinctly historical retrospect. Noth claims these four books were written together to answer a question asked by those in the Exile: How did we get here? Noth sees the Jewish separation of Joshua, Judges, Samuel, and Kings into a separate classification, the Former Prophets, to be a key to answering this question. The answer: the Israelites are now in Exile because they have sinned against God and have been led astray by the wicked kings of Israel and Judah. According to Noth, the Former Prophets were collected and finalized during the time of the Exile. They tell the story of how the Israelites came into Canaan with great promise, grew into a nation, and then were led away into captivity because of their sin. The name used to identify this history is the "Deuteronomistic History."

The Deuteronomistic History was so named because each of the four books found within this framework reflect a theological understanding in concert with the Book of Deuteronomy. The main theological feature of these books is called Retribution Theology. This can be simply stated as "If I am good God blesses me, but if I am bad God punishes me." In every book of the Deuteronomistic History Israel's rebellion against God is met with swift retribution. The central theme of Deuteronomy, "Remember the Lord your God," whispers throughout the books of Joshua, Judges, Samuel, and Kings. Ultimately, the Israelites do not remember the God of Abraham, Isaac, Jacob, and Joseph. Nor do they remember the law given to Moses, nor the covenant they have made with God to honor God's laws and ways—thus their ultimate defeat and captivity.

Joshua. Joshua can be said to represent the *idealistic* view of the conquest of Canaan by the Israelites. Joshua opens with the Israelites camped on the plains of Moab about to enter the land of Canaan. Moses, the experienced leader of the Exodus, is gone. The author of the Book of Joshua draws a constant comparison between Moses who is identified repeatedly as the "servant of the Lord," and Joshua who is called "son of Nun, Moses' assistant." The reader is constantly reminded that Joshua is no Moses. Only at the very end of the book of Joshua after recording Joshua's death does the author describe Joshua as a "servant of the Lord" (Joshua 24:29). The dating of Joshua and the Conquest can be inferred from our dating of the Exodus. The Wandering in the Wilderness is described as having lasted for forty years. Therefore, based on the dating of the Exodus the Conquest probably took place as a historical event sometime between 1400 and 1200 BCE. The more popular argument today dates the events of the Conquest from 1250 to 1200 BCE. The Book of Joshua can be divided into three distinct parts. In Joshua 1–12 the Conquest is described as a series of three swift military campaigns resulting in the Israelites taking total control of the land of Canaan. Joshua 11:23 records:

> So Joshua took the whole land, according to all that the LORD had spoken to Moses; and Joshua gave it for an inheritance to Israel according to their tribal allotments. And the land had rest from war. (NRSV)

Signs and wonders accompany the Israelites journey into the land of Canaan. The waters of the Jordan are parted, the walls of Jericho come tumbling down, and, according to Joshua 10, the sun stands still, allowing Joshua and the Israelites to defeat the Amorite kings. Joshua 13–21 records the distribution of the land to the various tribes. The land is divided under the supervision of Joshua, Eleazar the High Priest, and the heads of the tribal families. Lots are cast to determine the selection process. In the concluding chapters, 21–24, the Israelites confirm the covenant God made with their forefathers culminating with the death and burial of Joshua. Thus, the Book of Joshua introduces the reader to the beginning of the Deuteronomistic History. There is optimism throughout the introduction: God fulfills the promise made to Abraham and Moses.

Judges. Judges is sometimes described as the *realistic* view of the Conquest. The Israelites have not successfully driven the inhabitants of Canaan from their land, and often find themselves in continuous life-and-death struggles for possession of the land of promise. Judges 2:11–3:6 provides the reader with an overall framework for understanding the Book of Judges. The primary literary device in the Book of Judges is the so-called Judges Cycle. The Judges Cycle is a repeating paradigm for the successive rise and fall of each Judge. It is characterized by six elements: Apostasy (Israel sins); Oppression (God allows an enemy to oppress the tribes of Israel); Repentance (the people cry aloud to God for deliverance); a Deliverer (God raises up a judge to lead the people against the oppressors); Deliverance (God delivers the people out of oppression); and Peace. Each Judge's story follows this basic paradigm.

The years 1200–1020 BCE provide the backdrop for these accounts of the judges. This time period is often described as the "dark ages" of Israelite history because so little is actually known about this era. The only other biblical reference to this time period is found in the Book of

Ruth, which begins its story with the phrase, "In the days when the judges ruled" (Ruth 1:1).

Judges are categorized as major and minor judges. The only criterion for being a major judge is participation in military conflict. Most of the judges lead or participate in battles, including Othniel, Ehud, Shamgar, Deborah, Gideon, Jephthah, and Samson. Minor judges include Tola, Jair, Ibzan, Elon, and Abdon. Various features characterize the judges. Most of the judges were charismatic figures who are described as being filled with a special endowment of God's spirit. Judges were also usually identified with selected local tribes and never led the collective tribes of Israel (despite the general impression in the text that they ruled in succession). Thus, many of the judges probably ruled concurrently with one another in different regions of Israel.

THE JUDGES CYCLE

Apostasy
Oppression
Repentance
Deliverer
Deliverance
Peace

(Judges 2:11–3:6 provides a framework for each succeeding judge.)

These action stories are some of the greatest stories in the Old Testament. The great courage of Deborah—the only female judge in Israel—or the tragic waste of strength witnessed in the life of Samson are memorable tales of the indomitable spirit of the Israelites who were trying to possess the land given to them by God. The author/editor of Judges prepares the reader for the arrival of the monarchy, depicted in the following book of 1 Samuel. The phrase, "In those days there was no king in Israel" appears four times in Judges 17–21.[1]

First and Second Samuel. The rise of the monarchy is the subject of the Book of Samuel. The narrative of Samuel is drawn from the stories

---

[1]See Judges 17:6, 18:1, 19:1, and 21:25.

passed down concerning Samuel, Saul, David, and the Ark of the Covenant. The Deuteronomistic History records two divergent perspectives on the development of a king in Israel. One voice within the text is generally favorable to the idea of kingship. A competing voice rejects the idea of kingship, arguing the God of Israel alone should hold the place of king over Israel. Unlike the other texts in the Deuteronomistic History, Samuel is filled with repetitions and doublets (compare 1 Samuel 18:10-11 to 1 Samuel 19:9-10). The character Samuel plays an important role in the narrative. He functions as priest and prophet and is the last of the judges in Israel. Finally, Samuel anoints the first two kings of Israel, Saul and David.

Saul is an impressive choice as the first king of Israel. He is described as standing "head and shoulders above everyone else" (1 Samuel 9:2). Saul reigned from 1020 to 1000 BCE. Saul leads the Israelites against their enemy the Philistines who are also struggling to control Canaan. The Philistines are entrenched along the Mediterranean Sea in five city-states: Gaza, Gath, Ekron, Ashdod, and Ashkelon. Saul eventually dies while in battle with the Philistines. After being injured by an archer's arrow, Saul falls upon his own sword. David is a young man/warrior, who has grown in favor with the people of Israel while serving in Saul's court. He succeeds Saul as King.

David becomes the most beloved king in Israel's history. His reputation precedes him wherever he goes. He is well known for his musical ability, beginning his service in Saul's court as a royal musician. David is also well known for his bravery in slaying the taunting Philistine giant Goliath while only a teenager. David's first seven and one-half years as king are spent ruling from his capital in Hebron. The problems facing David were formidable. The tribes of Israel were badly divided between the ten tribes in the North and the two Southern tribes. David's lineage springs from the tribe of Judah, a Southern tribe, and he had the difficult task of trying to procure support from the North. Following a few years of struggle with the remnant of Saul's descendants, David is made king over all twelve tribes of Israel. David begins immediately solving the task of unification. He selects a new city to be his capital, Jebus, a Canaanite city the Israelites had not yet taken. There were distinct advantages to the choice, first it was a good geographical location lying between the tribal territories of the North and South. Second, it provided a politically neutral site to start anew. David and his men capture Jebus and rename the city Jerusalem, still known today as the "city of David." Moreover, Jerusalem becomes the site for religious unification. David relocates the Ark of the Covenant to Jerusalem from its resting place in Kiriath-Jearim. The Ark is Israel's most sacred object dating back to the days of Moses and the wanderings in the wilderness. The Ark was revered by all the tribes of Israel and served as a further tool of unification. David reigned in Jerusalem for thirty-three years. Combined with his first seven years as king in Hebron, this means David ruled a total of forty years, from approximately 1000 to 960 BCE.

The Deuteronomistic Historian is consistent in describing the genuine humanity of the characters mentioned in the narrative. The description of David is no different. David is a king worthy of respect and honor, but David also had his foibles. His indiscretions as well as his mighty deeds are treated in the texts. First Samuel 11 outlines the misconduct of David as he plays the role of Peeping Tom watching a beautiful young maiden, Bathsheba, as she was bathing. David's indiscretions accumulate as he sends for Bathsheba, who is married to Uriah the Hittite, and commits adultery with her and she conceives. The narrative describes David's attempts to cover his misdeeds. He sends for Uriah from the battlefield hoping perhaps Uriah will be with his wife so as to believe the child is his. Uriah foils David's attempt at subterfuge, refusing to sleep with his wife when his fellow soldiers are on the battlefield. David's sins progress as he has Uriah murdered in battle and brings Bathsheba into the royal harem. God shows his disapproval of David's conduct by requiring the life of the newborn infant. David's favor is never recovered throughout the narrative. He is later plagued with external problems and internal parental conflicts.

First and Second Kings. The Book of Kings completes the Deuteronomistic History, showing the wickedness of the Israelite kings and how the people were led farther and farther away from God's statutes and ways. Kings spans a lengthy period of time beginning with the reign of Solomon around 960 BCE and ending with the emergence of King Jehoiachin from prison in captivity in exile in Babylon around 561 BCE. The text names several sources used in its production, for example, the "Book of the Acts of Solomon" (1 Kings 11:41) or the "Book of the Annals of the Kings of Judah" (1 Kings 14:29). Prophetic sources in the Book of Kings include stories detailing the activity of Elijah and Elisha, interspersed throughout 1 Kings 17 to 2 Kings 9, and lesser-known prophets such as Micaiah ben Imlah.

The Book of Kings can sometimes be confusing because it covers the histories of Israel (the ten Northern tribes) and Judah (the two Southern tribes) after their separation from one another following the death of Solomon. The compilers of Kings switch back and forth between these two nations without much warning. The reader must be careful to identify which nation is being discussed in reference to a given king. This is further confused because in a number of cases the same name belongs to different kings though fortunately none rule concurrently. Indeed sometimes the same name belongs to two kings in the same kingdom. One example of this is King Jeroboam, the first king of Israel. There are actually two Jeroboams, Jeroboam I following the time of Solomon in the tenth century, and Jeroboam II who reigned in the eighth century. The Book of Kings refers to each of these kings as Jeroboam. The reader must understand the context, including the century being discussed, to rightly understand and interpret the story.

The Book of Kings begins by demonstrating the inability of David to continue reigning as King. The succession of Solomon to David's throne is the focal point at the outset. The process of finding a new king affirms the covenant God made with David in 2 Samuel 7 that a Davidic heir would reign on the throne continuously. A Davidic heir would remain on the throne in Judah until its demise in 587 BCE. Solomon's ascendancy to the throne is the first step in the fulfillment of God's promise to David. The task is made more difficult because there were no clearly established guidelines or precedents for the monarchy. David had become king when King Saul was wounded in battle and ultimately took his own life with his sons dying with him in battle against the Philistines. Solomon is forced to depose his half-brother Adonijah after Adonijah's supporters establish him as a claimant to the throne. Thus, the Davidic succession has now begun.

According to the Deuteronomistic Historian, wisdom is Solomon's greatest legacy. Solomon is credited with the flowering of the wisdom movement in Israel. The wisdom tradition was already well established in other cultures such as Egypt and Mesopotamia, but Solomon is seen as the great patriarch of wisdom in Israel in the first half of the tenth century BCE. Solomon's involvement in the wisdom movement is reflected in his association with the wisdom books of the Hebrew Bible. He is named in the superscription of Proverbs ("Solomon son of David, king of Israel") and apparently is alluded to in Ecclesiastes 1:1 ("the son of David, king in Jerusalem"). Solomon's business prowess also reflects his wisdom. Wisdom in the ancient Near East is often reflected by one's favorable level of affluence. Solomon is portrayed in the Deuteronomistic History as a successful horse and chariot trader, building great wealth through his management.

The building of the temple for the God of Israel is considered Solomon's greatest achievement. The building, which took seven years to complete, is described in specific detail in 1 Kings 6. Construction of the temple was started in the fourth year of Solomon's reign, or around 958 BCE, and after completion stood until its destruction by the Babylonians in 587 BCE. The temple became the rallying point for the people of Israel. First Kings 7 describes another one of Solomon's building projects, the royal palace. Solomon spent thirteen years constructing the royal palace.

As with David, the Deuteronomistic Historian displays the weaknesses of Solomon for the reader to plainly see. Solomon's policies of harsh taxation are seen as a horrible burden upon the people. Solomon divides the people of Israel into twelve separate tax districts requiring each district to provide revenues for the state one month of the year. Forced labor was another example of Solomon's improprieties: artisans and craftsmen were required to work for the king one out of three months without compensation. Solomon's most dishonorable act recorded by the Deuteronomistic Historian is found in 1 Kings 11: Solomon began to be led astray by his foreign wives. He built temples for the gods of his foreign wives and allowed religious syncretism[2] to pervade the nation of Israel. In the eyes of the Deuteronomistic Historian this action was clearly interpreted as unfaithfulness to the God of Israel. Solomon's harem included 700 wives and 300 concubines, but the Deuteronomistic Historian takes Solomon to task for his allowance of the worship of his wives' foreign gods, not for the sheer number of wives and concubines.

The death of Solomon brought an end to the United Monarchy. The twelve tribes who were united under David began to show signs of division throughout Solomon's reign. Rehoboam succeeded his father Solomon as heir to the throne. Rehoboam retained the support of the two

---

[2]Religious syncretism is the pluralization of multiple religious beliefs or practices in a given belief system or society. The practice seen throughout the Old Testament in Israel and Judah is in direct violation of the first two commandments, "No other gods" and "No graven images." When religious syncretism is present, the worship is so polluted with outside influences one is unable to differentiate between pure or defiled worship.

Southern tribes, but his claim to the throne was questioned by the ten Northern tribes. The ten Northern tribes inquired of Rehoboam as to what model of leadership he would choose. Would he continue the severity of

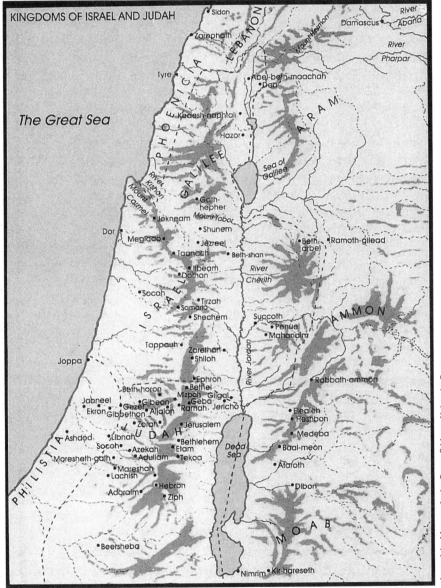

Map of the Divided Kingdoms showing borders and overall tribal areas

his father Solomon, or would he lessen the heavy burdens of taxation and conscription levied upon the people? Rehoboam responded that he would uphold the policies of his father Solomon, even going beyond his father in his taxation and forced-labor policies. The ten Northern tribes were outraged by his response. They withdrew their support for Rehoboam, and rallied around Jeroboam I, a leader who had been anointed by the prophet Ahijah before the death of Solomon. This separation created a new state and ushered in the period of the Divided Monarchy. The ten Northern tribes became known as Israel with Jeroboam I as their first king. The two Southern tribes were known as the Kingdom of Judah, continuing to pledge allegiance to the Davidic heir, Rehoboam.

Most of the Book of Kings recounts the history of the Divided King-doms, its civil wars, and struggles for survival. One theme is constant throughout the text: the wickedness of the kings of both Israel and Judah. The kings repeatedly lead the descendants of Abraham farther and farther away from the covenant their forefathers made with God. The Deutero-nomistic Historian assesses the kings of Israel and Judah by references to their treatment of the "high places," altars used as worship sites for foreign gods. Those kings who destroyed the high places received a favorable report; those kings who allowed the high places to exist were condemned. To permit the high places was tantamount to the sanction of unfaithfulness. The cycle of mostly wicked kings continues until Assyria destroys Israel in 722 BCE. The Book of Kings continues to record the history of Judah alone until its destruction at the hands of the Babylo-nians in 587 BCE.

Thus, the Deuteronomistic History is ended. How did we get here in Exile? The people of Israel and Judah are in exile and removed from their promised homeland because they have turned away from the God of Abraham, Isaac, Jacob, and Joseph. They did not heed the words of Moses recorded in the Book of Deuteronomy—"Do not forget the LORD your God."[3]

---

[3]Deuteronomy 8:11 is one example of multiple references to this admonition given by Moses to the Israelite community before they entered into the Land of Promise.

THE CHRONICLER

First Chronicles through Nehemiah presents an alternate view of the history of Israel. At the start, a genealogy is presented, beginning with Adam and ending at the conclusion of Nehemiah in the postexilic period in Palestine. In recent days it has been fashionable to posit a single editor or school of editors as responsible for collecting, editing, and finalizing 1 Chronicles through Nehemiah as a unified whole. Those taking this approach name this presumed editor or school the "Chronicler." Some have ascribed the authorship or the editing of this literary collection to Ezra the scribe. Several problems arise when trying to establish a clear unity between these works. A major obstacle to this view is the fact that Chronicles follows Ezra-Nehemiah in the tradition of the Hebrew Bible rather than preceding them as in Protestant Bibles. Though the presentation of Chronicles with Ezra-Nehemiah provides a convenient framework for an overall history of Israel, there are numerous differences between these two works.[4] There are, however, similarities between these works as both at least appear to be dependent on the works of Joshua-Kings as source material for their writing.

First and Second Chronicles. The core of Chronicles forms a parallel history to that found in the Deuteronomistic History. Close inspection reveals some noticeable differences. One major difference is the content treated in the differing works. The Deuteronomistic History follows the narrative history of the Israelites beginning with the Conquest as related in the Book of Joshua and ending with the release of Jehoiachin from prison in Babylonian captivity (2 Kings 25:27-30). The first nine chapters of Chronicles are occupied with a listing of genealogical records. These records focus on the ancestral genealogy of Israel's forefathers, inhabitants of Jerusalem, and the lineage of the Levites. The bulk of 1 Chronicles (chapters 10-29) focuses on the reign of David, passing over the periods of the Conquest and the time of the judges. Second Chronicles 1-9 details the reign of Solomon as the continuation of the house of David, and is followed by the story of the remaining Judean kings, treated in 2 Chronicles 10-36, but with only scant references to the Israelite kings in the North as they relate to the actions of Judah.

---

[4]See John Hayes, *An Introduction to Old Testament Study* (Nashville: Abingdon Press, 1979) 243-47, for a full treatment of these differences.

Detailed information about David is another point of departure between the two histories. The Deuteronomistic Historian shows the humanity of King David, allowing the reader to see David's strengths and weaknesses. The compiler of Chronicles provides an "antiseptic" history of the house of David. Many of the stories found in Samuel are missing in Chronicles. For example, the stories about David's reign in Hebron, the conflict with Saul's heirs, the Bathsheba affair, and the difficulties David faced with his sons are all omitted in Chronicles. David is also portrayed in Chronicles as the great designer of Israel's worship as opposed to the valiant warrior pictured in the Deuteronomistic History. Chronicles takes great pains to show the key role David played in the development of the temple and the priesthood.

Ezra/Nehemiah. Ezra and Nehemiah provide information concerning the period known as the Restoration, 538–333 BCE. The elite of Judah suffered for years in exile in Babylon following three waves of deportations from their homes in 598, 587, and 581 BCE. The Restoration is initiated with the fall of Babylon to Cyrus the Persian king in 539. The Cyrus decree, ordering the return of the captives and rebuilding of localized sites of worship, is attested to in Ezra 1:2-4. Isaiah 44:28 and 45:1 hail the coming of Cyrus, calling him the *messiah*, which means "anointed one." Cyrus allows the Israelites, along with the other nations relocated by the Babylonians, to return to their native lands, and encourages them to reinstitute localized worship. The first band of refugees returned to Palestine under the direction of Sheshbazzar sometime after 538 BCE. They were greatly disappointed with what they found in Jerusalem and the surrounding area. The Babylonians had leveled all the towns and they had not been rebuilt by those who now possessed the land. Obadiah states nomadic tribal groups from the desert took possession of the border regions of southern Judah. The books of Haggai and Zechariah describe the poverty and severe economic conditions awaiting those who returned from exile.

A second group of exiles returns during the reign of the Persian King Darius I (521–485 BCE). Zerubbabel, a descendant of David and a Persian-appointed governor, led this second wave of refugees with the aid of Joshua the high priest. Haggai and Zechariah record the events of this return, focusing on the rebuilding of the temple in Jerusalem. Construction began around 520 BCE; the temple was completed in 516 BCE and rededicated in 515 BCE.

A third group of deportees returned under the watchful eye of Ezra the scribe. Ezra is often called the second lawgiver because he brings a copy of the "law of Moses" with him from exile, presumably this "law" was the first five books of the Hebrew Bible. This is the first time the Pentateuch is mentioned in the texts, giving rise to the widely held view it was given its final form during the Exile. Ezra is charged with reforming the religious life of the people. The reform included the following elements: reading the law in a public assembly and providing an Aramaic translation for the masses who no longer spoke pure Hebrew; decreeing the divorce of all foreign wives in Judah; and leading in a

---

IMPORTANT DATES IN THE HISTORY OF ISRAEL

(all dates are BCE)

2000–1500	The Patriarchs
1290–1250	The Exodus
1250–1200	The Conquest
1200–1020	The Period of Judges
1020–922	United Kingdom
922–587	Divided Kingdom
922–722	Israel as Northern Kingdom
722	Israel's capital Samaria destroyed
922–587	Judah as Southern Kingdom
587	Judah's capital Jerusalem destroyed
587–539	Exile in Babylon
538–333	Restoration: Persian Period
333–167	Hellenistic Period

---

national fast. Though strictly speaking Ezra was a priest and not a governor, he did bring about national reform for a beleaguered people.

Nehemiah, the cupbearer to the Persian king Artaxerxes,[5] led the fourth major wave of returnees. He vowed to rebuild the walls of Jeru-

---

[5]There is much debate concerning exactly which "Artaxerxes" Nehemiah served under. Was it Artaxerxes I (464–423 BCE) or Artaxerxes II (404–358 BCE)? The textual and secondary evidence does not offer a clear solution to this problem.

salem, but faced heavy opposition by the existing residents, including
three major leaders: Sanballat, the governor of Samaria; Tobiah, known
as "the Ammonite"; and Geshem the Arab. The book of Nehemiah
chronicles the dangers faced by the party led by Nehemiah who,
according to Nehemiah 6:15, completed the project in fifty-two days.
Nehemiah returns to Jerusalem on a second occasion assuming the
position of governor over Judah.

Thus, the history sometimes attributed to a Chronicler comes to an
end. It began with genealogies from the primeval period and extends into
the Persian period during the times of Ezra and Nehemiah. It offers an
alternative reading for much of the Former Prophets, adding new material
when pertinent, or adding a varying perspective in other places.

RUTH, ESTHER, AND DANIEL

Other books help fill in the gaps left from the general overviews of
Israel's history as told by the Deuteronomistic Historian and the
Chronicler. Three little works, Ruth, Esther, and Daniel, provide rich
insights into particular historical periods in Israel. Though each book is
probably written much later than the time period described, the novellas
do provide interesting insight into the respective time periods. The
context of Ruth is the period of the judges. Esther describes a beautiful
story set in the Persian period. The first half of Daniel (1–6) finds its
context in the heart of the Exile in Babylon, while the second half of
Daniel (7–12) is dominated by cryptic language referring to the Maccabean Revolt in 167 BCE. All three novellas are also significant because the
Hebrew canon categorizes them in a different order than the Protestant
canon. The home for these works in the Hebrew canon is the *Ketuvim*,
the Writings. Ruth and Esther are listed with three other festal books, or
books set aside to be read during annual festivals: Song of Songs,
Ecclesiastes, and Lamentations. Ruth and Esther are associated with the
feasts of Pentecost and Purim, respectively. Daniel is located in the
Hebrew Bible between the five festal books and the works of Ezra/
Nehemiah. In the Protestant canon, by contrast, Ruth and Esther are
placed within the category of historical books and Daniel is listed among
the prophets.

Ruth. Ruth presents a beautiful love story revolving around an
Israelite, Naomi, who lives in the land of Moab; Ruth, a Moabitess,
Naomi's daughter-in-law; and Boaz, a relative of Naomi who lives in
Israel. Naomi and Ruth return to Naomi's native land, Israel, after a time

of economic hardship, mainly involving the loss of their husbands. Ruth demonstrates her faithfulness to her mother-in-law and the God of Israel by seeing to Naomi's needs even after the death of her husband. Upon arrival in Israel, Ruth encounters Boaz, a relative of Naomi who acts in the role of Kinsman-Redeemer. Boaz eventually marries Ruth and provides for the security of both Ruth and Naomi. The Book of Ruth ends with a genealogy of David, demonstrating Ruth to be the great-grandmother of the most revered king of Israel—and a Moabitess of all things!

Esther. Esther is an Israelite living in Persia who wins a beauty contest established by the Persian King Ahasuerus (Xerxes I, reigned 485–464 BCE), who is seeking a new wife. The plot of the book involves a scheme by Haman who is planning to exterminate the Jewish people from Persia. His plot is foiled by the courageous efforts of a Jewish man named Mordecai and the central figure, Esther, who risks her life in pleading for the security of her people. The place of Esther in the canon of the Hebrew Bible and Old Testament is not without criticism. The major disagreement many have with the book is that though Esther is a religious book, the text itself never mentions God.

Daniel. Daniel 1–6 is a story of survival. Daniel, Hananiah, Mishael, and Azariah are uprooted from their home in Judah and relocated in Babylon as part of the exile. Each is given a Babylonian name: Daniel is renamed Belteshazzar, Hananiah is now Shadrach, Mishael is Meshach, and Azariah is called Abednego. These four men, along with the leading elite of Judah, must now make a new life in a foreign land. The book of Daniel provides a paradigm for living in the midst of persecution. Daniel 3 and Daniel 6 detail different stories with similar story lines: allegiance to God with the threat of execution. The execution is carried through, and finally God miraculously delivers those who are faithful. Daniel 3 shares the famous story of the three men in the fiery furnace. Daniel 6 recounts Daniel in the lions' den. God's deliverance in times of persecution is the repeated theme of Daniel 1–6.

Daniel 7–12 is often misunderstood and misinterpreted. A dramatic shift takes place between Daniel 6 and 7. The story no longer focuses on four young men in exile, but instead uses cryptic language in carrying over the theme of perseverance in the face of persecution for those who are living during the tumult of the Maccabean Revolt. It is generally held that the Book of Daniel uses the historical figures of the four young men and their story to encourage those facing the horrors of religious persecution by a Syrian emperor culminating in the Maccabean revolt following 167 BCE. One striking example of such encouragement, Daniel 12:2-3, mentions life after death, an infrequent theme for much of the Old Testament, but integrally important to those facing death rather than renouncing their faith.

> Many of those who sleep in the dust of the earth shall awake, some to everlasting life, and some to shame and everlasting contempt. Those who are wise shall shine like the brightness of the sky, and those who lead many to righteousness, like the stars forever and ever.
>
> (Daniel 12:2-3 NRSV)

CONCLUSION

Joshua through Esther provides the careful reader with an overview of the history of the people of Israel from the Conquest to their relative freedom granted by the Persians. This history is filled with colorful characters, fast-paced action, and engaging narrative. The early recorders of Israel's history tell their contemporary readers of the power of the God of Israel, and the responsibility that comes with God's covenant. The sons and daughters of Abraham are not allowed to remain in control of their land of promise because of their unfaithfulness to the covenant they made with God.

Chapter 3

POETIC LITERATURE OF ISRAEL

I will sing to the LORD, for he has triumphed gloriously;
horse and rider he has thrown into the sea. (Exodus 15:1b, NRSV)

This verse in Exodus 15 serves as the introduction to the hymn popularly known as the "Song of the Sea," or the "Song of Moses." It sounds very different from its narrative counterpart in Exodus 14:28:

The waters returned and covered the chariots and the chariot drivers, the entire army of Pharaoh that had followed them into the sea; not one of them remained. (NRSV)

The basic content is the same, but these two verses convey two differing expressions of the same event. Exodus 15:1b fashions the story in poetic form. It expresses the inner thoughts and feelings of the writer who is recounting this event. Exodus 14:28 gives the basic details of the event but offers a "valueless" account of the event. Prose narrative is the more popular literary device used by the Israelites in communicating their stories for subsequent generations, but when the writers wanted to express more than just factual details, they often used poetry. Exodus 14 and 15 is one of two places in the Old Testament where a story is told first in narrative form and then retold in picturesque poetic form. The second occurrence of this phenomenon is in Judges 4 and 5. These passages describe for the reader the destruction of Sisera at the hands of two women, Deborah and Jael, following the pattern of placing the narrative first and then adding the poetic account—often described as the "Song of Deborah"—immediately after the narrative.

Hebrew poetic form occurs extensively in the Old Testament; as much as one-third of the Old Testament is poetry. Some books, such as the Psalms, Proverbs, Song of Solomon (Songs), and Lamentations, are written exclusively in poetic form. Other books are written largely in poetic form with only small departures recorded in narrative. One example of a book containing mostly poetry is Job: Job is all poetry except for its narrative framework in Job 1, 2, and 42:7-17. Most of the prophetic books are also written in poetic form. There are also examples of books containing mostly narrative forms, but which periodically include hymns or poetry, such as the aforementioned Exodus or Judges.

Parallelism and *meter* are the two dominant features in Hebrew poetry. The basic unit of Hebrew poetry is a line, with each line expressing at least one thought or idea. A verse is created when two or more lines are placed alongside each other. Parallelism can be described as the relationship that exists between the lines in a Hebrew verse. Parallelism is made manifest by the use of the rhyming of thoughts rather than sounds or words. Three major types of parallel relationships are found in Hebrew poetry. The most common form occurs when the two lines express the same general thought or idea. This is called *synonymous parallelism*. One example is Psalm 26:4:

> I do not sit with the worthless,
>> nor do I consort with hypocrites; . . .   (NRSV)

Sometimes the subsequent lines contrast the thought expressed in the first line. This is called *antithetic parallelism*, as in Psalm 1:6:

> for the LORD watches over the way of the righteous,
> but the way of the wicked will perish.   (NRSV)

Synthetic or formal parallelism occurs when the thought of the first line is carried out or completed in the second. Two examples of synthetic parallelism are Psalm 27:10:

> If my father and mother forsake me,
>> the LORD will take me up.   (NRSV)

and Proverbs 22:6:

> Train children in the right way,
>> and when old, they will not stray.   (NRSV)

Hebrew meter can be described as the number of beats per line in a given verse. The number of beats is determined by counting the number of stressed syllables in the line. The most common formula of Hebrew meter is three beats in both the first and second lines, often designated as 3+3. Laments and funeral dirges, known by their Hebrew term *qinah*, follow a 3+2 formula.

Ancient writers in Israel often chose poetry for expressing their message when narrative did not sufficiently serve their task. Hebrew poetry expresses the passion, emotion, pathos, and spirit of the writer in ways narrative is simply unable to achieve. One need only read once again our two verses Exodus 15:1b and Exodus 14:28 to grasp the power of poetry. This chapter will provide an overview of the poetic literature in the Old Testament. The poetic material will be subdivided into three major areas: the Psalms, the Wisdom texts, and other poetry.

THE PSALMS

The collection of hymns found in the book of Psalms is probably the most beloved and cherished literature of the entire Old Testament. Many New Testaments are published with Psalms added for good measure. Not many New Testaments have been published with Leviticus or Lamentations as additions for Christian audiences. The Psalms enjoy a special place in the Christian community. There are many reasons for our affection for this wonderful book. The Psalms contain the largest number of prayers found anywhere in the Bible, expressing the innermost thoughts of the writers of these hymns. They are shockingly honest at times, laying before the reader or hearer their cries of pain and whoops of joy. The Psalms are also theocentric, focusing on our relationship to God as individuals and as a community of faith.

For centuries, Davidic authorship has been the traditional assumption of both Jewish and Christian communities, but close reading of the texts reveals the presence of multiple authors and editorial activity in the final shaping of the Psalms. Chronicles portrays David as the great patriarch of worship. The Deuteronomistic Historian in the Book of Samuel also pictures David as a writer of hymns and a musician who is introduced to King Saul initially as a singer of songs to ward off the evil spirit which menaced him. Many of the psalms are attributed to David by their titles, or superscriptions. Psalm 23 is probably the best known of all the "David" psalms.

> *A Psalm of David.*
> The Lord is my shepherd, I shall not want.
> He makes me lie down in green pastures;
> he leads me beside still waters;
> he restores my soul.
> He leads me in right paths
> for his name's sake.
> Even though I walk through the darkest valley,
> I fear no evil;
> for you are with me;
> your rod and your staff—
> they comfort me.
> You prepare a table before me

in the presence of my enemies;
you anoint my head with oil;
my cup overflows.
Surely goodness and mercy shall follow me
all the days of my life,
and I shall dwell in the house of the LORD
my whole life long.   (NRSV)

Other psalms such as Psalm 137 reflect a historical time period long after David lived in Israel. Psalm 137 describes the animosity and humiliation suffered by the Israelites at the hands of the Babylonians following the destruction of Jerusalem in 587 BCE and the subsequent period of captivity.

It is difficult to outline a book like the Psalms. It is akin to making an outline of a modern hymnal. The book in its present-day form represents a continuous work of compilation begun during the time of David, but not completed until after the rebuilding of the second temple in the period of the Restoration. Thus, the psalms reflect the theological concerns of various hymn writers in Israel beginning in the tenth century through at least the fourth century BCE. There are categories one can use to order the psalms, but the process of selecting which hymns fall under which categories is ultimately subjective. Categorizing the psalms by types, however, can be helpful in terms of designating the various forms of literature found throughout the collection. Fortunately, the text itself provides a basic outline for the material found in Psalms. The Book of Psalms in its Hebrew form is divided into five distinct sections. Though no titles of description are used to distinguish individual sections of material, each section concludes with a doxology, a brief statement of praise alerting the reader to the end of the present body.

There are other collections demonstrably present in Psalms, such as the Davidic psalms, the Elohistic psalms, and the Psalms of Asaph but

---

	DIVISIONS IN THE PSALMS
Book I	Psalms 1–41
	Doxology in Psalm 41:13
Book II	Psalms 42–72
	Doxology in Psalm 72:18-20
Book III	Psalms 73–89
	Doxology in Psalm 89:52
Book IV	Psalms 90–106
	Doxology in Psalms 106:48
Book V	Psalms 107–150
	All of Psalm 150 is a doxology

space does not allow further investigation of these and other possible collections.

There are many theological themes present in the Psalms. First and foremost, the Psalms speak to the presence of God as a reality in the lives of the writers. The awareness of God is intimately expressed in a pervasive way throughout the words of the Psalms. Another theme is the great paradox of humanity. God is infinite, but humanity is finite, limited, and often responsible for disobedience or unfaithfulness before God, yet humanity is described as the crown and joy of God's creative activity. Sin is another of the major themes addressed in the Psalms. Sin is defined in the Psalms as disobedience or rebellion against divine sovereignty. The *Torah* as divine revelation is another major theme in the Psalms. God's words of instruction are to serve as a lighthouse to the surge of humanity adrift in life's perilous sea. The Psalms also frequently address the nation of Israel and their home, Zion,[1] as the people of God. Zion is pictured as the citadel of national and spiritual life, or the center of the universe.

The Psalms are a deeply emotive and personal collection of hymns and songs. They portray life on a vivid canvas of imagery projecting the boldest use of language and vocabulary to be found anywhere in the Hebrew Bible.

THE WISDOM WRITINGS

Proverbs, Job, and Ecclesiastes are examples of ancient Israelite Wisdom Literature. The category of "wisdom literature" refers to writings that are centered around the Hebrew terms *hokmah*, "wisdom," or *hakam*, "wise man." Neither the Hebrew Bible nor the Protestant Old Testament canon qualifies the wisdom writings in a special category designated as "wisdom literature." Instead, the wisdom writings are found in the Hebrew Bible in the *Ketuvim*, or Writings, and they are placed in the Protestant canon under the broad category of Israelite poetry. Each of the aforementioned wisdom books reflects the growing understanding of a

---

[1]"Zion" is used throughout the Psalms as a symbol for the place where Israel ultimately communes with God. It does not necessarily refer to a physical place, but rather it embodies life in the dwelling place of God. In the Psalms it often refers to the place of interaction between the people of Israel and God as it describes this encounter in the Jerusalem temple.

larger wisdom movement that developed in nations throughout the Fertile Crescent.

Wisdom writings flourished in Egyptian and Mesopotamian cultures centuries before the wisdom movement occurred in Israel. For these cultures, wisdom is often defined as successful living, or living well. Egyptian wisdom writings often focused on the training of young Egyptian males who were learning the craft of leading or ruling in Egypt. *The Instruction of Amen-em-ope*, with its close parallel to Proverbs 22:17–24:22, is one example of a text filled with instruction for a young noble who is learning valuable lessons to aid in his eventual leadership in Egypt. *The Instruction of Amen-em-ope* is an example of practical wisdom, or wisdom that gives instruction for successful living. Many of the wisdom texts in the ancient Near and Middle East focused on living well by aligning oneself with the existing order of the universe. Other wisdom writings focused on the philosophical issues of existence, such as trying to answer the question of the meaning of life or the purpose for one's existence. This wisdom is often described as speculative wisdom. Speculative wisdom has been identified in most ancient cultures of the Fertile Crescent but is perhaps most well known in the area of Mesopotamia. There are several parallels in Mesopotamian texts to the story detailed in the Book of Job dealing with the suffering of the righteous. Several texts found in ancient Mesopotamia discuss the contemplation of the meaning of life similarly to the query in the Hebrew text of the Book of Ecclesiastes.

The wisdom movement as evidenced in the Old Testament is focused on one central figure, Solomon. First Kings 10:23 describes Solomon as one who "excelled all the kings of the earth in riches and in wisdom" (NRSV). Solomon's great wisdom is explained in 1 Kings 3 as a gift from God based on the wise choice Solomon makes when asked to wish for anything and it would be granted. According to the text, Solomon asks for wisdom in order to rule the people of Israel with wisdom and justice. Proverbs and Ecclesiastes are both attributed to Solomon. Proverbs names Solomon in its superscription (1:1). Ecclesiastes implies Solomonic authorship in the assertion that its writer is "the son of David, king in Jerusalem" (1:1) and in the writer's descriptions of the great privileges that serve as props in his search for meaning in life.

Proverbs. The Book of Proverbs is a collection of various forms of wisdom material gathered together and piece-woven into its present, final form. While Solomon is traditionally credited as the author of Proverbs, internal evidence demonstrates the presence of multiple authors and editors who played major roles in the book's composition. Several names are mentioned in Proverbs as contributing to the book's development. Chapters 25–29 are attributed to the editing work of the sons or "officials of King Hezekiah of Judah" (25:1) during the late eighth or early seventh century. Proverbs 30 is attributed to a certain "Agur son of Jakeh" of unknown origin. Proverbs 31 mentions "King Lemuel," a non-Israelite king, as the author of Proverbs 31:1-9. "The words of the Wise" in Proverbs 22:17–24:22 demonstrate a close affinity with the Egyptian writing known as *The Instruction of Amen-em-ope*.

Like the book of Psalms, Proverbs is a collection, in this case a collection of wisdom writings gathered together and forged into a "digest" of wisdom writings. The Septuagint, or Greek translation of the Hebrew Bible, arranges the proverbs in a different order, perhaps indicating that portions of Proverbs circulated as separate collections prior to their being established as part of the book of Proverbs. Though the proverbs associated with Solomon must be dated to the tenth-century BCE, the final composition of the Book of Proverbs was probably not completed until the fourth century BCE.

The heart of the book of Proverbs is the *mashal*, or simple proverb. *Mashalim*, the Hebrew name for the Book of Proverbs, is the plural form of *mashal*. The *mashal* is a short pithy, aphoristic statement expressing a truth or maxim. Proverbs 13:11 is one example.

> Wealth hastily gotten will dwindle,
>   But those who gather little by little will increase it.   (NRSV)

The material known as the first and second collection of Solomonic proverbs, Proverbs 10:1–22:16 and 25:1–29:27, is comprised of various proverbs that are often unrelated to the proverbs that come before or after.

The content of Proverbs is not limited to *mashalim*. Proverbs 1–9, an introduction to the Book of Proverbs, contrasts Wisdom, who is personified as a lady, to Folly, who is personified as a woman of indiscretion. Dame Folly is portrayed as a prostitute drawing the foolish into her temporal pleasures and misdeeds. Lady Wisdom equally calls for young men to remain faithful to their marital commitments and to live wisely by remaining faithful to the instructions of God.

Proverbs 30 contains numerical sayings that are also distinguishable from typical proverbs or maxims.

Three things are too wonderful for me;
four I do not understand:
the way of an eagle in the sky,
    the way of a snake on a rock,
    the way of a ship on the high seas,
and the way of a man with a girl.   (Proverbs 30:18-19 NRSV)

The collection of Proverbs is drawn to a conclusion with a beautiful acrostic[2] poem (Proverbs 31:10-31) extolling the value of a wonderful wife or woman.

In broad terms, the wisdom of Proverbs is distinctly religious. Many proverbs are concerned with moral behavior and service to God and humanity. In narrow terms, the wisdom of Proverbs is distinctly utilitarian. Success comes from living the right way. One is ultimately successful by aligning oneself with the order present in the world. But underlying the wisdom literature in Israel is the belief that the God of Israel is ultimately responsible for the ordering of all that is, including creation, natural law, and the Torah. Therefore it can be stated that "the fear of the LORD is the beginning of knowledge" (Proverbs 1:7 NRSV).

Ecclesiastes. A second body of wisdom literature traditionally ascribed to Solomon is the book of Ecclesiastes. "Ecclesiastes" is from the Greek title given to the Hebrew book named *Qoheleth*.[3] The word *Qoheleth* is often translated as "preacher," but this conceals the real meaning of the word—"the leader of an assembly." The Book of Ecclesiastes describes a teacher of wisdom who is gathering together disciples to ponder the meaning of life. Unlike Proverbs, with its focus on practical wisdom, Ecclesiastes utilizes speculative wisdom in probing the vexing issues involved in the pursuit of meaning in life. The author of Ecclesiastes offers an unconventional and skeptical view of life that runs counter to the accepted principles of pragmatic wisdom. "Meaninglessness" or "vanity" (Ecclesiastes 1:2 and 12:8) is an *inclusio* in Ecclesiastes that serves as a literary framework and a *leitmotif* for the entire book.

---

[2]An acrostic poem is a poem that uses letters of a given alphabet sequentially for the beginning of each successive line or verse. An English parallel would be a poem using A–Z to begin each verse or line.

[3]*Qoheleth* is also spelled as *Koheleth*. The final "h" is silent in pronunciation.

The author of Ecclesiastes describes his pursuit for meaning in life. He systematically describes his pursuit of all avenues available to one in a position of privilege. Women, wealth, and work have all proved unsuccessful in providing ultimate fulfillment and happiness. The conclusion of this pursuit for meaning is attested in Ecclesiastes 12:13: according to the author of Ecclesiastes, the end of the matter is to "fear God and keep his commandments." All other pursuits are meaningless, empty, vain.

Job. The Book of Job is the only wisdom book in the Old Testament that is *not* related to Solomon according to tradition. Much debate surrounds the origin of the Book of Job. Some scholars claim Job is the oldest document found in the Old Testament while others claim Job was completed relatively late in Israel's history. Debate also surrounds the nationality of Job. Nowhere in the text is Job called an Israelite, though he does worship God, is described as a "righteous" man, and even offers sacrifices on his children's behalf. Many parallels to the Book of Job have been discovered in the ancient Near East. The theme of the suffering of the righteous is a universal theme in many ancient cultures. Job is also considered a masterpiece of world literature; thus, the story of Job has found its way into many modern anthologies of world literature.

The Book of Job is also unique in that it has two distinct literary components. The first component is its narrative framework found in Job 1–2 and 42:7-17. The story of Job is narrated by a storyteller who sets the stage for the poetic dialogues in Job 3:1–42:6. The familiar story describes a certain man named Job who is qualified as upright and complete, a righteous man who honors God in all he does. A heavenly council is described in Job 1:6 where an adversary or court accuser called "the Satan" accuses God of providing a hedge of well-being or protection around Job and his family. The court accuser maintains Job would not serve God if this divine protection were removed. God advocates Job's faithfulness and allows "the Satan" to advance an assault against Job, resulting in Job's loss of his possessions, his children, and his health. In all these attacks Job remains steadfast against these onslaughts. The narrative framework provides an introduction to the ensuing dialogue that takes place between Job and his friends about the proper response to suffering. The narrative concludes in Job 42 by a reinstatement of all that was taken away from Job including newfound wealth and children and renewed health.

The second major literary component of Job is the poetic dialogue between Job and his three friends, Eliphaz, Bildad, and Zophar, followed later by comments by Elihu, a younger person who joins the dialogue along the way, and God's response to Job beginning in Job 38. Job's three friends all advocate a belief in Retribution theology. According to their counsel, Job must be guilty of some egregious sin for God to be punishing him in this manner. Each one of Job's friends advises Job to confess his heinous sin and ask for God's forgiveness. Perhaps a proper confession would allow for healing and the reinstatement of Job's relationship with God that obviously has been broken by Job's sin. Job maintains his innocence despite his friends' insistence on his secret sin. This dialogue continues until God intervenes and ultimately ends the discussion. God upbraids Job for his challenges made against God in the crisis, but he exonerates Job over and against the accusations made by Job's friends.

If the Book of Job is perceived as only a response to the question of why the righteous suffer, the book must ultimately be classified as a failure. Job is never told why the calamities have befallen him, and suffering is described as the result of a gambling God who manipulates the lives of humans at God's whim. The Book of Job does provide a deeper meaning than the one generally ascribed to the work. The theme of the Book of Job can be viewed as maintaining a relationship with God. The story of Job begins with Job portrayed as a worshiper of God who carried out the expectations of religiosity to perfection. Even in the midst of tumultuous circumstances Job did not sin against God or abandon his faith. At the conclusion of Job, however, Job has much more than mere religiosity or the easy explanation that all was returned to him in time; Job now has a relationship with God. The poetic section ends with this tremendous affirmation from Job's lips.

> I had heard of you by the hearing of the ear,
> but now my eye sees you; . . .   (Job 42:5, NRSV)

This powerful wisdom story, then, is a reminder to all that in the midst of struggles and tribulations, God is there. Every saint of God is not promised the restoration of all that is taken from one in this life. In fact, many saints die stricken with horrible illnesses or diseases, so the claims of Retribution theology are ultimately unsatisfying. Job reminds us through any storm, circumstance, or period of pain, however, that God is there.

OTHER POETRY

In addition to the Psalms and the Wisdom Literature, two other books are written in Hebrew poetry: Song of Solomon (also Song of Songs) and Lamentations. These two books are often overlooked in the Protestant tradition. Few sermons or Bible studies are derived from these two works.

Song of Solomon. Song of Solomon focuses on the issue of human sexuality using beautiful love poetry. King Solomon is traditionally described as the author of this work. Though Solomon is mentioned in the first verse, and his chariots are described in 3:6-11, Solomonic authorship is questioned by many. One major challenge to Solomonic authorship is the issue of integrity within the writing. The Song of Solomon describes a monogamous relationship between a lover and beloved. It is hard to imagine Solomon in any context being described as entering into a monogamous relationship, knowing his harem consisted of 700 wives and 300 concubines.

Song of Solomon provides the Jewish and Christian guardians of canonical credentialing with much to consider. These ancient communities ultimately interpreted the Song of Solomon in an allegorical sense in order for it to gain admission into the Jewish and Christian canons. The Jewish community regarded the Song of Solomon as an allegory of God's love for Israel. The Christian community viewed the Song of Solomon as an allegory of Christ's love for the church. In annotations to the text, many English Bibles today include notation and commentary regarding the Christian allegorical approach to the Song of Solomon. The Song of Solomon has also been interpreted as a cultic myth or drama used in Israelite worship services. Its inclusion in the *Megilloth* or festal scrolls in the Hebrew Bible confirms its ongoing use at the Passover festival each year.

Many modern readers are returning to the face value of the poem itself. Song of Solomon is a solitary love poem, or at the least a collection of love poetry dating back to the times of ancient Israel. Its simplicity and beauty affirm the divine blessing human sexuality can be in a proper relationship between husband and wife before God.

Lamentations. Lamentations details the misery the people of Israel underwent during and following the siege of Jerusalem in 587/586 BCE. It is a superb example of Hebrew acrostic poetry. Chapters 1, 2, and 4 are single acrostic poems with each verse beginning with a subsequent letter of the Hebrew alphabet. Chapter 3 is a triplet acrostic with three verses allotted to each subsequent letter of the Hebrew alphabet. Chapter five has twenty-two verses, the number of letters in the Hebrew alphabet, but it is not an acrostic poem. Lamentations represents a highly detailed form of Hebrew poetry. It is remarkable that a writer suffering such great atrocities would undertake the painstaking task of recording in such a highly stylized manner the laments of his people. The Protestant canon places Lamentations at the conclusion of Jeremiah who is traditionally named as its author. The Hebrew Bible, however, places Lamentations with the other festal scrolls of the *Megilloth*. It is used during the observance of the Ninth of Ab, an annual festival of mourning during July or August of each year. During this commemoration, the Jewish people remember the atrocities afflicted against them throughout the centuries.

CONCLUSION

Israelite poetry enabled the writers of ancient Israel to express ideas they otherwise would have been unable to communicate to their readers. From the praises and laments of the Psalms, to the didactic words of wisdom in Proverbs, to the flowering of human sexuality in the Song of Solomon, to the cries of despair in Lamentations, poetry enables the reader to look deeply within the soul of the writer. Poetry allows us to "remember" in fresh ways the pilgrimage of those who lived many centuries ago in a world far removed from our experience today. If we miss the beauty of the form or the skill of these ancient writings, we may ultimately miss the meaning intended by the authors.

Chapter 4

Prophetic Voices in Israel

The Prophets, the final division in the Protestant canon of the Old
Testament, has the greatest number of books of the four major sections
and comprises forty percent of the total books of the Old Testament. The
Prophets division is subdivided into two subgroupings, Major Prophets
and Minor Prophets. Based solely on their length, the three prophetic
books of Isaiah, Jeremiah, and Ezekiel are considered Major Prophets.
The Minor Prophets are made up of the twelve prophetic books known
in the Hebrew Bible as the Book of the Twelve: Hosea, Joel, Amos,
Obadiah, Jonah, Micah, Nahum, Habakkuk, Zephaniah, Haggai, Zechariah, and Malachi.[1]

Navi is the Hebrew word for "prophet" throughout the Hebrew Bible.
It refers to one who is a spokesperson, or one who pours forth God's
message for all to hear. *Ro`eh*, meaning "seer," is an older term for
prophet that was sometimes employed in ancient Israel. It apparently had
become passé even before the time of the United Kingdom under Israel's
first king, Saul. First Samuel 9:9 records that

> (Formerly in Israel, anyone who went to inquire of God would say,
> "Come, let us go to the seer"; for the one who is now called a prophet
> was formerly called a seer.) (NRSV)

This parenthetical note in the text is part of a description of Samuel
during an encounter with Saul. The term is also used in a pejorative way
in the confrontation between Amos and Amaziah at the shrine at Bethel.
Amaziah accuses Amos of being an "old time" prophet, a *chozeh* (a syno-
nym of *ro`eh*) or seer (Amos 7:12). This ancient description and defini-
tion is important because it reflects a presupposed definition many Christian readers bring to these ancient Jewish texts. Many presuppose that the
prophets were principally concerned with seeing the future or predicting
future events. In reality, however, the prophets were primarily concerned

---

[1]As previously discussed in chapter 2, Daniel is considered a "Minor
Prophet" in the Protestant canon, but not in the Hebrew canon. The Hebrew
canon places Daniel in the *Ketuvim*, or Writings. Therefore, Daniel will not be
addressed in this overview of the Minor Prophets.

with providing God's message for the people and times in which they lived. The prophets of ancient Israel were also involved in social activism, often rallying support for those who had no voice in Israel. They faced severe persecution because of their condemnation of common social injustices and economic practices that kept the poor impoverished while the rich continued to live off the plight of the powerless.

The prophets in ancient Israel were also mediators of the covenant made between God and Israel. The prophets carried the responsibility of confronting the people when their lifestyles failed to reflect their covenant commitments. The prophets were also responsible for making sure the king ruled the nation in accordance with God's covenant and laws. Intercession was also considered a task of the prophets. The prophets were charged with taking the plight of the people before the God of Israel, crying out for relief and justice.

Although all the prophetic books are named for male prophets, women did serve as prophets, proclaiming God's message for the people. Five separate texts in the Old Testament describe women as prophets: Exodus 15:20 calls "Miriam, Aaron's [and Moses'] sister," a prophet. Deborah is called a prophet in Judges 4:4. Huldah is called a prophet and provides a prophetic message for King Josiah in 2 Kings 22:11-20 (see also 2 Chronicles 34:19-28). Isaiah's wife is also called a prophet in Isaiah 8:3. Noadiah is identified as a false prophet in Nehemiah 6:10-14. In describing the coming outpouring of God's spirit, the prophet Joel states that sons *and* daughters will prophesy:

> Then afterward
>   I will pour out my spirit on all flesh;
> your sons and your daughters shall prophesy,
>   your old men shall dream dreams,
>   and your young men shall see visions.   (Joel 2:28, NRSV)

Though only a minority voice, it is clear that women did serve as prophets in ancient Israel, proclaiming God's word for the people of their day.

Every nation of the ancient Near East had prophets or religious leaders who served as messengers of their gods for the people. A major feature of ancient prophetic activity was ecstatic prophecy, characterized by bizarre behavior on the part of the prophets. This behavior included unexplainable trances, wild flailing fits of rage, or other unique physical manifestations. Though not commonly recorded by the Israelite prophets this behavior did exist in Israel, as evidenced in 1 Samuel 10. Samuel anoints Saul to be Israel's first king and tells him to travel a predetermined route until he meets up with a band of prophets who are engaged in a prophetic frenzy. Saul is told to join with the band and to participate in the frenzied activity characteristic of ecstatic prophecy and afterwards to do all that he is led to do.

Many of the prophets of ancient Near Eastern nations were associated with a particular shrine. Those wishing to receive a message or direction from a god would come with a gift for the prophet and await the message of their god. The message would often be attained through divination, the act of "divining" the will of a god through an outward manifestation such as pouring oil over water or reading one's palm. In Mesopotamia, a common method of divination was hepatoscopy, the reading of a divine message through the creases and folds of the liver of an animal. Dream interpretation was another common practice. Israelite prophets were primarily concerned with proclaiming God's messages to the people of Israel, but they also shared many of the features characteristic of their ancient Near Eastern neighbors. There is no evidence to suggest, however, that some acts of divination such as hepatoscopy were ever practiced in Israel.

The prophets in Israel are sometimes designated as Classical or Preclassical Prophets. The Classical Prophets are those prophets also known as the writing prophets who are associated with books bearing their names. The Preclassical Prophets refer to a group of prophets who were active in the early history of Israel but did not have books bearing their names. Prophets such as Elijah and Elisha have more material associated with their stories and messages than many of the Classical Prophets but do not have books bearing their names. Instead, the information about these prophets is subsumed in the Book of Kings along with the record of the kingly activities in Israel and Judah. Some of the Preclassical prophets mentioned in the Old Testament include Moses (who, Deuteronomy 34:10 suggests, was the greatest of all the prophets), Deborah, Nathan and Gad (professional prophets who served in David's court, see 2 Samuel 12:1-12), Elijah and Elisha (see 1 Kings 17–2 Kings 13; 2 Kings 6 mentions the development of a prophet's school under the leadership of Elisha), and other professional prophets. There were also many false prophets mentioned, such as the prophets of Baal who challenged Elijah at Mount Carmel (1 Kings 18). This is only a representative list of the Preclassical Prophets. Many more prophets and prophetesses are called by name, and probably many more were never mentioned by the compilers of the written record of the prophetic history of Israel.

MAJOR PROPHETS

The eighth, seventh, and sixth centuries BCE provide the backdrop for the golden age of the Classical Prophets of Israel. The three Major Prophets, Isaiah, Jeremiah, and Ezekiel, serve as representative voices for these three time periods respectively, from the time of the Divided Monarchy to the Exile in Babylon. The Book of Isaiah begins by describing events of the eighth century BCE before later focusing on events in the sixth century. The Book of Jeremiah opens a window to its readers into the late seventh and early sixth century, beginning with the reign of Josiah and ending with Jeremiah's migration to Egypt during the time following the destruction of Jerusalem by the Babylonians. Ezekiel offers a voice from the Exile in Babylon during the sixth century.

The prophet Isaiah serves as a fair sampling of the messages of the eighth-century prophets. Amos, Hosea, and Micah also lived and ministered to the needs of the people during the eighth century alongside Isaiah. The central message of these prophetic books is the theme of social justice. The middle years of the eighth century brought about a period of great prosperity in both Israel and Judah. Under the leadership of Jeroboam II (Israel) and Uzziah (Judah) the people lived in relative peace and prosperity from 780 to 740 BCE. In the midst of great economic growth the eighth-century prophets offered words of warning to those who were abusing others within their own society by unjust economic and social practices. Isaiah 1:16-17 reflects the general call to focus on social concerns as a matter of faith:

> Wash yourselves; make yourselves clean;
> remove the evil of your doings from before my eyes;
> cease to do evil,
> learn to do good;
> seek justice,
> rescue the oppressed,
> defend the orphan,
> plead for the widow.   (NRSV)

This call is echoed by other eighth-century prophets, for example, in Amos 5:24, Hosea 6:1-6, and Micah 6:8.

Isaiah. As recorded in Isaiah 6, God's call to Isaiah takes place in the temple. Isaiah consistently describes God in transcendent terms. He sees God "sitting on a throne, high and lofty" or as "holy, holy, holy," fundamentally apart or different from humanity. Isaiah, the eighth-century prophet, begins his work as a prophet in the year of King Uzziah's death in 742 BCE, serving as a national prophet under the reigns of Jotham (742–735 BCE), Ahaz (735–715 BCE), and Hezekiah (715–687 BCE). There are three major historical events of the eighth century recorded by Isaiah and described from the perspective of a prophet serving as an advisor to the king of Judah. The first event is the Syro-Ephraimitic War of 734–732 BCE involving the attack of Judah by Syria and Israel as a defensive measure to attempt to bolster their defenses against the coming Assyrian invasion. The Immanuel Prophecy of Isaiah 7:1-17 is given in response to the shrinking courage of King Ahaz. Facing the threat of invasion, Isaiah speaks of the coming of a young boy to be born in his day who would serve as a sign to King Ahaz that God is with him. Thus, the name *Immanu-El,* which literally means "God with us." A second major historical event mentioned in the book of Isaiah is the Ashdod Rebellion in 714 BCE. Isaiah responds to this event in Isaiah 18–20. Isaiah 20 pictures the prophet Isaiah parading naked through the streets of Jerusalem for three years as a word of warning to the people of Judah of what will become of them if they join this rebellion against the nation of Assyria. The last event associated with Isaiah is the Sennacherib Crisis (705–701 BCE), sometimes called the Assyrian cycle, detailed in Isaiah 28–32. Assyria, led by Sennacherib, conquered all of Judah except for the city of Jerusalem spared by God's hand by the forethought of King Hezekiah who builds an underground tunnel to supply water for its inhabitants in case of a siege by a foreign army. The dates for the ministry of Isaiah of Jerusalem can be established with relative certainty from 742 to 701 BCE. The record of the activities of Isaiah, the eighth-century prophet, is concluded by chapter 39 of the Book of Isaiah.

There is much debate concerning a proper interpretation of the remaining 27 chapters of Isaiah. Isaiah 40:1-2 begins with a new call to its writer:

Comfort, O comfort my people, says your God.
Speak tenderly to Jerusalem,
    and cry to her
that she has served her term,

that her penalty is paid,
that she has received from the Lord's hand
double for all her sins.   (NRSV)

Gihon Spring from which "Hezekiah's Tunnel"
transported water to the Pool of Siloam within the walls of the city

The transcendence of God so prominently displayed in Isaiah 1–39 is now replaced by the immanence of God. Isaiah 40–66 portrays God as tenderly caring for God's people; words of judgment are replaced by words of encouragement and hope. The Jerusalem temple prominent in the call and life of Isaiah is now described as lying in ruins and devastation, reflecting the time after the destruction of Jerusalem by the Babylonians (see Isaiah 64:10-12). Uzziah, Jotham, Ahaz, and Hezekiah, eighth-century kings of Judah frequently mentioned by name in Isaiah 1–39 are noticeably absent in Isaiah 40–66 and are replaced by a single reference, in Isaiah 44:28–45:1, to Cyrus, a sixth-century Persian king who destroyed Babylon and allowed the exiles of Judah to return to their homeland. Also noteworthy is that the name Isaiah, so prominent throughout Isaiah 1–39, is missing from Isaiah 40–66.

Some interpreters of Isaiah maintain solitary authorship of the book by the eighth-century prophet Isaiah. They maintain if there are indeed references to the sixth century then God must have given Isaiah special revelation to understand and interpret the coming future events. Other interpreters see multiple authors for the Book of Isaiah, frequently arguing for the presence of at least two, but perhaps three major divisions of the book, reflecting writings in the eighth century combined with later writings in the sixth century BCE. Regardless of one's interpretive perspective, Isaiah remains a timeless treasure for understanding how the people of Judah relied upon the God of Abraham in the midst of historical uncertainties. From the Syro-Ephraimitic War to the Exile, God never abandons the faithful, or even the unfaithful.

Jeremiah. Jeremiah serves as a prophet in Judah in times of uncertainty at the end of the seventh and the beginning of the sixth century BCE. His ministry begins in the thirteenth year of the reign of King Josiah (circa 627 or 626 BCE) and continues through his forced migration from Jerusalem to Egypt around 585 BCE. His messages span the reigns of Kings Josiah, Jehoahaz, Jehoiakim, Jehoiachin, and Zedekiah. He is often described as the "Weeping Prophet" because of the great compassion evidenced in the messages throughout the book bearing his name. The late seventh and early sixth centuries BCE saw the decline and final destruction of Judah, followed by their leaders being deported in three separate waves into Exile in Babylon. Jeremiah ministered in a difficult time, often being asked by God to deliver messages counter to the wishes of the king and the people.

His call is recorded in Jeremiah 1. He describes his call as being extended while still inside the womb, relating God's plan to use him from the beginning of his existence. Also related to his personal call is the nationalistic nature of that divine call. Jeremiah describes in his call a boiling pot spilling over from the north. He interprets this boiling pot to be an invading army, later identified as Babylon, which will come and invade Judah. Another famous message from the Book of Jeremiah is the "Temple Sermon" recorded in Jeremiah 7:1-15. In this brief sermon, Jeremiah counters the message of Isaiah, who claims the inviolability of Jerusalem because of God's protection of the temple. Jeremiah warns his hearers not to trust solely in the temple to preserve the nation of Judah. He calls the people to act in responsible, moral ways by being faithful to the covenant made with God by their forefathers. Jeremiah describes God's impending destruction of the temple and the nation of Judah if the people do not return to God with contrite hearts. The people respond violently to Jeremiah's message by seizing him and threatening execution. He is spared when his defenders argue that the destruction of Jerusalem was previously foretold by the eighth-century prophet Micah (3:12) and Micah was not executed for his bold statement. Jeremiah withstands the challenges of his enemies, but is still faced with the monumental task of ministering to his fellow countrymen during the devastation of Judah in 587/586 BCE.

The extant text of Jeremiah is significant because two different versions of Jeremiah are represented by the Hebrew version (represented by most of today's English translations) and the Greek version (also known as the Septuagint, dating to circa 250 BCE). The Hebrew version is approximately 2,700 words or one-third longer than its Greek counterpart. Most of the differences are attributable to words added in the Hebrew version like "Jeremiah *the prophet*" rather than simply "Jeremiah," but one whole section (now Jeremiah 33:14-26) is omitted in the Greek version. Repetitions in the Hebrew text are also omitted in the Greek version. Jeremiah 6:13-15, for example, is repeated in the Hebrew text in 8:10b-12, but 8:10b-12 does not occur in the Greek text. No suitable explanation has been offered for these diverging texts, but many believe there were two early Hebrew versions of the writing of Jeremiah, one transmitted by the Hebrew version followed today, and the second recorded, preserved, and transmitted by the Greek version. Jeremiah is also significant because of his use of a scribe named Baruch who helped record the message of the prophet.[2]

Ezekiel. Ezekiel details life in Babylonian captivity prior to and after the destruction of Jerusalem at the hand of the Babylonians. Ezekiel was taken in the first wave of deportations in 597 BCE, thus demonstrating his high standing in Israelite society. His group of deportees settled at Tel Abib beside the Chebar River (Ezekiel 1:1, 3:15). Ezekiel's name means "God strengthens" in Hebrew. He was a descendant of the priestly families in Israel. Ezekiel is commissioned by God to minister to the battered community of exiles who have lived through the utter devastation of their homeland and now face the daunting task of living in a strange culture far from their homeland, families, and the temple in Jerusalem.

To say Ezekiel was eccentric is to grossly understate the obvious. The texts of Ezekiel are filled with unbelievable descriptions of wild, weird behavior more characteristic of the ecstatic prophets of the ancient Near East than the classical prophets of Israel. In fact, this behavior has led many scholars to view Ezekiel as attempting to revive the traditions of the Preclassical prophets, such as the great miracles of Elijah and Elisha. Others hold to the opinion that Ezekiel suffered from obvious physical maladies such as epilepsy. Ezekiel 4 provides a trilogy of his eccentricities for the reader. In Ezekiel 4:1-3, the prophet is described as playing in the sand (with a brick) building siege works against a city he has made representing the city of Jerusalem. In 4:4-8, Ezekiel is instructed to lie on his left side for 390 days, then turn over and lie on his right side for forty days, representing years of punishment ascribed to Israel and Judah respectively. Finally, in 4:9-17 Ezekiel is instructed to make bread using human excrement for fuel. He protests, based on his priestly lineage, stating this act would prove to be an act of defilement and something not befitting a priest. The text records God's relenting, allowing him instead to use cow dung for fuel. These three scenes typify the activity found in the remainder of Ezekiel.

The message of Ezekiel is summarized in two stages. First, Ezekiel proclaims to those in Exile that Jerusalem will be destroyed. In Ezekiel 1–24, the prophet details the doom coming to the inhabitants of Jerusalem. Apparently, several of those in the exiled community believed their

---

[2]See Jeremiah 36 for a description of Baruch's role in the transmission of the words of Jeremiah.

stay would be a minimal one because the Jerusalem temple still stood. Their hopes rested upon the concept of the inviolability of Jerusalem. Ezekiel encourages the exilic community to prepare for the worst, and to build new lives in their days of bondage. The second and larger section of Ezekiel's message came after the destruction of Judah. His message shifts from a message of doom to a message of hope and restoration. Two great images dominate this shift. Ezekiel 37:1-14 is perhaps the most famous text in the book of Ezekiel. In this text Ezekiel describes in a vision God raising a great army from a valley of dry bones. The message is clear, if God can raise an army of dry, decayed bones to life then there is indeed hope for the exiles in Babylon. Ezekiel 40–48 is another beautiful image of hope. These chapters describe in great detail the creation of a new Jerusalem. Christian readers cannot miss the parallels between Ezekiel 40–48 and the description of the new heaven and new earth in Revelation 21–22. The message of Ezekiel is parallel to most of the prophetic texts of the Hebrew Bible. Wicked activity will be punished, but there is always hope in the faithfulness of the God of Israel. The book of Ezekiel is unique among the prophetic books of Israel. Unlike other prophetic books that give very scant chronological information or data, Ezekiel provides the reader with a well-detailed chronology of the events detailed in the book. Six different verses offer a chronological time line for the events recorded in the pages of Ezekiel: 1:2 begins in 593 BCE; 8:1 in 592 BCE; 20:1 in 591 BCE; 24:1 in 588 BCE; 33:21 in 586 BCE; and 40:1 in 573 BCE. In the pages of the prophets of Israel and Judah, only the Book of Zechariah even remotely approximates this display of chronological concerns.

MINOR PROPHETS

The use of the word "minor" in relation to apportioning value to items or events can sometimes be misleading. This is certainly the case with the Minor Prophets. Though termed "minor," these prophetic texts are invaluable for their understanding of the role and nature of the prophets in Israel. The Minor Prophets are called minor solely for their brevity as compared to Isaiah, Jeremiah, and Ezekiel. In some cases their writings fill less than two pages (for example, Obadiah) while others are significantly longer (Hosea and Zechariah). Collectively, in the Hebrew Bible these books are known as the Book of the Twelve.

(As mentioned earlier, the Hebrew and Protestant canons differ with regard to the Book of Daniel. Daniel is included in the prophets in the

Protestant canon, but found in the Hebrew canon nestled among the Writings.)

In a few cases the Minor Prophets offer very little in the form of historical information or markers for the modern reader to use in the process of knowing the historical context for their writing. Some of the books offer detailed superscriptions that suggest the historical occasion for the writing of the book: Hosea 1:1, Amos 1:1, Micah 1:1, Nahum 1:1, Zephaniah 1:1, Haggai 1:1, and Zechariah 1:1. Other Minor Prophets are relatively obscure regarding their contexts in Israel's history: compare Joel 1:1, Obadiah 1:1, Jonah 1:1, Habakkuk 1:1 and Malachi 1:1.

The themes of the Minor Prophets vary as widely as the different lengths of each book. Some of the Minor Prophets focus on judgment on the nations of Israel and Judah due to their unfaithfulness to God. Hosea illustrates the coming of God's judgment and God's great love for Israel by comparing Israel's relationship to God with the spousal relationship between Hosea and Gomer, a woman of ill repute whom Hosea was instructed to marry. Just as Hosea repeatedly demonstrates his love for his unfaithful wife throughout the story of their relationship, God faithfully demonstrates love for the nation of Israel though Israel is unfaithful to God. Amos and Micah offer words of judgment upon Israel and Judah, respectively, in the eighth century.

Other books in the corpus of the Minor Prophets focus on God's judgment on other nations of the ancient Middle and Near East. Obadiah offers words of condemnation on Edom presumably for pillaging Jerusalem and Judah during the destruction of Jerusalem in 587 BCE. Nahum offers venomous words towards the nation of Assyria, the ruthless nation responsible for the destruction of Israel, who also served as a constant threat to Judah. Joel and Zephaniah both emphasize the coming of the Day of the Lord. Haggai and Zechariah both emphasize the need to rebuild the temple in Jerusalem and reflect the circumstances in Jerusalem following the return of the exiles around 520 BCE. Living by faith is emphasized in the short book of Habbakuk. Habakkuk 2:4 states:

> Look at the proud!
> Their spirit is not right in them,
> but the righteous live by their faith.   (NRSV)

Malachi uses a series of disputations to call the people of Israel back to faithfulness to the God of Israel following the waning of the newness of the rebuilt temple during the middle of the Restoration period. Jonah is unique among the collection of the Minor Prophets. Rather than being a collection of prophetic messages or sermons, Jonah takes the form of a short story based on the account of an actual eighth-century prophet mentioned in 2 Kings 14:25. In this fantastic story, the love of God is demonstrated as available for all nations, including the hated enemies of Israel and Judah, the Assyrians. These varied themes displayed throughout the Minor Prophets all follow similar patterns for writing prophetic literature as found in the Major Prophets.

MESSIANIC PROPHECY AND THE COMING OF CHRIST

Many students of the Bible today view the prophets of the Old Testament only through the interpretive lens of messianic prophecy. In fact, less than two percent of the material in these books is even remotely Messianic in nature. Nevertheless, a common perception today is that the prophets of Israel all held a vision of a young Jewish boy named Jesus who would come and be the founder of the Christian faith. Though most of the prophetic texts speak to the times at hand, there are some texts that do look forward to a better day or age to come.

Israel's hope for a righteous and just king provides the historical background for the development of the concept of the coming of *Messiah*, a term commonly translated in the biblical text as "anointed one." Beginning with Saul, the kings of Israel were ceremonially anointed[3] to serve as God's adopted "son" and official representative on earth. They were commissioned to be the guarantors of peace and justice for the people of Israel. Each king came to the throne of Israel and Judah with the anticipation his reign would usher in an era of peace, prosperity, justice, and righteousness. Rarely did the kings live up to these heavy expectations. These expectations are evident in Psalm 72, a coronation psalm probably written to commemorate the installation of a new king.

The prophets, serving as covenant mediators between the people and God, held the kings of Israel and Judah responsible to the expectations of an anointed one. When these expectations were left unmet, the prophets articulated the future hope of a new day when the king would rule in a manner worthy of his high calling. Thus, messianic hope was

---

[3]"Anointing" in the Hebrew Bible denotes a ritual in which a person is set apart for leadership or service by oil being poured over the person's head. Each king of Israel and Judah was "anointed" by a priest denoting God's blessing or choice for the current leader. See 1 Samuel 10:1-8 or 1 Samuel 16:1-13.

born. The messianic texts were not simply texts telling of the coming of Jesus, but were texts born out of frustration and providing words of encouragement for a new day that, hopefully, would soon come. Following the fall of Judah in 587 BCE, the Jewish people struggled with their national identity and longed once again for self-rule. As they struggled with the task of rebuilding their lives in postexilic Judah, the hope for the coming of a righteous leader began to intensify. Many hoped for a royal anointed one, a messiah who would come as a political figure leading the nation of Israel in throwing off the tyrants who ruled over Palestine and their native lands. Some hoped for a priestly messiah who would lead the people in a religious revival.

The writers of the New Testament along with the early Jewish Christian community believed these messianic expectations were fulfilled by the arrival of the earthly ministry of Jesus Christ[4] around CE 26–30. Following the death of Jesus Christ, the early Christian community poured over the Jewish Scriptures looking for evidence to strengthen their claims against the Jewish community that Jesus was indeed *the* Messiah who came to be the righteous and just King of Israel. This claim is no more apparent than in the later ordering of the Protestant Old Testament canon that ends with the Book of Malachi as opposed to the Book of 2 Chronicles in the Hebrew canon. Malachi 4:5-6 states:

> Lo, I will send you the prophet Elijah before the great and terrible day of the LORD comes. He will turn the hearts of parents to their children and the hearts of children to their parents, so that I will not come and strike the land with a curse.   (NRSV)

Thus, the Protestant Old Testament ends with the expectation of the coming of one—later identified as John the Baptist—who will proclaim the arrival of the long-awaited Messiah—Jesus Christ.

CONCLUSION

The prophetic books found in the Old Testament all speak to the faithfulness of the God of Israel and the continued unfaithfulness of the people of Israel. Though God is often portrayed as willing to destroy Israel for her sin, judgment is always tempered with hope for restoration. The prophets offered the words of the unseen God for the people to know

---

[4]The Greek word *Christos*, or English "Christ," is the translation of the Hebrew word *Messiah*, and means "anointed one."

how to walk properly before their God. The summary words of the eighth-century prophet Micah provide a standard for living that is applicable for every age and generation.

> He has told you, O mortal, what is good;
>   and what does the LORD require of you
> but to do justice, and to love kindness,
>   and to walk humbly with your God?   (Micah 6:8 NRSV)

Part Two

THE NEW TESTAMENT

Chapter 5

The Gospels: Introduction and Context

As we turn to the New Testament, we will be dealing with the very bed-rock of the Christian faith. The New Testament tells the story of Jesus and the rise of the Christian church in response to his life. Moreover, the New Testament was written by Christians for Christians. It contains the earliest Christian writings and has become "sacred" Christian scripture. Of course, it must not be forgotten that the New Testament presupposes the Old Testament and stands in continuity with it. For Christians, the God supremely revealed in Jesus is the same God already revealed in Moses and the prophets, and the Old Testament rightly remains a part of the Christian Bible. Yet, because the New Testament is explicitly Christian, written in response to the coming of Christ, it has shaped, and continues to shape, the Christian faith even more directly than the Old Testament.

Over the next four chapters, we will use the New Testament to examine the origin and early formation of Christianity, but at the same time we will also survey the testament that Christians call uniquely their own. The purpose of the present chapter is twofold. First, we will discuss the nature of the Gospels as sources for knowledge of Jesus. Then we will set the stage for the New Testament story by exploring the historical setting in which Jesus was born.

The Origin and Character of the Gospels

The founder and central figure of the Christian faith is Jesus Christ, a Palestinian Jew known to his contemporaries as Jesus of Nazareth. Born about 6 BCE, he conducted a brief ministry of teaching and healing and was executed by the Roman governor Pontius Pilate about 30 CE. After-wards, his disciples came to believe that God had raised him from the dead, that he was the Messiah ("Christ" in Greek) and Son of God, and that in him the long-awaited age of salvation had dawned. For knowledge of the ministry and teaching of Jesus, we are largely dependent on the New Testament Gospels.[1] The word "gospel" means "good news." In

---

[1] There are a number of additional sources, but they do not add substantially

Christian usage, it was first used to refer to the good news of salvation which God had wrought in Christ. Secondarily, it came to refer to the written accounts of Jesus' ministry—Matthew, Mark, Luke, and John. Inquisitive readers of the New Testament may wonder why it includes four Gospels instead of just one. And why do the four Gospels differ from one another in the way they tell the story of Jesus? And which version is "correct"? A brief introduction to the origin and character of the Gospels will shed some light on such questions and enable a more perceptive reading of the Gospels.

1. *Origin of the Gospels.* As perplexing as the presence of four Gospels in the New Testament may be, it is equally amazing to ponder the fact that at first there were no Gospels at all. Since those who knew Jesus were still living and the early Christians believed themselves to be living in the last generation, there seemed to be no need for written Gospels. For some three to four decades after the death of Jesus, the memory of his words and deeds was preserved primarily in oral tradition. For example, a parable or miracle story would be told in the context of a sermon, a saying of Jesus would be repeated in the instruction of new members, or the story of the Last Supper would be retold during a Lord's Supper celebration. This process had a profound impact on the nature of the material in the Gospels.

For one thing, the tradition preserved only those aspects of Jesus' ministry that had continuing significance for the early Christians, leaving huge gaps in what a historian would like to know about Jesus. For instance, what was he doing between age twelve and the time of his baptism? Also, the tradition was often preserved in isolated fragments with the result that often the original sequence of events and the original setting of Jesus' sayings have been lost. The sequence of events and the grouping of sayings provided by the Gospel writers may often be based on thematic considerations rather than purely chronological or historical concerns. It also seems that the traditions were shaped to address the

---

to the information found in the Gospels. Several early, non-Christian sources confirm the existence of Jesus as the originator of the Christian movement. Numerous apocryphal (noncanonical) Christian gospels are widely considered too late and legendary to provide useful information, although some scholars believe that the Coptic *Gospel of Thomas* may preserve some sayings of Jesus independently of the canonical Gospels. Apart from the Gospels, the New Testament itself contains scant information about the ministry of Jesus.

changing needs of the Christian communities in which they were used. For example, a parable created by Jesus to disarm his critics might be retold and applied to Christian conduct in the church.

Eventually, as the Christian movement spread beyond its Palestinian origins and the eyewitness generation began to pass away, the need was felt to have written materials. Possibly there were some written collections of miracle stories or of the sayings of Jesus along the way. Most scholars believe that the earliest of our Gospels to be written was Mark. Close comparison of the Gospels reveals that Matthew, Mark, and Luke are quite similar to one another. Hence, scholars call them "Synoptic" (meaning "viewed together"). The Synoptic Gospels follow a generally similar outline of Jesus' ministry and contain a large amount of overlapping content with close verbal similarities. John, by contrast, follows a very different chronology and includes very few passages with parallels in the Synoptics, and even those do not display the degree of verbal similarities seen among the Synoptics. Most scholars account for the similarities among the Synoptics by assuming that Mark, the shortest and least polished of the Gospels, was written first and that it then became a source for Matthew and Luke, both of which include most of Mark's material. As a second source, Matthew and Luke seem also to have incorporated a hypothetical written collection of sayings of Jesus, commonly referred to as "Q" (perhaps so named after German *Quelle*, "source"). In addition, Matthew and Luke each include a significant amount of unique material drawn from each writer's distinctive sources or traditions. This overlapping use of sources by the Synoptic Gospels accounts for the close similarities, as well as the differences, among them. Meanwhile, John is not based on the Synoptics or on their sources but was written out of its own sources and traditions, explaining why John is so different from the Synoptics.

Because all of the Gospels were written anonymously, we do not know for sure the names of any of their authors. The titles now associated with the Gospels are not original but were added in the late second century as the Gospels were being collected. They reflect traditions about authorship which were current at that time. While scholars debate the accuracy of the traditional identifications, honest scholarship must admit less than certainty. Nevertheless, it is customary to refer to the Gospels by their traditional titles even while acknowledging uncertainty about their actual authorship.

In any case, the identity of the Gospel writers is less important than recognition of the nature of their role. They functioned not as individual authors composing their own memoirs but as redactors (that is, final editors) editing earlier sources and traditions into final form. The writers worked as skilled theologians who each took the sources and traditions which had come down to them and artistically wove them into a rich tapestry. Their purpose was not to produce objective accounts of precisely what happened but to tell the "good news," that is, to interpret the story of Jesus for the edification of their readers. Each Gospel was written in and for a particular Christian community and was shaped by its author to address the concerns of that community. Each writer selected and arranged the materials to be included, made subtle alterations in wording, and provided an editorial framework—all aimed at producing an account with the distinctive emphases demanded by the situation of the author's readers. The Gospels are not intended to be bare, historical chronicles but rich, theological portraits of Jesus, each bringing out the significance of Jesus for a particular set of readers. This helps explain why we have more than one Gospel and why they tell the story in different ways.

2. *Four Portraits of Jesus.* Mark, our earliest and shortest gospel, was written about 65–70 CE. Traditionally attributed to Mark, who was not a disciple of Jesus but a companion of Peter, the book seems to be addressed to Christians facing the possibility of suffering on account of their faith, possibly in connection with Nero's persecution (64–65 CE) or the Jewish War (66–70 CE). Mark presents a fast-paced narrative with far less teaching material than the other Gospels. After a hurried, itinerant ministry of teaching and healing in Galilee, Jesus journeys to Jerusalem. There the narrative slows and focuses sustained attention on a one-week Jerusalem ministry which climaxes in Jesus' crucifixion and resurrection. Mark strongly emphasizes that Jesus was a suffering Messiah, whose death was "a ransom for many" (10:45), and calls his readers to be willing to take up their own crosses and follow him (8:34-35).

Matthew's Gospel, traditionally attributed to Jesus' disciple of that name who was known as a tax collector, was written about 75–90 CE. Matthew basically follows Mark's narrative, preceding it with a birth narrative (which Mark lacks) and interspersing it with five large blocks of teaching material. The longest and best-known of these five discourses is the Sermon on the Mount (chaps. 5–7). Overall, Matthew was composed with a strong appeal to Jewish readers, emphasizing that Jesus fulfills prophetic expectations and that he did not come to destroy the Torah commandments but to reveal their true intention. The teaching of Jesus is presented as a definitive statement of God's will, obedience to which is of ultimate importance.

The Gospel of Luke and its sequel, the Book of Acts, are also dated about 75–90 CE. Both books are traditionally attributed to Luke, a physician and Gentile Christian sometimes found in the company of Paul. The two books are tied together by prefaces (Luke 1:1-4; Acts 1:1-2) which dedicate the two-volume work to an unknown person named Theophilus. Like Matthew, Luke has a birth narrative and generally follows Mark's outline of Jesus' ministry (although omitting nearly half of Mark). Almost half of Luke is material unparalleled elsewhere, most of which is inserted into the journey to Jerusalem (chaps. 9–19). Luke is written with an appeal to Gentile readers and emphasizes the inclusiveness of the gospel. Jesus is good news for the poor, sinners, outcasts, women, Samaritans, and Gentiles. In the book of Acts, it becomes the task of the church to continue Jesus' work by taking the gospel to the whole world.

The Gospel traditionally attributed to the disciple John is the latest of the canonical Gospels, written about 90–100 CE. Transposing the story of Jesus into a higher key, it allows the early Christian theological understanding of Jesus to come through much more explicitly. Whereas the Synoptic Jesus preaches the kingdom of God and avoids attention to his own identity, the Johannine Jesus rarely speaks of the kingdom and focuses entirely on his role as the heavenly Revealer. John's story begins before creation, alluding to the role of the Word of God in creation and maintaining that the same Word of God was incarnated ("enfleshed") in Jesus. As the Son of God, Jesus was sent by the Father to reveal God to the world. His death on the cross embodies and reveals God's love for the world and provides the means by which he returns to the Father. Repeatedly, Jesus invites his listeners to believe in him as the way to eternal life with God.

Not surprisingly, the Gospel of John has long been considered "the spiritual gospel." Clement of Alexandria (about 200 CE) maintained that after the Synoptics had recorded the "bodily facts" about Jesus, John was inspired to write a "spiritual gospel" to interpret their spiritual significance.[2] It would be an oversimplification to say that the Synoptics are historical while John is theological. All the Gospels contain both

---

[2]Quoted by George R. Beasley-Murray, in *John*, Word Biblical Commentary 36, ed. David A. Hubbard et al. (Waco TX: Word Books, 1987) lxvii.

historical memory and theological interpretation. Yet it remains true that in John the theological interpretation is more thorough and explicit. It is clear that, on the whole, the Synoptics' portrait of Jesus is closer to the historical Jesus. Therefore, the sketch of Jesus' ministry in chapter 6 below will be based primarily on the Synoptic Gospels.

THE WORLD OF JESUS AND THE NEW TESTAMENT

Before turning to the story of Jesus and the rest of the New Testament, it is necessary to set the stage by taking account of the historical and cultural context of that story. The New Testament did not appear in a vacuum. Jesus was a first-century Jew. Christianity emerged out of Palestinian Judaism, then slowly spread around the Mediterranean world, embracing Gentiles imbued with Hellenistic culture. The remainder of this chapter, therefore, will discuss some of the more salient aspects of the New Testament world. We will begin by looking at the political and religious situation of Palestinian Judaism, then we will zoom out to bring Diaspora Judaism and the larger Hellenistic world into the picture. This will not only bring the New Testament to life and help us to understand it historically, but it also will enable us to take more seriously the Christian doctrine of the Incarnation, namely, that in Christ, God entered into human history in a definite time and place.

1. *The political situation.* At the time of Jesus, Palestine, like most of the Mediterranean world, was controlled by Rome. By this time, the Jewish people, with only one brief respite, had already labored under a succession of foreign regimes for nearly six centuries. It was a condition in stark contrast to the promises of the prophets and the hopes of the people. The following survey will provide a sense of the national frustration that developed during those centuries.

a. *Babylonian period (587–539 BCE).* As discussed above in chapter 2, in 587 BCE the Babylonians had conquered Judah (all that remained of the kingdom of Israel), bringing the Davidic dynasty to an end, demolishing the magnificent temple built by Solomon, and taking thousands of Judeans into exile. In spite of this national disaster—which, according to the prophets, had resulted from the peoples' breaking their covenant with God—the Jews survived, reorganized their traditions to form the religion that would now be known as Judaism, and looked forward to a time of restoration and renewal of the covenant (see Jeremiah 31:31-34).

b. *Persian period (539–333 BCE).* By 539 BCE, the Persians had wrested power from Babylonia and gave the Jews in Babylonian captivity opportunity to return to their homeland. Restoration, however, was painfully slow and partial. Many Jews stayed in Mesopotamia, and those who returned to Palestine found very meager conditions. Eventually, the temple was rebuilt and a Jewish community took root, organized around the recently compiled Torah which was brought by Ezra from Babylon to Jerusalem during the Persian period. Yet Judah remained a province of the Persian Empire under the authority of Persian appointees.

    c. *Hellenistic period (333–166 BCE).* Persian control ended in 333 BCE when Alexander the Great, the conquering general from Macedonia, added Palestine to his vast Hellenistic empire, which ultimately reached to the borders of India. Following Alexander's premature death in 323, Palestine was torn between rival Hellenistic kingdoms, coming first under the control of the Ptolemies (Egypt) and then of the Seleucids (Syria). It had been Alexander's ambition to unify the world through a common Greek language and culture, and indeed, during the centuries after his death, Hellenistic culture permeated the Mediterranean world and Greek became the language of international communication. Greek-speaking Jews in Alexandria translated their Hebrew scriptures into Greek, producing a translation known as the Septuagint (250–100 BCE). By New Testament times, the Greek language had become so widely known that it served as a ready-made vehicle for the spread of Christianity. Most of the early Christian churches adopted the Septuagint as scripture, and all of the New Testament books were written in *koine* ("common") Greek, the most commonly recognized language of the time.

KEY DATES IN THE NEW TESTAMENT CONTEXT

587–539 BCE	Babylonian period: Jews in Babylonian Exile
539–333 BCE	Persian period: Jewish return and restoration
333–166 BCE	Hellenistic period: Greek influence and oppression
166–63 BCE	Maccabean Revolt and Hasmonean period: Jewish independence
63 BCE–135 CE	Roman period: New Testament times
6(?) BCE	Birth of Jesus
30(?) CE	Death of Jesus
35(?)–64(?) CE	Missionary work of Paul
66–70 CE	Jewish War with Rome
70 CE	Fall of Jerusalem; destruction of temple
132–135 CE	Second Jewish Revolt

d. *Maccabean Revolt (166–141 BCE)*. Although Alexander intended Hellenism to unify the world, it did not unify the Jews. Many aristocratic Jews eagerly embraced Hellenistic culture, while many ordinary Jews, including a group known as Hasidim ("the pious ones"), devoutly resisted it. In 167 BCE, the issue came to a head when the Seleucid ruler Antiochus IV Epiphanes outlawed traditional Jewish practices on penalty of death and desecrated the temple with an altar to Zeus on which swine were sacrificed. A horrifying persecution followed. These actions ignited the Maccabean Revolt, a quarter-century conflict which, against all odds, managed to win total Jewish independence. This story, which can be read in 1 and 2 Maccabees (found in the Apocrypha), forms the context in which the book of Daniel was written as a call for faithful resistance to the oppressive Seleucid regime.

e. *Hasmonean period (141–67 BCE)*. The Maccabean family (also known as the Hasmoneans) founded a dynasty which ruled for almost a century over a resurgent Jewish kingdom. The Hasmonean rulers assumed the office of high priest and also claimed the title "king." Their military conquests, including Galilee in the north and Idumaea in the south, where the inhabitants were forcibly converted to Judaism, resulted in a Jewish kingdom nearly as large as that ruled by David and Solomon. In 128 BCE, the Jews destroyed a temple of the Samaritans, a rival religious group which claimed to preserve the religion of Moses more purely than the Jews. This contributed to the bitter animosity which characterized relations between Jews and Samaritans from that time on.

In spite of the resurgence of Jewish power, however, many Jews did not see the Hasmonean kingdom as the arrival of the long-awaited golden age. Some objected that the high priesthood had been usurped by a family not of proper lineage; others were offended by the combination of high priest and warring king in one office. Moreover, the Hasmonean dynasty quickly devolved into a morass of self-aggrandizement, Hellenizing lifestyle, and palace intrigue. It is not surprising that several of the Jewish parties known to us from New Testament times had either their origin or early development in this period, as Jews of various persuasions reacted in different ways to the policies of the Hasmonean rulers.

f. *Roman period*. The last period of Jewish independence until modern times came to an end in 63 BCE when the Roman general Pompey took control of Palestine, adding it to the ever-expanding conquests of Rome. By the first century CE, the Roman Empire embraced most of the Mediterranean world and much of Europe. Because all New Testament events take place within the Roman Empire, we will look a bit more closely at this period.

(1) *Administration and Taxes.* Rome allowed the Jews a measure of local autonomy. At various times there was a puppet king or governor appointed by Rome, who was expected to maintain order, tend to Roman interests, and ensure the smooth flow of revenue to Rome. The Sanhedrin, a Jewish ruling council presided over by the high priest, was allowed to administer affairs primarily in Jerusalem on the basis of the Jewish law. Roman control was felt mainly in the presence of Roman troops and in the burden of Roman taxes. Taxes were high and the system of collecting them was corrupt. Most notorious were the duties levied on goods in transit. The privilege of collecting duties in a given district was awarded to the highest bidder, who paid Rome in advance, then made a profit by

---

The exact date of Jesus' birth is unknown. Confusing as it may seem, the best scholarly estimate is 6 BCE, give or take one or two years. This is based largely on the impression given in Matthew and Luke that the birth of Jesus took place shortly before the death of Herod the Great in 4 BCE. Theoretically, of course, according to our calendar system, Jesus' birth should be dated 1 CE. (There is no year 0 in our calendar system. The traditional notation AD stands for *anno Domini*, "in the year of the Lord.") The anomaly was introduced in the sixth century when a calendar was first devised based on Jesus' birth; the calendar makers simply miscalculated. Based on more accurate calculations, we now leave the calendar as is and revise the date.

---

collecting the duties plus a commission. The system was easily abused simply by overestimating the value of goods. Tax collectors were despised by the Jews both because they were assumed to be dishonest and because they collaborated with Rome.

(2) *The Herods.* Most prominent among the puppet rulers of Palestine under Roman control were several generations of the Herods, an aristocratic Jewish-Idumaean family who curried favor with Rome and got themselves appointed to various positions of authority. The earliest and foremost of the Herods was Herod the Great, who was given by Rome the title "King of Judea," an office he exercised from 37 to 4 BCE. He was a strong, capable ruler who maintained order and conducted a strong building campaign throughout Palestine. Besides the building of palaces, fortresses, cities, and a harbor (Caesarea Maritima, which became the

Roman capital of Judea), he rebuilt the Jerusalem temple into a magnificent structure surrounded by acres of courtyards which were enclosed by colonnaded porticoes. At the same time, Herod was a ruthless ruler, more enamored with Roman culture than with Jewish law, who earned a reputation for readiness to assassinate anyone—even members of his own family—perceived to threaten his authority. According to Matthew 2:1-19, Jesus was born shortly before Herod's death in 4 BCE. Upon learning of it, Herod slaughtered the male infants in Bethlehem in an attempt to eliminate this prospective new rival. This episode cannot be confirmed historically, but it graphically illustrates the kind of behavior people had come to expect from their king. Such brutality must have contributed to the perennial longing for a different kind of rule.

At Herod's death, Rome divided Palestine among three of his sons, all of whom were governors, rather than kings. Philip (4 BCE–34 CE) ruled territories to the northeast of the Sea of Galilee, where the population was largely non-Jewish. Herod Antipas (4 BCE–39 CE) ruled Perea, east of the Jordan River, where John the Baptist was active, and Galilee in the north, where Jesus grew up and conducted much of his ministry. It was Antipas who imprisoned and then beheaded John after he criticized Antipas's illicit marriage to his former sister-in-law; he was also suspicious of implications Jesus' ministry might have for his own rule. Archelaus (4 BCE–6 CE) was made governor of Idumaea, Judea, and Samaria—the heartland of biblical Palestine—with the prospect of becoming king if he ruled well. His brutal tyranny, however, elicited such vehement protests that Rome deposed him and placed his territory under the direct control of a Roman procurator.

(3) *The procurators.* Also known as prefects or governors, the procurators were a series of Roman administrators who governed various parts of Palestine beginning in 6 CE. This shift to direct Roman rule was accompanied by a census for purposes of assessing a new tax, all of which provoked a wave of nationalistic unrest. Judas the Galilean, motivated by devotion to God as the only Lord and King, led an uprising which was met by quick Roman reprisal and the crucifixion of some 2,000 Jewish rebels. Sporadic popular rebellions—sometimes led by figures making prophetic, messianic, or royal claims—met a similar fate, as the Romans responded with quick, brutal retaliation. Pontius Pilate (26–36 CE), the fifth procurator of Judea, was involved in several conflicts with the Jews and attacked a band of Samaritans he mistook for revolutionaries. He is best known, of course, as the procurator who

ordered the crucifixion of Jesus (about 30 CE), probably because he feared Jesus was stirring up sedition.

(4) *The Jewish War and its aftermath.* Three decades later, the hostility escalated into a full-scale, open rebellion, the Jewish War with Rome (66–70 CE). Despite some early successes, the Jewish rebels were no match for the Roman legions. The Romans first subdued Galilee, then headed south to Judea. After a long siege, Jerusalem fell in 70 CE, with a horrific slaughter and a total destruction of Herod's magnificent temple. In many ways, Jewish history had come full cycle since 587 BCE—once again the Jews were a people without a state and without a temple. A Second Jewish Revolt against Rome (132–135 CE), led by an alleged Messiah (Simon bar Kochba), failed miserably. Jerusalem was demolished and a Roman colony was established on its site. Meanwhile, near the end of the first century an academy of Jewish scholars in the little town of Jamnia near the Judean coast (sometimes referred to as the "Council of Jamnia") was busy reorganizing Judaism around scripture, tradition, and synagogue.

2. *The religious situation.* With this framework of political events in view, it is necessary also to look at some religious developments in Judaism during this period. Only the most important features can be touched on here.

a. *Synagogues.* Synagogues were gathering places for study, instruction, prayer, and worship. The exact origin of the synagogue is obscure. None appear in the Old Testament but they are presupposed in the New. Most likely they emerged during the Babylonian exile, developed among Jews scattered outside the homeland, and eventually became established throughout Palestine as well. Unlike the temple, which was centralized in Jerusalem, synagogues were found wherever Jews were living in sufficient numbers. Synagogues also functioned quite differently than the temple. Whereas temple activity revolved around the priestly function of sacrifice, which was offered twice daily as well as on special occasions, no sacrifices were performed in the synagogues. Synagogue worship rather involved the reading, translation, and interpretation of scripture along with the recital of prayers. The informality of the synagogues and their openness to lay participation provided a setting in which the early Christians could present and discuss their gospel. The pattern of synagogue worship also influenced the development of early Christian worship.

b. *Jewish diversity.* Judaism at the time of Jesus was much more diverse than it would come to be in the period after 70 CE. Certainly there were central tenets maintained by all Jews: the one God of creation who

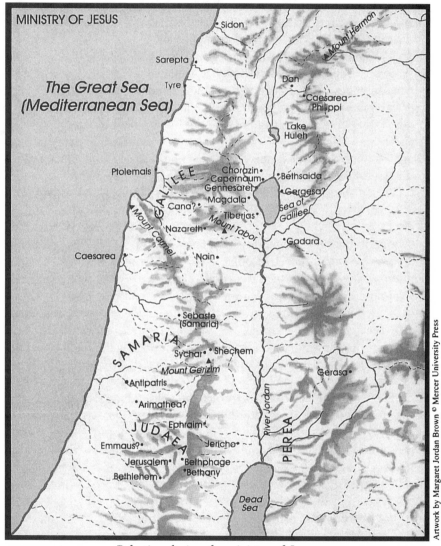

Palestine during the ministry of Jesus

chose Israel, entered into covenant with them, and gave them the Torah (the Jewish law) as guidance for living as God's people. Beyond these, there were many issues open to debate: the content and interpretation of the Torah, how to relate to Gentiles and unfaithful Jews, and, not least, the solution to the problem of foreign domination. Within Judaism there emerged many competing groups with differing views and agendas. Among these, the first-century Jewish historian Josephus describes the following three or four as the most important.

(1) *Pharisees.* The Pharisees were a party of Jewish laymen who had devoted themselves to meticulous observance of the Torah as it was interpreted by the scribes, scholars who studied and interpreted the scripture. Scribal interpretation sought to take the law seriously by working out the rules by which the commandments could be applied to every aspect of daily life and adapted to changing circumstances. During many generations of scribal activity, there had accumulated a significant body of rulings pertaining to various aspects of Jewish customs and piety, such as Sabbath observance, tithing, ritual washings, prayers, and fasting. This cumulative body of material came to be called the "tradition of the elders" or the "oral law." Characteristic of the Pharisees was their devotion to both the written law (Pentateuch) and the oral law. Although numerically small, they had popular influence and were revered as the most exacting interpreters of the Torah. Nevertheless, they were not stick-in-the-mud conservatives but progressive, open to new ideas which are not explicit in the scripture but which could be deduced by interpretation. They accepted such doctrines as the resurrection of the dead, final judgment, and rewards and punishments in the afterlife. They appear to have nurtured the hope for a royal Messiah to redeem and restore Israel. They may also have believed that Israel's subjugation to the pagans resulted from neglect of the law and that the coming of the Messiah depended upon returning to the law. This would account for the Pharisees' contempt for "sinners," flagrant violators of the law, and for the ignorant "people of the land" who had neither time nor resources for studying and applying the meticulous finer points of the Law. It also explains why the Pharisees are so prominent in the Gospels as vocal opponents of Jesus. From their perspective, Jesus not only did not keep the law properly but also was engaged in behavior which would delay Israel's redemption.

(2) *Sadducees.* The Sadducees were drawn from the wealthy ruling families in Jerusalem, including both the priestly and nonpriestly aristocracy. They controlled the temple and dominated the Sanhedrin, which also included a minority of Pharisees. Firmly entrenched in positions of

power and privilege, they had a vested interest in cooperating with the Romans to maintain order. They typically urged caution in protesting Roman policies and warned that rebellion could prove disastrous. Theologically, they were conservative, insisting on not going beyond a literal reading of the Torah. On this basis, they rejected not only the oral law as a whole but also the concepts of resurrection, judgment, and the afterlife. The Sadducees viewed Jesus as a potential troublemaker and were instrumental in arresting him and turning him over to the Romans. With the destruction of the temple and the demise of the Jewish government in 70 CE, the Sadducees ceased to function. The rabbinic Judaism reorganized at Jamnia was largely shaped by Pharisaism.

(3) *Essenes.* The Essenes were a highly sectarian Jewish party, known to us from several ancient accounts. The Dead Sea Scrolls, discovered beginning in 1947 in caves overlooking the western shore of the Dead Sea, are believed by most scholars to have belonged to an Essene group. The ruins at the nearby site called Qumran seem to be the remains of an Essene settlement. If these identifications are correct, then the scrolls and the ruins give us a more complete picture of who the Essenes were. They appear to have emerged in the Hasmonean period in protest of the Hasmoneans' control of the temple. Their "Teacher of Righteousness" led them to withdraw into the wilderness, where they lived in isolation as the "true Israel." Members of the sect surrendered their personal possessions to the group upon entrance and bound themselves together under a hierarchical structure of ranks and a rigid code of discipline. They practiced strict ritual purity, took daily baths of purification, and ate sacred meals. They awaited the appearance of two messiahs, one royal and the other priestly. They expected to participate in a final cosmic war between light and darkness which would establish them in control not only of Israel and the temple but also of the world. The Essenes are not mentioned by name in the New Testament, but many of their beliefs and practices are comparable to those of the early Christians. Their existence shows just how diverse Judaism was at the time of Jesus.

(4) *Zealots.* "Zealots" is a term used to refer to the militant freedom fighters who were ready to use violence to oust the Romans. It is now considered doubtful that there was a single, continuous Zealot party throughout the period of the procurators. Josephus reserves the term for a faction which appeared soon after the beginning of the Jewish War, refused to allow a negotiated settlement, and fought on to the bitter end. Even apart from the existence of an organized party, however, it is clear

that there was a tradition of zeal for God and the Torah which led many to take up arms from time to time. The so-called "fourth philosophy" founded by Judas the Galilean in 6 CE was devoted to the principle that no one but God can be Lord and King, motivating his group's rebellion against the Roman census and tax. There were many royal, prophetic, or messianic pretenders who agitated for violence, apparently hoping that God would honor their efforts by divine intervention. Among the disciples of Jesus was one known as "the Zealot" (Luke 6:15) and two others known as "Sons of Thunder" (Mark 3:17). Among the crowds that followed him there were no doubt many who wished him to lead a zealot-type rebellion (see John 6:15). Jesus steadfastly refused.

It should also be pointed out that there were a number of lesser Jewish parties and, above all, that most Jews belonged to none of these parties. In the midst of this diversity, there were soon to appear some new voices announcing a new day and a different agenda for God's people— the voices first of John the Baptist, then of Jesus and the early Christians.

c. *Jewish future hopes.* It is impossible to understand the New Testament without some awareness of the intense Jewish interest in a decisive future action of God to redeem Israel. The technical term for this concept is "eschatology," literally "the doctrine of last things" or "of the end time." The oppressive conditions of the closing centuries BCE accentuated the development of eschatological hopes. Given the great diversity of Judaism in other regards, it is not surprising to find a variety of future expectations as well. In general, there were two strands of eschatological thought, the messianic hope and apocalypticism, which were often complementary and interwoven.

The Jewish hope for a *Messiah* (from the Hebrew word meaning "anointed one") has already been discussed in chapter 4 as growing out of prophetic longings for an ideal king who would fulfill the royal ideology. During the long centuries of Gentile domination after the Exile, these hopes had grown more urgent but also quite diverse. Probably dominant was the nationalistic hope for a royal Messiah, descended from David, who would liberate the Jews from their oppressors, restore the kingdom of Israel, and rule over it. During the New Testament period, a number of messianic claimants appeared with militant aspirations. The Qumran community expected both a royal Messiah and a priestly Messiah. No one was looking for a Messiah whose role would be to suffer and die. Thus, when the New Testament calls Jesus "the Christ" (from the Greek word meaning "anointed one") it is claiming that he fulfills the messianic hope but, at the same time, allowing that he redefines the concept of Messiah and fulfills it in unexpected ways.

Alongside this nationalistic hope, and sometimes intertwined with it, there arose a more radical, cosmic hope today referred to as apocalyptic eschatology. Apocalyptic writings, most of which are nonbiblical, appeared between 200 BCE and 200 CE, usually in response to some intense persecution or upheaval. Purporting to give visions of the heavenly world or of the end time, the apocalyptic seers typically look not for the coming of a Messiah to restore the nation but for the end of the world as we know it. This evil age is destined to be replaced by a glorious new age to come. The present world order is viewed as hopelessly corrupt. Satan is in revolt against God and has temporarily achieved dominance. This accounts for the many evils in the world, above all for the injustices being inflicted upon God's people by the wicked pagans. No improvement is expected in this age; rather, as the end of the age draws near, it must degenerate into a period of terrible tribulation, an intense outbreak of evil. Since the crisis that prompts the writing of the apocalypse marks the beginning of the tribulation, it ironically is a hopeful sign, signaling that the end is near. Soon God will intervene—either directly or through a heavenly "Son of Man" figure who will appear as cosmic Judge—to set things right. This world will meet a cataclysmic end and a new creation will take its place. A resurrection of the dead and final judgment according to deeds will rectify the injustices of this world. In a reversal of fortunes, the wicked, who prospered in this age, will be doomed to eternal punishment or annihilation; the righteous, who suffered in this age, will be rewarded with eternal life in a new age of bliss. Thus, the oppressive pagan kingdoms of the world are doomed to be swallowed up by the coming Kingdom of God.

The persistence and variety of the Jewish eschatological hopes testify to the deep yearnings of a people who longed for freedom and who looked to their God for redemption. It is important to see the Christian movement against the background of Jewish eschatology not only because the New Testament takes up and presupposes many of its concepts, but also because the early Christians saw Jesus as God's answer to these longings.

3. *Diaspora Judaism.* Our background study so far has focused on Judaism in Palestine, for that is the context in which Jesus and the first Christian church appeared. Before turning to that story, however, we must briefly broaden our scope because New Testament Christianity quickly

moved out into the larger Mediterranean world where it encountered both Diaspora Jews and Gentiles imbued with Greco-Roman culture.

"Diaspora" means "dispersion" or "scattering," and refers to the many Jews who had come to live in scattered places outside Palestine. Sometimes through forced displacement, sometimes through voluntary migration, Jews had come to live in Mesopotamia, Egypt, Syria, Asia Minor, Greece, and Italy. Most major cities had at least one synagogue. Though the difference should not be exaggerated, Diaspora Jews tended to absorb more of the Hellenistic culture than Palestinian Jews did. They typically spoke Greek and read scripture from the Septuagint, the Greek translation produced in Alexandria (250–100 BCE). Some Jews assimilated into the surrounding culture; those who did not assimilate kept the commandments as well as they could, making concessions when necessary.

Although Jews were sometimes ridiculed for their peculiar customs, Judaism also proved attractive to a number of Gentiles, who were drawn to its strict monotheism and high moral standards. Gentiles who actually converted to Judaism—a process involving circumcision, a bath of purification, and sacrifice at the temple—are called "proselytes." Gentiles who loosely attached themselves to the synagogues, supporting Judaism and adopting many of its beliefs but without converting, are called "God-fearers." Both groups appear in the New Testament. The existence of Diaspora Judaism is of tremendous importance to the development of early Christianity. As the Christian missionaries took the gospel around the Roman Empire, the many Jewish synagogues served as natural starting points. The New Testament churches outside Palestine also inherited from the synagogues the Septuagint as their "Bible."

4. *The Larger Greco-Roman world.* The Christian mission, of course, was not confined to Jews, but soon embraced not only proselytes and God-fearers but also Gentiles with no previous knowledge of Israel's God. This brought Christianity into ever closer contact with strange new cultures. The Christian faith had to find ways to relate to these cultures and was itself transformed in the process. Many of the New Testament books reflect this process, along with efforts to guard against losing the essence of the gospel as well. Here we can only be suggestive of the bewildering variety of movements which filled the first-century Roman Empire.

The *Pax Romana* ("Roman Peace") established by Augustus (27 BCE–14 CE), the first Roman emperor, brought the Mediterranean world together in an unprecedented way. The great Roman army maintained order throughout the empire. A network of roads, built and maintained to transport the army, facilitated ordinary travel and communication as well. A Roman navy patrolled the Mediterranean, making shipping relatively safe from piracy. For all of this, Augustus was hailed by the Roman poets as a savior, temples were built in his honor, and a cult of emperor worship was inaugurated. Even under Roman rule, the underlying culture continued to be Hellenistic. Greek was still the language of literature and of international discourse—hence, the writing of all the New Testament books in Greek.

The early Roman Empire witnessed a great proliferation of religions. By contrast with the optimistic spirit of classical Greece, it was an age of much pessimism and despair. People felt lost and powerless in a vast, impersonal empire in which they had no meaningful voice. They seemed to be at the mercy of dark, mysterious forces which controlled their destiny. Superstition, magic, the use of amulets and charms, augury, and astrology were prevalent as ways of trying to gain an edge. The old official civic religions were still practiced, of course, and were believed to be a source of Rome's great power, but they were increasingly irrelevant to the personal lives of individuals. Of growing significance was a vast array of religions and philosophies which were oriented more toward the needs and well-being of individual adherents. Many of them were created by "syncretism" (the "blending together" of beliefs or practices from different religions), as religions from the eastern provinces were borrowed, adapted, and combined with Greek elements to provide a virtually endless supply of new religions.

Among the intellectual class, old Greek philosophies such as Platonism, Stoicism, and Cynicism, having been transformed into popularized, semireligious philosophies of life, enjoyed wide currency. As wandering philosophical teachers would lecture to crowds in the marketplace or in rented halls, they also had a certain mass appeal. Stoicism in particular soared to great heights of ethical challenge.

Even more popular were the so-called mystery religions, which offered the prospect of personal salvation. The many mystery cults were devoted to various gods and goddesses and frequently centered around the myth of a dying and rising deity. Initiation took place through participation in secret rites through which the initiate ritually experienced the death and rebirth of the god. The initiate was thereby assured of security and blessing in this life and of immortal happiness after death. Especially popular and influential were the Eleusinian mysteries, native to Greece;

the cult of Isis, from Egypt; and Mithraism, a Persian import which was extremely popular among Roman soldiers and eventually became Christianity's main rival. When it moved into the Hellenistic world, Christianity adopted some patterns similar to those of the mysteries. Baptism, for example, was conceived as dying and rising with Christ and coming to share his new life. Therefore, care had to be taken to distinguish Christianity from the mysteries. It is rooted not in a myth but in a historic person, Jesus Christ, who lays exclusive claim to believers and makes ethical demands unknown in the mysteries.

A final category that deserves mention is Gnosticism (from the Greek word *gnosis*, "knowledge"), a highly syncretistic, philosophically oriented group of religions which sought salvation through knowledge. Rooted in a radical dualism which defined spirit as good and matter as evil, Gnosticism rejected the material world as a cosmic mistake. Human beings are essentially divine spirit trapped in material bodies, alienated from and forgetful of their true origin in the realm of spirit. Salvation comes through revealed knowledge, which consists of both the Gnostic myth, explaining the origin of things, and secret formulas by which at death the spirit may escape the physical world and return to God. Gnostic ethics tended either toward ascetic rigorism, designed to subdue the evil flesh, or toward libertine immorality, justified by the irrelevance of the material body. Christianity already interacted with Gnostic ideas in the New Testament period, and their interaction became particularly acute in the second century when fully developed Gnostic systems emerged.

This great proliferation of religions indicates that people were looking for something that could provide security in the midst of all the dangers and uncertainties of life, something that could give purpose and hope to an otherwise mundane or miserable existence. Into this maelstrom of movements came one more—Christianity, from the tiny eastern province of Palestine, proclaiming that God in Christ had acted to meet the deepest needs of humanity.

Chapter 6

THE MINISTRY AND MESSAGE OF JESUS

But when *the fullness of time* had come, God sent his Son, born of a woman, . . . so that we might receive adoption as children.

(Galatians 4:4-5)

The previous chapter described something of "the fullness of time." The stage is now set for the birth of the Messiah. This chapter presents a sketch of Jesus' ministry based primarily on the Synoptic Gospels. Because Mark's account is the earliest and simplest, its outline will be followed wherever possible.

BEFORE THE PUBLIC MINISTRY

Jesus' birth is recounted only in the captivating narratives found in the opening two chapters of Matthew and Luke, both of which are primarily concerned to set the story of Jesus in the context of the long history of God's dealing with Israel and to evoke in their readers a sense that God is about to act again in a decisive way for the salvation of God's people. In spite of the very different ways the two accounts develop these themes, they both agree on the essential facts: Jesus was born to a young Jewish woman named Mary, who was engaged to a Jewish man named Joseph, though the marriage had not been consummated; the birth took place in Bethlehem, a little town just south of Jerusalem, but Jesus grew up in Nazareth, an obscure village in Galilee. Both accounts give witness to the "virgin birth" (or "miraculous conception") of Jesus, which is a way of affirming his special relationship with God, but which should not be construed to mean that Jesus is less than fully human (as if he were half-god and half-human, as in Greek mythology, for example). Jesus' birth in Bethlehem, King David's hometown, connects him to the hope for a Messiah, a new David (see Micah 5:2).

We have scant traditions related to Jesus' childhood and early adulthood. We get the impression he grew up in Nazareth in a religious Jewish family. Luke 2:41-52 tells the story of a family pilgrimage to the Jerusalem temple when Jesus was twelve. He had four brothers and at least two sisters (Mark 6:3). He followed Joseph into the carpentry trade (Matthew 13:55; Mark 6:3). As Nazareth is only about six miles from

Sepphoris, a splendid Roman-style city which served as Antipas's capital, Jesus would have had ample opportunity to witness the luxury the powerful were able to enjoy by oppressing the poor. It is even possible that Joseph and/or Jesus were employed in the rebuilding of Sepphoris, which was razed in 4 BCE after an uprising.

All four Gospels connect the beginning of Jesus' ministry with the mission of John the Baptist, a fiery eschatological prophet who warned of impending judgment which was about to visit God's wrath on the ungodly (Mark 1:1-8; Matthew 3:1-12; Luke 3:1-20; John 1:19-28). John urged people to repent (turn from sin) before it was too late, and those who did repent he baptized, immersing them in the Jordan River as a symbol of their repentance. He warned his fellow Jews not to depend upon their descent from Abraham, for what was required was genuine repentance which results in changed living. John viewed his work as preparation for one greater than he, whose coming would bring salvation for the repentant but judgment for the unprepared. Thus, the Gospels depict him as a forerunner of the Messiah. John's message created quite a stir. People were flocking to him for baptism. Perhaps many saw in John a sign that God was about to purify and renew Israel.

Among those who came to John for baptism was a young Jewish man from Nazareth named Jesus. That Jesus was baptized by John is considered historically certain, since the early Christians would never have invented an event that could seem to imply Jesus' subordination to John. Apparently, Jesus submitted to John's baptism because he agreed with the message that Israel must repent. At his baptism Jesus experienced God's call to a mission of his own and the Spirit of God empowered him for the task (Mark 1:9-11).

Immediately he found himself in the wilderness for a time of temptation (or testing), where he says No to the misuse of his divinely given power for personal benefit, for winning fame, or for gaining political power (Mark 1:12-13; Matthew 4:1-11; Luke 4:1-13). These initial confrontations with Satan seem to foreshadow later pressures on Jesus to be a militant-political Messiah, leading a revolt against the reigning powers and setting up a theocracy (see John 6:15; Mark 8:31-33; 11:9-10; Matthew 26:51-52). That was not to be his mission; the shape his mission *would* take remained to be seen.

THE GALILEE MINISTRY

After the imprisonment of John the Baptist, Jesus returned to Galilee and began an itinerant ministry of teaching and healing. The Synoptics do not say how long this lasted. John's Gospel gives the impression of a three-year ministry punctuated by three visits to Jerusalem. No attempt will be made here to trace a sequence of events. Rather, we will summarize key aspects of Jesus' message and activity.

1. *Preaching and Teaching.* a. *The Arrival of the Kingdom of God.* Mark's Gospel opens its account of Jesus' ministry by summarizing his message as an announcement of the arrival of God's long-awaited kingdom:

> Now after John was arrested, Jesus came to Galilee, proclaiming the good news of God, and saying, "The time is fulfilled, and the kingdom of God has come near; repent, and believe in the good news."
>
> (Mark 1:14-15)

"Kingdom of God"[1] is an eschatological concept, referring to the end-time reign of God which will set things right and bring salvation for God's people. It is widely agreed that this was the key theme not only of Jesus' teaching but also of his whole ministry. Although scholars have debated whether for Jesus the kingdom is present or future, there is a sense in which it is both. In essence, and certainly in its fullness, the kingdom still lies in the future, as when Jesus teaches his disciples to pray, "Your kingdom come. Your will be done on earth as it is in heaven" (Matthew 6:10; see also Luke 11:2). Yet, on occasion, Jesus dares to speak of the kingdom as already present in his own ministry. "But if it is by the finger of God that I cast out the demons, then the kingdom of God has come to you" (Luke 11:20). The kingdom has drawn so near that its power is already breaking into the present as Jesus announces good news to the

---

[1]"Kingdom of heaven," which is frequently found in the Gospel of Matthew, is synonymous with "kingdom of God." Matthew frequently uses "kingdom of heaven" in passages where the parallels in Mark or Luke have "kingdom of God." He is simply being sensitive to the concerns of his Jewish readers. Pious Jews, out of reverence, tended to avoid direct reference to God, using circumlocutions instead. Another example is the high priest's question to Jesus in Mark 14:61, "Are you the Messiah, the Son of the Blessed One?"

desperate and heals the infirm (see Matthew 11:2-6). Thus, Jesus himself embodied the coming kingdom.

In Jesus, the kingdom has come so near that it shapes the present by demanding a response.[2] Jesus invites people to enter the kingdom by repenting and believing the good news (Mark 1:15). To "repent" means "to turn around." Individually this involves turning away from sin and toward God; corporately, it involves abandoning the many alternative paths to national restoration, such as legal and ritual purification (Pharisees, Qumran) or armed resistance (Zealots).[3] Such paths are not only futile but unnecessary, for "believing the good news" means trusting God to establish his own reign. Jesus neither charges his listeners to "bring in" the kingdom nor to qualify themselves for entrance—except by receiving the kingdom and its salvation as a gift in childlike trust (Mark 10:15). "Do not be afraid, little flock," he assures them, "for it is your Father's good pleasure to give you the kingdom" (Luke 12:32).

b. *The Good News of the Kingdom.* The arrival of God's kingdom is good news because it brings forgiveness for sinners and justice for the poor and oppressed. Jesus turned his ministry toward the lowly, the marginalized, and the outcasts of society. He preached "good news to the poor" (Luke 4:18-19; Matthew 11:5-6), the oppressed, the hungry, the powerless. His ministry embraced the sick, the blind, the lame, the lepers. Above all, he was "a friend of tax collectors and sinners" (Matthew 11:19). This label designated a category of sinners whose lifestyle or occupation left the possibility of their repentance and forgiveness in serious doubt. Because poverty and disease were widely believed to be signs of God's displeasure, the boundaries between the categories of the poor, the sick, and the sinners tended to blur, and Jesus' ministry embraced them all.

To many of Jesus' contemporaries, this was the most startling and offensive aspect of his ministry. Rather than targeting a righteous remnant for inclusion in the kingdom, he welcomed sinners freely. An unprecedented time of salvation had dawned in which God was restoring Israel not by purging the wicked but by offering forgiveness to any and all, a

---

[2]See Leander Keck, *Who Is Jesus? History in Perfect Tense* (Columbia: University of South Carolina Press, 2000) 79, 81-89.

[3]On this meaning of "repentance," see N. T. Wright, *The Challenge of Jesus: Rediscovering Who Jesus Was and Is* (Downers Grove IL: InterVarsity Press, 1999) 43-44.

sort of general amnesty, so to speak. Occasionally, Jesus is reported to have said directly, "Your sins are forgiven" (Mark 2:5; Luke 7:48), meaning "God has forgiven them." More frequently, forgiveness is portrayed in word pictures: rejoicing over finding something that was lost (Luke 15:5-6, 9, 23-24); large or small debts being freely canceled (Matthew 18:27; Luke 7:42); the sinful tax collector being justified rather than the pious Pharisee (Luke 18:14).[4] Jesus told the chief priests and elders, "the tax collectors and the prostitutes are going into the kingdom of God ahead of you" (Matthew 21:31). He told the Pharisees, "I have come to call not the righteous but sinners" (Mark 2:17). Even more remarkable is the way Jesus not only declared forgiveness verbally but also enacted it in his treatment of people, most notably in his table fellowship with "tax collectors and sinners." Jesus' table fellowship was highly symbolic. On the one hand, it symbolized acceptance and forgiveness of those with whom he ate. On the other, it celebrated in advance the joy of the coming kingdom because it acted out in advance the "messianic banquet" which was expected at the end time. But as far as Jesus' critics were concerned, he was celebrating with the wrong crowd (Mark 2:16: Luke 15:1-2).

　　c. *The Demand of the Kingdom.* "Your kingdom come. Your will be done, on earth as it is in heaven" (Matthew 6:10). This line from the Lord's Prayer shows that the coming of the kingdom is synonymous with the doing of God's will. The kingdom of God, therefore, not only offers unconditional forgiveness but also demands radical obedience to the will of God. Nobody enters the kingdom by qualifying through righteous deeds; entrance is only by accepting God's forgiveness. Nevertheless, belonging to God's kingdom implies submission to his lordship and, accordingly, demands total obedience.

　　Jesus sets his own proclamation of God's will over against the Jewish law. He does not dismiss the Torah as irrelevant but calls for a kind of radical obedience that transcends it. His ethical teaching tends to simplify, intensify, and internalize the commandments. Like other Jewish teachers of his day, he simplifies the Torah, quoting two passages from the Old Testament itself to reduce its many provisions to the all-embracing Great Commandment:

---

[4]See Joachim Jeremias, *New Testament Theology: The Proclamation of Jesus,* trans. John Bowden (New York: Charles Scribner's Sons, 1971) 114.

He said to him, " 'You shall love the Lord your God with all your heart, and with all your soul, and with all your mind.' This is the greatest and first commandment. And a second is like it: 'You shall love your neighbor as yourself.' On these two commandments hang all the law and the prophets."   (Matthew 22:37-40)

For Jesus it is impossible to love God without also loving one's neighbor. Ritual acts of piety directed toward God are not acceptable unless matched by kindness towards others. So important is love of neighbor that Jesus even reduces the Torah to the Golden Rule—"In everything do to others as you would have them do to you" (Matthew 7:12)—which in itself fulfills the commandments.

Yet this does not mean Jesus was watering down the law to make it easier. Often he intensifies the commandments almost unimaginably, for love often demands more than what the law requires. For example, whereas the law requires love of neighbor, Jesus expects love for the enemy as well (Matthew 5:43-47) and even redefines "neighbor" to include the enemy (Luke 10:29-37). Again, whereas the law allows measured retaliation against an offender, Jesus counsels "turning the other cheek" and even urges aid to the offender (Matthew 5:38-42). In an occupied land, where every act of resistance was met with increasingly brutal oppression, Jesus' way was to break the cycle of violence through willingness to return love for hate. Jesus' words would later inspire the nonviolent resistance of, for example, Mahatma Gandhi and Martin Luther King, Jr.

Jesus also internalizes the law. It is not only one's actions that count, but also the inward motivation and attitude of the heart. For example, whereas the law prohibits murder and adultery, Jesus is concerned about anger and lust as well (Matthew 5:21-22, 27-28). He de-emphasizes the meticulous rules of Sabbath keeping, tithing, ritual purity, and the like to which the Pharisees were devoted and subordinates them to ethical concerns. The purity that counts is not a matter of mere ritual cleansing but of right character and conduct (Mark 7:1-23; Luke 11:38-42).

Jesus insists that his followers must treat others the way God has offered to treat them. To be recipients of God's mercy and forgiveness, they must be willing to forgive others (Mark 11:25), renouncing the judgmental spirit that so readily condemns in others faults conveniently overlooked in oneself (Matthew 7:1-5). He charges them to live now in ways that correspond to the values of the coming kingdom of God, which will turn worldly values upside down. Thus, he urges them to have a detachment from possessions which enables generosity toward the poor (Matthew 6:24; Luke 12:33-34; Mark 10:21); a spirit of humility which declines to seek status and honor but confers dignity on all alike (Luke 14:7-14); an attitude which finds greatness not in domination and power over others but in service to them (Mark 10:42-44). It is not that by adopting such a lifestyle Jesus' followers can make the kingdom come, but that, because in Jesus it has in some sense *already* come, they can enter into it and live now by its standards.

d. *The "Fatherhood" of God.* Nevertheless, because God's kingdom has not fully come, living by its rules in the midst of this evil age can be dangerous. It makes disciples vulnerable to those who would take advantage of them. Indeed, Jesus frequently warns of suffering and persecution. The disciples' reassurance is Jesus' teaching about the "fatherhood" of God.[5] The God whose kingdom is coming is compared to a loving, benevolent father who knows and cares for his children. Jesus assures that God knows our needs even before we ask; that God is more ready than any earthly father to "give good things to those who ask him"; that the same God who feeds "the birds of the air" and clothes "the lilies of the field" is even more eager to supply our needs (Matthew 6:8; 7:7-11; 6:25-34). Jesus addressed God with the intimate word "Abba" (Mark 14:36), an Aramaic word used by children for their own fathers. It expresses Jesus' sense of special intimacy with God (Matthew 11:25-27), an intimacy he also sought to convey to his disciples, for he taught them to pray with the same intimate form of address (Galatians 4:6; Romans 8:15). It is likely that this Aramaic word lies behind the more formal "our Father" of the Lord's Prayer. In this prayer, Jesus teaches his disciples to pray for the coming of God's kingdom. The prayer petitions God for the forgiveness of sins and for provision of daily needs. At the same time, the prayer acknowledges the petitioner's obligation to do the will of God and to pass on God's forgiveness by forgiving others. Turning over to God all anxiety about future salvation as well as about daily needs frees disciples to live in the present according to the values of the coming kingdom.

---

[5]It should not be assumed that Jesus is attributing male gender to God. Rather, he is using an image taken from his culture to express the benevolence of God. In Matthew 23:37 and Luke 13:34, Jesus expresses benevolence in feminine imagery, describing his own desire to care for the wayward people of Jerusalem "as a hen gathers her brood under her wings."

e. *Jesus' Manner of Teaching.* In some ways, Jesus' manner of teaching was as remarkable as its content. Two aspects stand out: parables and authority. Approximately one-third of Jesus' teaching in the Synoptic Gospels is in the form of parables, brief scenes or stories which function metaphorically. Far from mere teaching illustrations, they are works of art which capture the imagination and compel new insight. Jesus used parables both to give glimpses into the nature of the kingdom and to disarm his critics. Two of the best-loved parables of the Prodigal Son and the Good Samaritan.

The Prodigal Son (Luke 15:11-32) is a two-part parable. The first part describes how the younger of two sons shamefully leaves home, emigrates, squanders his inheritance, then returns begging for mercy; the father's lavish, joyful reception of his wayward son—surprising but also understandable—depicts God's forgiveness of sinners who return. The second part shows the loyal older son scornfully refusing to join the celebration of his brother's return; his attitude is like that of the Pharisees who scorned Jesus' table fellowship with sinners, suggesting that the parable may have been told for their benefit (see Luke 15:1-2).

THE LORD'S PRAYER

[This familiar version of the Lord's Prayer is from Matthew 6:9-13. A briefer and less familiar version appears in Luke 11:2-4.]

Pray then in this way:
Our Father in heaven,
hallowed be your name.
Your kingdom come.
Your will be done,
    on earth as it is in heaven.
Give us this day our daily bread.
And forgive us our debts,
    as we also have forgiven our debtors.
And do not bring us to the time of trial,
    but rescue us from the evil one.*

---

*The familiar doxology—"For the kingdom and the power and the glory are yours forever. Amen."—is not found in the best Greek manuscripts. It was probably added later, based on 1 Chron 29:11-13, to round out the prayer for liturgical use. Most modern versions print it only in a footnote.

The Good Samaritan (Luke 10:29-37) is told in response to the question, "Who is my neighbor?" The story tells of a Jewish traveler, mugged and left dying beside the road. Listeners may be amused as a priest and a Levite, fellow Israelites, pass by without helping, but they are shocked when a Samaritan, a despised enemy, out of deep compassion does everything humanly possible to care for the victim. By identifying with the victim who was rescued by the enemy, the hearer of the parable is led to the remarkable insight that even one's enemy must be considered a neighbor. For those rescued by God's mercy, love of neighbor must not exclude anyone, even those who are outside one's own ethnic, racial, religious, or social group.

A frequent response to the teaching of Jesus is astonishment at the authority with which he taught. "They were astounded at his teaching, for he taught them as one having authority, and not as the scribes" (Mark 1:22). With authority he commanded unclean spirits and forgave sins (Mark 1:27; 2:10). He placed his own "but I say to you" over against the word of scripture (Matthew 5:21-48). His use of the solemn formula, "amen [usually translated "truly, verily"] I say to you" (for example, Matthew 10:15—"truly I tell you" in NRSV), to claim certainty and finality for his own words was unparalleled. He claimed to speak directly for God, demanded total commitment from his followers, and implied that entrance into God's kingdom depended on acceptance of his mission.

2. Gathering Disciples. As Jesus went about teaching and healing, great crowds turned out to see him. From among these crowds he singled out a smaller group to be his disciples. A "disciple" is literally a "learner," hence a pupil or follower. The Synoptic Gospels focus special attention on a group of disciples known as "the Twelve." Four of this group were two pairs of brothers—Simon (also known as Peter) and Andrew, James and John—who were fishermen. Jesus called them away from their nets and invited them to "follow me and I will make you fish for people" (Mark 1:16-20). By various accounts, the Twelve also included both a tax collector named Matthew (Matthew 10:3) and a second Simon who was known as "the Zealot" (Luke 6:15). Little is known about most of the Twelve, and even the names of several differ among the various listings (Matthew 10:1-4; Mark 3:16-19; Luke 6:12-16; Acts 1:13). Even so, it is evident that Jesus chose not the educated elite, but the ordinary, the disreputable, and even a few "hotheads." We can also be sure that the number twelve is not accidental but intended to symbolize the twelve tribes of Israel. Jesus' mission is to restore Israel as a renewed people of God. The task of the Twelve is first to spend time with Jesus, learning from him, and then to be sent out to gather others into the kingdom of God (Mark 3:13-15). Hence, the same group came to be known also as "apostles," those who are "sent out" as authorized messengers.

It should also be recognized that Jesus' disciples were not limited to the Twelve. There was a broader group of followers from whom they were chosen. Among these there were some who traveled with Jesus and others who remained behind in their homes. It is especially remarkable that the disciples included a number of women. Luke 8:1-3 mentions by name Mary Magdalene, Joanna, and Susanna, as well as "many others" who traveled with Jesus on a tour through "cities and villages" and "who provided for them out of their resources." On a visit in the home of Mary and Martha, Jesus allowed Mary to sit at his feet as he taught and commended her for doing so (Luke 10:38-42). The inclusion of women among the disciples of a Jewish teacher is highly unusual.

While Jesus does not appear to have organized a "church" in any institutional sense, his band of disciples formed a new community of those who broke ties with the past and devoted themselves wholeheartedly to the kingdom of God. This community later constituted the nucleus of the early Christian movement. Discipleship has also become an important symbol of the Christian life. Being a Christian means more than believing certain things about Jesus. It means following him, living according to his teaching and his example.

3. *Performing Miracles.* The Bible speaks not of "miracles" but of "signs, wonders, and mighty deeds," unusual events which point to the power of God at work. Many such deeds are attributed to Jesus in the Gospels. They can be classified as *healings*, such as the cure of a leper (Mark 1:40-45); *exorcisms*, such as the restoration of the Gerasene demoniac (Mark 5:1-20); *resuscitations*, such as that of Jairus's daughter (Mark 5:21-24, 35-43); and *nature wonders*, such as the feeding of the five thousand with five loaves and two fish (Mark 6:30-44). Jesus had great compassion for people whose lives were broken by disease or infirmity. Such conditions were often regarded as a sign of God's disfavor and sometimes, as in the cases of leprosy and physical deformity, resulted in exclusion from society and/or from worship in the temple. Jesus' healings demonstrate that the kingdom of God is concerned not only with "spiritual" needs but with restoration of the wholeness of life in all its dimensions—physical, spiritual, and communal. The exorcisms

show Jesus as God's agent routing Satan's demons and breaking Satan's subversive power over God's creation (Mark 3:22-27). Jesus' miracles are signs that in his ministry the kingdom of God is breaking into this world. "But if it is by the finger of God that I cast out the demons, then the kingdom of God has come to you" (Luke 11:20). In Jesus, God was at work, setting right the brokenness of the world.

One should not think of these miracles, however, as unique events which prove the truthfulness of Christian claims about Jesus. For one thing, they are not unique. Many Jewish and Hellenistic teachers are said to have performed similar deeds. For another, they do not actually *prove* anything. Jesus' critics witnessed his miracles and could not deny them, yet they accused Jesus of operating by satanic power (Mark 3:22). This is strong evidence that Jesus really performed miracles, for his opponents would have denied them if they could; but it also indicates that miracles in themselves do not settle the matter. More than once Jesus' critics demanded a sign of his authority to teach and act as he did, but he refused (Mark 8:11-12; Luke 11:16, 29-32). To see God at work in Jesus requires an act of faith, and that is what Jesus' critics could not produce because he did not fit their presuppositions.

4. *Engaging in Controversy with the Religious Leaders.* Jesus' Galilee ministry involved a number of clashes with Jewish religious leaders—especially with a group labeled "the scribes and Pharisees"—over a variety of issues. Jesus and his disciples did not observe the regular, biweekly times of fasting advocated by the Pharisees (although Jesus himself fasted in times of spiritual need and did not condemn the practice when performed out of true motivation). When confronted, he explained that it was not a time for fasting, a sign of mourning, but for rejoicing over what God was doing in his ministry (Mark 2:18-22). On several occasions, Jesus gave a more lenient interpretation of the Sabbath rules than was customary among the Pharisees, allowing his disciples to harvest and eat grain and performing cures even when life was not in danger. When challenged, he argued that the need to satisfy hunger and the requirement to perform deeds of mercy took precedence over the prohibition of work on the Sabbath (Mark 2:23–3:6). He took issue with the Pharisees' emphasis on purity rules, for example, in the ritual cleansing of utensils and hands before eating, declaring that even the most meticulous observance of such rules amounts to hypocrisy (mere role playing) if not accompanied by purity of heart as expressed in deeds

of obedience, justice, and kindness (Mark 7:1-23; Matthew 23:25-26; Luke 11:37-44).

Perhaps the most significant area of dispute involved Jesus' attitude toward sinners. When Jesus pronounced that a paralyzed man's sins were forgiven and demonstrated his authority to do so by curing him, some scribes who were present declared it blasphemous, since only God can forgive sins (Mark 2:3-12). Some scholars believe the real offense here was that Jesus totally bypassed the temple and its rituals, which were designed to mediate God's forgiveness, thus presenting himself as a substitute for the temple. Similarly, Jesus' table fellowship with sinners came under fire from the Pharisees because it was diametrically opposed to their own program, which called for restricting table fellowship to those who were ritually pure. From the Pharisees' point of view, Jesus' open table fellowship was celebrating the joy of the coming kingdom with those who ought to be excluded in order to purify the community. Jesus defended his conduct by comparing his role to that of a physician. Just as a doctor is not needed by the healthy but by the sick, so Jesus came "to call not the righteous but sinners" (Mark 2:15-17).

In the context of Judaism, the "righteous" meant not people who are perfect but those who honestly strive to keep the law properly and who make atonement for any failures through the prescribed rituals. As part two of the parable of the Prodigal Son makes clear, God's love seeks to embrace both sinners (the wayward son) and the "righteous" (the dutiful son). But for that to happen the "righteous" must be willing to accept God's merciful inclusion of sinners. Indeed, they must be willing to see their own need for mercy. The parable of the Pharisee and the Tax Collector (Luke 18:9-14) shows that it is not the one who depends on moral superiority to others but the one who says "God be merciful to me, a sinner" who is right with God. Jesus warned those who presumed themselves to be "heirs of the kingdom" that failure to embrace the good news of the kingdom would result in their exclusion from it (Matthew 8:12). At some point, Jesus determined that the challenge of the kingdom must be taken to Jerusalem and laid at the feet of those who regarded themselves as dutiful guardians of access to God.

THE WAY TO JERUSALEM

We do not know how long Jesus' Galilee ministry lasted and no one should claim to be able to reconstruct an exact sequence of events. Mark 6–8 suggests a period of growing tensions and temporary withdrawals from Galilee. Tension is in the air in two ways: Herod Antipas, the ruler of Galilee, has executed John the Baptist and is suspicious of Jesus' activity (Mark 6:14-29; Luke 13:31); and there is growing public inquisitiveness about who Jesus is (Mark 6:14-15). That Jesus had not explicitly been claiming any special role for himself but had been acting with great authority left his identity tantalizingly ambiguous. People were free to fill in the blanks in their own ways or to try to capitalize on his charismatic power and press him into their own agenda. Thus, on one of the withdrawals, some in the crowd saw messianic implications in the feeding of the five thousand (Mark 6:30-44) and, according to John's account, were "about to come and take him by force to make him king" (John 6:14-15), but he slipped away.

According to Mark's presentation, a critical turning point came during a withdrawal to the northeast, near Caesarea Philippi (Mark 8:27-33). As Jesus is questioning his disciples about his identity, Peter declares, "You are the Messiah" (the Greek text of course has "Christ"). This pronouncement, known as "Peter's confession," seems to be the first open declaration of Jesus' messianic identity. Jesus has not been claiming the title "Messiah," and when Peter blurts it out Jesus commands the disciples to silence about it and quickly changes the subject. Evidently, Jesus did not care about titles, probably because there was no existing title that exactly described his mission. He may have avoided "Messiah" in particular because, for many, it carried political and military implications with which he did not want to be associated. Immediately, now using the highly enigmatic term "Son of Man," he announces his intention to go to Jerusalem, where he expects to be rejected and killed. Peter's reaction (he "rebuked" Jesus) shows why titles are at this point premature. What Peter meant by "Messiah" and how Jesus understood his own role were totally incompatible. Only after Jesus' completed mission has redefined "Messiah" will the title become appropriate.

On the way to Jerusalem, the Gospels record Jesus predicting his fate two more times (Mark 9:31; 10:33-34), yet each time the disciples respond in ways that show they either fail to comprehend or refuse to accept it. It may be, as many scholars suppose, that Jesus' intimations were not so explicit as the present form of the "passion predictions" sound. It is surely the case that the disciples did not have the benefit of viewing Jesus' ministry from our vantage point on this side of the cross and resurrection. Yet, even if Jesus' predictions have been made more explicit in retrospect—and even disregarding the possibility of divine foreknowledge—there is every reason to believe that he really did reckon with a violent death. If there were sharp conflicts already in Galilee, they could only intensify in Jerusalem. In addition, Israel's rulers had a long history of rejecting and ill-treating God's prophets, of whom Jesus considered himself the last in a long line (Matthew 23:29-39; Luke 13:33-34; Mark 12:1-12). So Jesus set out for the holy city, aware of the danger that awaited him, but willing to die for the sake of the kingdom.

The Final Week in Jerusalem

Although John's Gospel reports extensive activity of Jesus on three visits to Jerusalem, the Synoptics compress his ministry there into the span of one week. This period is highlighted by a number of significant "symbolic actions" of Jesus in the style of the Old Testament prophets, who not only delivered their messages verbally but often acted them out in dramatic actions. Many of the events of the Jerusalem ministry are commemorated by Christians in "Holy Week" observances during the week before Easter.[6]

As Jesus and his followers approached Jerusalem on a Sunday, there was much anticipation in the air. It was the week of Passover, which brought great crowds of Jewish pilgrims to Jerusalem to celebrate the Exodus from Egypt. Hopes always ran high that this might be the year when God will act to liberate Israel again as in the days of Moses. In an event traditionally known as "the triumphal entry into Jerusalem" (Mark 11:1-11), Jesus made arrangements to ride into the city on a donkey in the style of the Old Testament kings (see 1 Kings 1:38), symbolically declaring himself "king." A crowd gives him a royal welcome, spreading their garments and leafy branches in the road, as we might roll out a red carpet, and hailing him as a royal Messiah. John 12:13 specifically mentions "palm branches," such as had been used in celebrations of the Maccabees' purging of Jerusalem and purification of the temple. If the crowd expects him to stage an overthrow and clean house as the Maccabees did, they will be disappointed. That the "king" rides a donkey, not a warhorse, indicates peaceful intentions, fulfilling the expectation in Zechariah 9:9-10

---

[6]The following account reflects the traditional chronology of the events of "Passion Week." In the Gospel accounts, there are a number of points at which it is unclear on which day an event occurred. There are also a number of discrepancies between accounts.

of a peaceful king who comes not to make war but to end war (Matthew 21:4-5). In Luke 19:42-44, Jesus laments that his nation is failing to recognize "the things which make for peace" and warns that rejection of the way of God's kingdom will put Israel on a disastrous collision course with her enemies. This event is commemorated on Christian calendars as Palm Sunday, which comes one week before Easter.

After spending the night with friends in Bethany, a small village just outside Jerusalem, Jesus and the disciples returned to the city on Monday for one of the week's more fateful events, the "cleansing" of the temple (Mark 11:15-19). In the outer courtyard, known as the Court of the Gentiles, Jesus attacked the money changers and pigeon sellers, overturning their tables and driving them out. The money changers were there to exchange Roman coins, with their idolatrous images, for the local coinage, which alone was acceptable to the temple. The pigeon sellers provided unblemished sacrifices for Jewish worshipers. Quoting the prophets, Jesus accused the temple authorities of turning the "house of prayer for all peoples" (Isaiah 56:7) into "a den of robbers" (Jeremiah 7:11). The action symbolically attacked the temple establishment, but the exact point of the protest is debated. It may have been an attack on the corruption and greed of the temple authorities, who exploited the worship system in order to live in luxury, or an assault on the exclusiveness of the temple, which the prophets had promised would one day have a place even for "the outcasts of Israel" and for foreigners (Isaiah 56:1-8; cf. 2:1-4). Matthew 21:14 has Jesus curing the blind and lame "in the temple," as if to include those the temple system would have excluded. Perhaps Jesus' temple action was an act of judgment against the temple itself; within days, Jesus will predict the destruction of the temple (Mark 13:1-2) and will be accused of threatening to destroy it (Mark 14:57-59; 15:29). In any case, it is not surprising that this event seriously disturbed the temple authorities and precipitated their decision to arrest and execute Jesus. They probably feared that he was about to provoke an uprising with the potential for harsh Roman reprisal.

On Tuesday, Jesus boldly returned to the temple, denouncing the religious leaders for rejecting his message and engaging in controversy with various delegations (Mark 11:27–12:44). Set just outside the temple is a lengthy "eschatological discourse" (Mark 13) addressed to the disciples. This "little apocalypse" outlines expectations for the future: suffering for the disciples of Jesus, the destruction of the temple and the nation, the cataclysmic end of the age, and finally the glorious coming of the Son of

Man with the fullness of the kingdom. Apparently Jesus was not arrested in this setting because the authorities feared that his sway over the crowds could be used to start a riot (Mark 14:1-2). They needed an opportunity to take him away quietly.

By Wednesday they had found such an opportunity. Judas Iscariot, one of the Twelve, went to the chief priests and volunteered to betray Jesus to them, apparently by agreeing to inform them whenever Jesus could be found in a vulnerable setting (Mark 14:10-11). Because Judas's motivation for this conspiracy is unstated, it has been the subject of much speculation. One reasonable suggestion is that Judas perceived Jesus as a reluctant military Messiah and betrayal would force him to make a move. If so, it certainly would not be the last time Jesus' cause would be betrayed by those who thought they were supporting him. In the meantime, while dining with friends in Bethany, Jesus was anointed by a woman with an expensive bottle of perfumed oil, an action Jesus interpreted with reference to his impending death (Mark 14:3-9).

On Thursday evening, Jesus and the Twelve gathered in a borrowed upstairs room in Jerusalem to eat the Passover together (Mark 14:12-25). Passover was the annual celebration of Israel's deliverance from bondage in Egypt; Jesus would give it a new significance. As the meal began, Jesus announced that one of the disciples would betray him but did not specify which one. During the meal, he blessed and broke a loaf of bread, saying,

"Take, eat; this is my body."   (Matthew 26:26; cf. Mark 14:22)

He then took a cup of wine, gave thanks, and said,

"Drink from it, all of you; for this is my blood of the covenant, which is poured out for many for the forgiveness of sins. I tell you, I will never again drink of this fruit of the vine until that day when I drink it new with you in my Father's Kingdom."
(Matthew 26:27-29; cf. Mark 14:23-25)

The meal anticipates Jesus' death the next day and interprets it as a sacrifice that will renew the covenant between God and his people. This "Last Supper" is commemorated by Christians whenever Communion (or the Lord's Supper) is observed and especially during Holy Week in Maundy Thursday services, which may include Communion and even a foot-washing ceremony (based on the account in John 13:1-38).

After the meal, Jesus led the disciples out to Gethsemane (Mark 14:32-42), an olive grove on the Mount of Olives overlooking the temple area. There Jesus wants to spend time in prayer. In a very human moment, he is struggling with what is to happen next. He prays, "Abba, Father, for you all things are possible; remove this cup from me; . . . " (Mark 14:36). Jesus could easily have slipped away into the refuge of the Judean wilderness or called upon crowds of followers for defense—not to mention "legions of angels" (Matthew 26:53), as suggested by the devil in Jesus' initial temptation (Matthew 4:6). But either course, even if successful, would have betrayed the cause of the kingdom. Jesus continued: "yet, not what I want, but what you want" (Mark 14:36). In an act of utter trust in God, Jesus chooses the way of the kingdom and embraces his destiny.

Meanwhile, Judas had slipped away and led a detachment of temple police to the place (Mark 14:43-52). He identified Jesus by kissing him on the cheek, and they arrested Jesus. One of the disciples drew a sword in defense, but Jesus stopped him. The disciples then abandoned him and scurried for cover (Mark 14:50).

Late Thursday night, Jesus was given a hasty hearing before the Sanhedrin, the Jewish ruling council (Mark 14:53-65). After an initial charge of threatening the temple does not stick because of disagreements among the witnesses, the high priest Caiaphas asks Jesus directly whether he claims to be the Messiah. Matthew 26:64 and Luke 22:67-68 report an evasive answer; only Mark 14:62 recounts an affirmative response. In any case, the high priest declares Jesus guilty of blasphemy (speaking words contemptuous of God), and the council concurs. Although blasphemy was a capital offense under Jewish law, punishable by stoning to death, under Roman administration the Sanhedrin seems to have lacked the authority to execute.

Therefore, on Friday morning the temple authorities bound Jesus over for trial before Pontius Pilate (Mark 15:1-15), the Roman governor, who normally resided in Caesarea but came to Jerusalem during feast days because of the potential for disturbances. Before Pilate, the charge against Jesus is sedition or insurrection. The chief priests accused Jesus of calling himself "the Messiah, a king" or "the King of Israel" (Luke 23:2; Mark 15:32), alleging that he was another of the rebel leaders with whom Rome had to deal periodically. Pilate interrogates Jesus as to whether he claims to be "King of the Jews," but his response is evasive and uncooperative. The governor is painted in the Gospel accounts as unconvinced that Jesus is guilty, yet he allows himself to be pressured into condemning him. Given the volatility of the Palestinian situation, the pressure on the governor to maintain order, and the consequences if he should be wrong, his decision is not surprising. In the end, he orders the crucifixion of Jesus and hands him over to the Roman soldiers.

Crucifixion was a horrifying method of execution inflicted by the Romans upon criminals whom they most wanted to make an example, especially provincial rebels and insubordinate slaves. Victims were typically flogged, sometimes so cruelly that death resulted from this alone. They were then fastened, by ropes or spikes, to a wooden cross and left to die from exposure, exhaustion, and suffocation. The process could be agonizingly slow, sometimes lasting several days. Jesus was flogged, mocked by the soldiers, and crucified outside the city at a place called Golgotha (Mark 15:16-41). His agony was comparatively brief; placed on the cross about mid-morning, he was dead by mid-afternoon. As Jesus died on the cross, the Twelve were nowhere to be seen, but a group of women who had followed him from Galilee stood watching from a distance. According to Mark 15:34, just before his death, Jesus cried out, "My God, my God, why have you forsaken me?" This is the opening line of Psalm 22, a lament of the righteous sufferer who is tormented unjustly but is confident of vindication by God. Had Jesus been abandoned not only by his disciples but even by the God in whom he had put his trust? On "Good Friday," as it is commemorated on the Christian calendar, the darkness was too thick to tell.

Late Friday afternoon, Jesus' body was secured by a certain Joseph of Arimathea, about whom little is known, and buried in a tomb, that then was sealed with a large, round stone (Mark 15:42-47). Sundown on Friday marked the beginning of the Jewish Sabbath, which was observed by resting through Saturday.

The closing chapters of all four Gospels, with varying details, report that at the crack of dawn on Sunday morning, some of the women who had been present at the cross went to the tomb, bringing spices to anoint Jesus' body according to the funeral customs. To their surprise, they discovered the tomb had been unsealed and the body was not there. An angel appeared and announced that Jesus had been raised from the dead. Thus, all the Gospels give witness to the discovery of the "empty tomb." There follows a series of appearances of the resurrected Jesus to various disciples in various places. Here the Gospels diverge considerably. In Mark and Matthew, the angel instructs the women to tell the disciples to return to Galilee, where Jesus will appear to them. The authentic text of

Mark ends abruptly at this point.[7] Matthew reports that Jesus appeared to the women outside the tomb and later to the disciples on a mountain in Galilee, where he commissions them to take the gospel to all nations (Matthew 28:16-20). Luke 24:13-35 reports an appearance to two disciples on the road to Emmaus, just outside Jerusalem, and subsequently to the disciples assembled in Jerusalem (Luke 24:36-53). John 20-21 records appearances both in Jerusalem and in Galilee.

It is difficult to arrange these experiences into a plausible chronological sequence. What is clear is that collectively they gave rise to faith in the resurrection of Jesus. This means that the final chapters in the Gospels mark not the end of Jesus' story but a whole new beginning. The resurrection is celebrated by Christians on Easter Sunday, the holiest day of the Christian calendar. It is also celebrated every Sunday, since the Christian practice of worship on Sunday (the Lord's Day)—rather than on the Jewish Sabbath (Saturday, the seventh day)—is rooted in recognition of Jesus' resurrection on the first day of the week. In the next chapter, we will see how this Easter faith became the starting point for the Christian movement.

---

[7]The various endings of Mark beyond 16:8 are considered by textual critics to be later scribal additions. It is also possible Mark had an ending which is now lost.

Chapter 7

RISE AND GROWTH
OF THE CHRISTIAN CHURCH:
THE BOOK OF ACTS

The Christian movement began among a band of Jesus' disciples as a response to his life, death, and resurrection. Christianity was at first essentially a sect of Palestinian Jews who believed Jesus was the Messiah. Soon the movement spread into the Jewish Diaspora and embraced Gentiles as well. Our task in the present chapter is to survey the rise and growth of the Christian church during its formative period, from its beginnings in Jerusalem through the work of the apostle Paul (about 30–65 CE).

The Book of Acts, a sequel to the Gospel of Luke, is our only narrative account of this formative period. Acts paints a picture of the Christian church arising in Jerusalem among Jewish followers of Jesus, moving out into the Greek-speaking world to embrace Gentiles, and finally arriving in Rome, the capital of the inhabited world. A key theme in Acts is that the message of Christ is good news for the whole world. Although written perhaps as late as 90 CE, Luke's account seems to be based on earlier sources and traditions and contains solid information about the earlier period. However, Acts is not an objective, comprehensive historical account in the modern sense but a "theological history," a selective account put together to commend the Christian faith to its readers. It leaves many gaps in what a historian would like to know about the early development of Christianity. Fortunately, Paul's letters, which begin about 50 CE, contain much information that supplements and helps interpret the picture found in Acts; for the period of Paul's ministry the letters are, of course, the primary sources.

THE EASTER FAITH AS A NEW BEGINNING

The Christian church arose on the basis of faith in the resurrection of Jesus. At his arrest and crucifixion Jesus' disciples fled in fear and disappointment (Mark 14:50). They "had hoped that he was the one to redeem Israel" (Luke 24:21), but apparently their hopes were misplaced. Yet soon those same frightened, disappointed disciples had reassembled in the city where Jesus had met his fate, now with a vibrant new hope and conviction. What made the difference is that they had become convinced that God had raised Jesus from the dead. And what convinced them was not so much the empty tomb, which is not mentioned in the earliest sources and traditions, but the resurrection appearances. They had seen him alive again! If he was no longer dead, then God must have raised him. The historian is not in a position to say what happened inside Jesus' tomb, but the transformation in the lives of his disciples is well documented.

Faith in the resurrection stands at the very heart of the earliest Christian confessions and preaching. One of our very earliest recorded Christian confessions is found in 1 Corinthians 15:3-8—written about 54 CE, perhaps before any of the Gospels—in which Paul passes on an early confession of faith which he had received from those who were in the faith before him. The confession, which Paul labels "as of first importance," affirms that "Christ died for our sins" and "was buried"—the burial confirms the reality of the death. It continues that he "was raised" and he "appeared"—six appearances of the resurrected Christ to various disciples attest the reality of the resurrection. The sermon summaries found in Acts, which may be based on traditions of the early Christian preaching, also have affirmation of the resurrection at their core (Acts 2:24, 32; 3:15; 5:30).

Even more important than this bold assertion of the death and resurrection of Jesus is the significance that came to be attached to it, how it was interpreted theologically. It should not be imagined that the full significance of this extraordinary event emerged immediately. Its implications grew and developed over time and were expressed in different ways against the background of various cultures. The following developments can be documented within the formative period and are foundational to the emerging Christian faith.

First, the resurrection meant that God had justified Jesus' mission and message. In spite of the crucifixion, which seemed to say No because no one had expected such a redeemer, Jesus was indeed "the one to redeem Israel" after all. The title "Messiah" (Hebrew), or "Christ" (Greek), which Jesus himself had tended to avoid, now became appropriate—albeit with a new meaning. Jesus' mission both fulfilled the hope and transformed the concept. A Messiah who dies, especially on a cross, was a paradox and a stumbling block to believing in Jesus. It took a tremendous act of faith to believe that the Crucified One was in fact God's way of redemption—the same kind of faith with which Jesus had entrusted himself to God in accepting his fate on the cross.

Not only "Messiah" but other honorific titles were applied to Jesus as well, most importantly, "Son of Man," "Son of God," and "Lord." In general, the tendency was in the direction of ever more lofty acclamations. Thus, the one who had preached the salvation of God's kingdom came to the center as the agent of God's salvation.

TITLES FOR JESUS IN NEW TESTAMENT CHRISTIANITY

(Of the many honorific titles applied to Jesus in the New Testament, four are of central significance. These terms are highly complex and tend to take on varying shades of meaning in different contexts. The following discussion is intended to be suggestive.)

Messiah (Hebrew) / *Christ* (Greek), both meaning "anointed one," identifies Jesus as the long-awaited new king, like David, who would redeem Israel. Jesus was viewed, however, as fulfilling the expectation in an unexpected way, transforming the concept in the process. Among the earliest Jewish Christians this was the most significant title. It was primarily the confession "Jesus is Messiah" which set them apart as a distinct group within Judaism. When the term was translated into "Christ" in Hellenistic Christianity, it tended to lose its force as a title and to be thought of as part of Jesus' name, "Jesus Christ" or "Christ Jesus."

Son of Man primarily identified Jesus as the cosmic Judge who would appear at the end time to pronounce final judgment and usher in the kingdom of God. In the Gospels the term is found frequently and only on the lips of Jesus and may have been Jesus' preferred self-designation. Yet, even if it was what Jesus' preferred, it is not clear in what sense he meant it. The phrase can mean "a human being" in the generic sense and can be a polite way of saying "I"; Jesus may have used it in that way on occasion. In other contexts, the term refers to the earthly Son of Man who has authority to forgive sins (Mark 2:10), the suffering Son of Man who is rejected and killed (Mark 8:31), and the eschatological Son of Man who will come in power (Mark 13:26-27). For Christians, the Son of Man had come and would come again in power at the *Parousia* of Christ.

Son of God depicts Jesus as standing in such close relationship with God that he reveals the character of God. "Son of God" should not be taken to mean that Jesus was physically descended from God (as in Greek mythology) or that he was in any way less than fully human. In

Jewish usage, the term need not imply divinity. In the Old Testament, it often refers to mere mortals—such as the nation Israel or the king—chosen by God for a particular task. In Semitic languages, "to be a son of someone" meant to be like that person. In that sense, to call Jesus the Son of God is to say that his manner of life and his sacrificial death are so God-like that they reveal the essence of God's nature. If we want to know what God is like, we should look at Jesus. In the Hellenistic world, "Son of God" might imply a person specially endowed with supernatural powers; there are echoes of that understanding in the Gospel miracle stories. An early confession quoted in Romans 1:4 holds that Jesus was declared Son of God by his resurrection. Mark 1:11 records a voice from heaven at his baptism calling him "my Son." In Luke 1:35, he is Son of God from birth. Both Paul and John think of Christ as the preexistent, heavenly Son sent by God into the world.

Lord acknowledges Jesus as the Master to whom believers are devoted as servants. In general usage, "Lord" referred either to a human master or to God as Master; it could also be a simple title of respect or polite address (compare "Sir"). In Jewish usage, "Lord" was substituted for the divine name "Yahweh" in reading or translating the biblical text and so came to be closely identified with God. In the Hellenistic world, "Lord" was a frequent title for the many deities worshiped in the various cults. In the New Testament, "Lord" is a very frequent title for Jesus, but it is not always clear in what sense it is meant. When Jesus is addressed as Lord in the Gospels, it is usually a title of respect. The Aramaic prayer *Marana tha* ("Our Lord, come!") recorded in 1 Corinthians 16:22 shows that the earliest Christians called Jesus "Lord," but not necessarily in the sense of equating him with Yahweh. In Hellenistic Christianity, "Jesus is Lord" became the most important confession, affirming Jesus over against the many pagan deities. Here "Lord" clearly takes on connotations of divinity, as when Old Testament texts in which "Lord" originally referred to God are quoted in reference to Jesus.

A second consequence of the Easter faith is that it revealed a positive significance of the crucifixion. There is evidence that the early Christians pondered deeply and searched the Old Testament for light on the paradox of a suffering Messiah. They found sufficient clues to conclude that the death of Jesus was not just a tragic mistake but was "in accordance with the scriptures" (1 Corinthians 15:3). It was, somehow, a part of God's plan of redemption. Perhaps because they were already familiar with the animal sacrifices in the temple and with the concept of a righteous martyr—both of which were thought to make atonement for the sins of the people—they interpreted Jesus' death in similar terms. Christ died "for us" (Rom. 5:8) or "for our sins" (1 Cor. 15:3). Early confessional language speaks of the death of Christ as "a sacrifice of atonement by his blood, effective through faith" (Rom. 3:24-25). This means that Jesus' death is God's way of dealing with sin, wiping it away, and offering forgiveness and a place in the new Israel.

Third, the death and resurrection of Christ signal the eschatological turn of the ages. Resurrection of the dead was not an ordinary event but an eschatological expectation. Jesus' resurrection was the "first fruits" (1 Corinthians 15:20) of the end-time resurrection, which, therefore, was already beginning. The early Christians had a strong sense of living in the last days or even in the overlapping of the ages. This evil age, they believed, is hurtling toward a close. Already the new age of salvation is dawning, and the Holy Spirit is being poured out on God's people. Jesus the Messiah is creating a new Israel of those who repent and receive forgiveness and who live now by the power of the Spirit as they wait for their final redemption.

A fourth implication of the resurrection is the *Parousia* expectation. Jesus has been exalted to the right hand of God as heavenly Lord. From heaven, he has already sent the Holy Spirit as a continuing presence with his people. Soon he will return in power and glory to establish the kingdom of God in its fullness. There was an intense expectation that the *Parousia* (literally, "coming" or "arrival") of Christ was imminent; it could happen at any moment. The New Testament never uses the phrase "second coming" but reserves the term "*Parousia* of Christ" for his future coming. Soon Christ will return from heaven in glory as eschatological Judge. The dead will be raised to face the final judgment, and Christ will gather those who by faith belong to him into the fullness of God's salvation. This gave a sense of urgency to the appeal to fellow Jews to repent and become a part of the new Israel destined for end-time salvation. Soon even non-Israelites (Gentiles) would be invited to join as well.

THE CHRISTIAN CHURCH IN JERUSALEM

The preceding analysis of theological insights unfolding out of the Easter faith gets us well ahead of the story, for those developments did not happen overnight. Here we come back to the beginning to survey the major stages in the evolution of the New Testament church. Acts 1–5, examined here, describes the rise and growth of a Christian community in Jerusalem. Subsequent sections will explore the emergence of

Hellenistic Christianity and its expansion into the Diaspora (Acts 6–12) and Paul's mission to the Gentiles (Acts 13–28).

1. *Birth of the Christian church.* As the book of Acts opens, the disciples are gathered in Jerusalem. Presumably there have already been resurrection appearances in Galilee—though Luke–Acts does not mention them—on the basis of which the disciples have reassembled and returned to the holy city. There, resurrection appearances occur for forty days during which Jesus instructs the disciples concerning their marching orders. In Acts 1:8, he commissions them to be his "apostles," those who are sent out to bear witness to the whole world:

> But you will receive power when the Holy Spirit has come upon you; and you will be my witnesses in Jerusalem, in all Judea and Samaria, and to the ends of the earth.

This thematic verse sets out an agenda which will unfold through the rest of the book. After Jesus' ascension to heaven (Acts 1:9; also reported in Luke 24:51), the apostles and others gather in an upstairs room in Jerusalem, choose Matthias as a replacement for Judas, who has committed suicide, to round out the Twelve, and spend time in prayer as they wait for the promised coming of the Spirit (1:12-26).

Acts 2 tells the story of the Day of Pentecost, a Jewish pilgrimage feast which came fifty days after Passover. The band of believers experience a dramatic outpouring of the Holy Spirit, which fills them with the ability to speak in "other languages." Generally speaking, "Holy Spirit" in the Bible signifies God's empowering presence. In the Old Testament, the Spirit is said to have come upon individuals temporarily to enable them to perform a given task. The New Testament connects an eschatological coming of the Spirit with the resurrection and exaltation of Jesus. The Spirit is now a permanent endowment of God's people, giving them a foretaste of the coming salvation and endowing them with power for righteous living and for performing the work of the church. Early Christianity was a charismatic, Spirit-filled movement. Throughout Acts, the author emphasizes that the church was guided and empowered by the Spirit at every important turn. Here the miracle of speaking in foreign languages symbolizes God's empowering the church to take the gospel to the whole world. Peter's sermon reported in Acts 2 interprets the outpouring of the Spirit as fulfillment of prophecy and a sign that the promised age of salvation has arrived.

Empowered by the Spirit, the apostles begin to preach the good news about Jesus. Acts records a number of sermons preached in the early days of the church. While these speeches in their present form seem to have been composed by Luke—a common practice in Hellenistic history writing—they also seem to be based on early traditions. The recurring themes in the apostolic preaching can be summarized in six main points.

(1) The long-awaited age of salvation has dawned (Acts 2:17, 21; 3:18, 24).

(2) In his ministry, death, and resurrection, Jesus has fulfilled the messianic prophecies (Acts 2:22-23, 30; 3:13-15).

(3) Jesus the Messiah now sits at the right hand of God as head of the new Israel (Acts 2:33-36; 4:11; 5:31).

(4) The presence of the Holy Spirit in the church is a sign of Christ's power as exalted Lord (Acts 2:17-21; 2:33; 5:32).

(5) Christ will soon return to bring the consummation of the Messianic Age (Acts 3:20-21; 10:42).

(6) Therefore, repent and receive forgiveness, the Holy Spirit, and the promise of salvation (Acts 2:38-39; 3:19, 25-26; 4:12).[1]

It is natural that, at first, this appeal was aimed at fellow Jews, inviting them to become a part of the new Israel.

Response to the Christian preaching was mixed. Some believed and joined company with the growing Jerusalem church. Acts 2:41-42 and 4:4 mention 3,000 and 5,000 believers, respectively, being added. Some interpreters have supposed that these numbers are exaggerated. In any case, they should be kept in perspective. Most Jews certainly did not become believers but either ignored or rejected the Christian message. Some, especially the religious authorities, were hostile to the new movement. Nevertheless, a vigorous Christian church was growing in Jerusalem.

2. *A Profile of "Palestinian Jewish Christianity."* The earliest Christians who constituted the Jerusalem church were Aramaic-speaking Palestinian Jews who confessed that "Jesus is the Messiah." They were, in essence, a sect of Judaism, since they did not have a sense of leaving one religion to join another. Basically, they were Jews for whom the Messiah had come. For them, the coming of the Messiah did not mean they should quit being Jews. They continued to participate in Jewish worship in the temple and in the synagogues, to reverence the Jewish scriptures, and to

---

[1]Based on C. H. Dodd, *The Apostolic Preaching and Its Developments. Three Lectures with an Appendix on Eschatology and History* (London: Hodder & Stoughton, 1944, 1956; New York: Harper & Row, 1964) 21-24. See Acts 2:14-39; 3:12-26; 4:8-12; 5:29-32; 10:34-43.

observe Jewish customs such as Sabbath, circumcision, and the food laws. Their reluctance to break with such observances, which marked the distinction between Jews and Gentiles, made it difficult for them to accept the inclusion of Gentiles once that issue presented itself.

As a special movement within Judaism, these earliest Christians seem to have thought of themselves as the new or renewed Israel (comparable to the Qumran sect's self-designation as "the true Israel"). Paul once uses the similar term "Israel of God" (Galatians 6:16). Acts several times refers to the Christian movement as "the Way" (Acts 9:2; 19:9, 23; 22:4; 24:14, 22). The term which became normative is "church," in Greek *ekklesia*, literally "gathering" or "assembly." In the New Testament, "church" refers not to a building, but to the assembly of believers in Christ wherever they happened to gather. In the New Testament period they met primarily in the homes of believers who had houses large enough to accommodate the group. Church buildings as such were a later development.

While continuing to participate in Jewish worship, the early Christians also developed two distinctively Christian rituals, baptism and the Lord's Supper (or Communion). Baptism was a ritual of initiation into the community of believers performed by immersion in water. Prerequisite for baptism were repentance and confession of faith in Jesus. The ritual symbolized cleansing from sin and was associated with forgiveness and the gift of the Spirit. This symbolism can be seen in the climax of Peter's sermon:

> Peter said to them, "Repent, and be baptized every one of you in the name of Jesus Christ so that your sins may be forgiven; and you will receive the gift of the Holy Spirit." (Acts 2:38)

Later, in Hellenistic Christianity, baptism would come to depict also the believer's dying and rising to new life with Christ, as seen in Romans 6:4:

> Therefore we have been buried with him by baptism into death, so that, just as Christ was raised from the dead by the glory of the Father, so we too might walk in newness of life.

The Lord's Supper was a communal meal in which Jesus' words over the bread and wine ("This is my body.. . . This is my blood.") at the Last Supper were recalled. The meal commemorated the saving death of Christ and anticipated the joy of the coming kingdom, as seen in an early tradition passed on by Paul in 1 Corinthians 11:23-26:[2]

> For I received from the Lord what I also handed on to you. . . . "Do this, . . . in remembrance of me." For as often as you eat this bread and drink the cup, you proclaim the Lord's death until he comes.

Acts describes the Jerusalem Christians as developing a remarkably close-knit fellowship. They practiced a community of goods in which the needs of any were met by the resources of all (Acts 2:43-47). Occasionally they encountered harassment from the Jewish authorities, who took issue with their proclamation that a crucified criminal was the Messiah. On several occasions various apostles were temporarily imprisoned and charged not to preach in the name of Jesus (Acts 4:1-22; 5:17-42).

THE EMERGENCE OF HELLENISTIC CHRISTIANITY

Acts 6–12 describes the emergence in Jerusalem of Hellenistic Jewish Christianity, which leads to internal and external conflict, to geographical and ethnic expansion, and ultimately to a Gentile mission.

1. *Diversity and Tension in the Jerusalem Church.* At some point there appeared in the Jerusalem church a group of Greek-speaking Jewish Christians. Their origin is not explained, but apparently they had roots in the Diaspora, where Jews tended to speak Greek. As Greek-speaking Jews they typically would have absorbed more of the Hellenistic culture and would have been less strict in the Jewish observances and more open to contact with Gentiles than Palestinian Jews were. When they became Christians, they began to interpret the new faith in ways differing from those of the Aramaic-speaking Jewish Christians. They eventually distanced themselves from certain Jewish practices and showed greater openness to the inclusion of Gentiles. Thus, the Jerusalem church now had two factions, with language, cultural, and theological differences between them. It is not surprising that this situation would lead to tensions.

Acts 6:1-6 describes a conflict within the Jerusalem church between the "Hebrews" and the "Hellenists," apparently referring to Aramaic-speaking and Greek-speaking Jewish Christians, respectively. The dispute

---

[2]It is unclear whether Acts references to "breaking bread" (e.g., Acts 2:42, 46) refer to the Lord's Supper or to common meals. In any case, Paul's letters are earlier than Acts and Paul passes on to the Corinthians a tradition that was earlier still.

has to do with charity relief for widows, with respect to which the Hellenists complain that their widows are being neglected. The issue is quickly resolved by the selection of seven men to oversee the charity operation. Interestingly, all of "the Seven" have Greek names and probably were leaders of the Hellenists. Stephen, in particular, stands out as a key leader, and the story now focuses on him.

2. *The Martyrdom of Stephen and the Persecution of the Church.* As Acts 6 continues, Stephen functions not merely as a coordinator of food distribution but as a powerful preacher of the gospel. His witness to Jesus in the Greek-speaking synagogues stirs up a hornet's nest of opposition among Diaspora Jews living in Jerusalem. Soon he finds himself hauled before the Sanhedrin on charges of speaking blasphemous words against the temple and the Torah and of advocating that Jesus will destroy the temple and change the Jewish customs (Acts 6:13-14). The accusation suggests that Stephen was questioning the necessity of certain Jewish rituals now that the Messiah has come. If so, it would readily account for the outrage against Stephen, which surpasses any opposition the Twelve had faced up to this point.

In Acts 7, Stephen makes a lengthy defense that turns into a harsh attack on his accusers. His speech, which rehearses a good bit of Old Testament history, calls into question the presumed Jewish privileges of Torah and temple—declaring that Israel has a long record of disobeying the former and that God is not confined to the latter. At this, Stephen's adversaries pounce upon him, drag him outside the city, and stone him to death (Acts 7:54–8:1). Thus, Stephen becomes, as far as we know, the first Christian martyr. Interpreters frequently draw attention to parallels between Stephen's execution and that of Jesus and to the Christ-like manner in which Stephen died with a prayer for the forgiveness of his attackers on his lips. Present and approving of this action is "a young man named Saul," who will become better known as the apostle Paul.

In the wake of the action against Stephen, an intense persecution broke out against the Jerusalem church, in which Saul/Paul again was active (Acts 8:1-3). This attack seems to have targeted in particular the Hellenistic Jewish Christians because of their more progressive stance in questioning Jewish practices and privilege. If they were already advocating freedom in Christ to abandon practices such as circumcision, the food laws, and Sabbath—the very rituals that marked Jews as distinct from Gentiles—they would have appeared quite offensive and threatening to the Jewish religious establishment. They would also have been preparing the way for the eventual inclusion of Gentiles. In any case, they apparently bore the brunt of the persecution and were scattered into the countryside, while "the apostles," representing the more conservative Palestinian Jewish Christians, remained in Jerusalem.

3. *Geographic and Ethnic Expansion.* Ironically, the persecution did not result in suppressing the movement but in forcing it to spread, as "those who were scattered went from place to place, proclaiming the word" (Acts 8:4). The next few chapters in Acts trace out the beginnings of the expansion of the gospel, mainly through the efforts of the Hellenistic Christians as they fled back into the Diaspora. Philip, one of the Seven, traveled to Samaria and began a successful mission there (Acts 8:5-25). This represented not only a geographical expansion but the crossing of a significant ethnic boundary, since Jews and Samaritans were distant cousins but bitter enemies. Subsequently, Philip broke additional barriers when he baptized an Ethiopian eunuch, who, because of his physical deformity, would not have been eligible for conversion to Judaism (Acts 8:26-40). From the story of Paul's conversion near Damascus (Acts 9:1-22), to be examined later, we learn that a church now existed in that Syrian city, likely also planted by Hellenistic Christians fleeing the persecution in Jerusalem.

Meanwhile, Acts interrupts the story of the Hellenists to show that the Aramaic-speaking church in Jerusalem also was taking some tentative steps toward expansion. After a tour through the coastal cities of Palestine (Acts 9:32-43), Peter took the bold step of evangelizing the Gentile Cornelius (Acts 10:1-48). Cornelius, a Roman army officer stationed in Caesarea, was a "God-fearer," a Gentile who revered Israel's God but had not converted to Judaism. As a Palestinian Jew, Peter considered Gentiles to be unclean, godless sinners, with whom he should avoid close contact. The Acts account dramatically describes how a series of visions overcome Peter's prejudice and bring Peter and Cornelius together. In Acts 10:28, 34-35, Peter's new insight is expressed in these words:

> "You yourselves know that it is unlawful for a Jew to associate with or to visit a Gentile; but God has shown me that I should not call anyone profane or unclean." . . . "I truly understand that God shows no partiality, but in every nation anyone who fears him and does what is right is acceptable to him."

Upon hearing the message of Jesus, Cornelius and his household receive the Holy Spirit and are baptized. Afterwards, the Jerusalem church reluctantly accepts what Peter has done but does not take up the cause of pursuing a Gentile mission (Acts 11:1-18). That cause would be championed, rather, by the Hellenistic Christians.

The first real Gentile mission came in Antioch, a large, cosmopolitan city in northern Syria (Acts 11:19-26).[3] Here Acts resumes the account of the progress made by the Hellenistic Jewish Christians as they fled the persecution in Jerusalem. Some of the Hellenists had traveled to places like Samaria, Damascus, Phoenicia, and Cyprus, still preaching to fellow Jews. Now others of them arrived in Antioch and began something new— a deliberate, concerted mission to the Gentiles. And it was successful. The Hellenists' openness to abandoning the rituals that defined Jewish distinctiveness finally issued in the full inclusion of Gentiles. There grew up in Antioch a church that freely included Jewish Christians and Gentile Christians together. Gentile converts were not required to be circumcised. Jewish and Gentile Christians ate together without regard for the Jewish food laws.

This was something new, and it may not be an accident that "it was in Antioch that the disciples were first called 'Christians' " (Acts 11:26). This new name, meaning "partisans of Christ"—which out of convenience we have already used anachronistically in describing the earlier period— appears to have been coined by outsiders. Found only twice more in the New Testament (Acts 26:28; 1 Peter 4:16), "Christians" was not embraced as a regular self-designation until the second and third centuries.

The Antioch church was the first church situated in a major cosmopolitan city. It quickly became a center of Hellenistic Christianity and the base of a broader Gentile mission. As the Christian movement penetrated the Hellenistic world, it would face the double challenge of fighting for the right to include Gentiles without imposing Jewish customs on them and of finding ways to express the gospel in terms of Hellenistic culture without compromising the essence of the faith in the process. When the Jerusalem Christians learned of the bold developments in Antioch, they sent Barnabas to work with the new church. He, in turn, recruited Saul/Paul, who by now had become a Christian apostle and perhaps was already engaged in evangelizing Gentiles. It is hard to imagine a better choice for spearheading the work which lay ahead.

---

[3]Chronologically, it is unclear whether the conversion of Cornelius or the Antioch mission to the Gentiles came first. Luke may have placed the Cornelius story first for thematic purposes. In any case, the Gentile mission in Antioch was the first deliberate, sustained effort.

PAUL AND THE SPREAD OF THE GOSPEL TO THE GENTILES

Apart from Jesus himself, nobody in the New Testament looms larger than the apostle Paul. About one-third of the New Testament is connected to his name, including thirteen Pauline letters and Acts 13–28, which details his missionary journeys. He is the most ambitious and successful missionary and churchplanter in this period of whom we have record. Paul is also widely regarded as the most profound theological thinker in the early church, and his letters have served as a major source of Christian theology.

1. *Paul's Background and Conversion.* Paul's background in two cultures ideally fitted him to become the "apostle to the Gentiles" (Romans 11:13). On the one hand, he was a native of Tarsus, a Greek city in southeastern Asia Minor, which was a center of Stoic philosophy and other schools of Greek learning. In many ways, Paul shows familiarity not only with Stoic ethical teaching and Greek rhetoric, but with Hellenistic culture more generally. His first language was Greek; he readily draws illustrations from the military and athletics; he was a Roman citizen, which provided a certain stature and legal rights. On the other hand, Paul was a devout Jew, probably more meticulous in observing the Torah than was typical in the Diaspora. He had become a Pharisee and had studied in Jerusalem under Gamaliel, perhaps the most eminent Jewish teacher at the time.

This dual cultural heritage is reflected in Paul's two names. There is a popular misconception that "Saul" and "Paul" are pre- and post-Christian names, as if Saul changed his name to "Paul" at his conversion. Rather, they are Jewish and Greco-Roman names, respectively, reflecting the two cultures in which Paul moved. Many Hellenistic Jews had such dual names. Acts 13:9, which first introduces the name "Paul" into the narrative, does not say Saul changed his name but that Saul was "also known as Paul," and the context here is not the conversion but more than a decade later on the first missionary journey.

Prior to his becoming a Christian, Paul had been a vehement opponent of the new movement. In Acts, he first appears playing a minor role in the stoning of Stephen (Acts 7:58), then as a leader of the persecution in Jerusalem (Acts 8:3), and finally is seen headed to Damascus looking for Christians there (Acts 9:1-2). In the letters, Paul attributes his persecution of the church to his "zeal" for the Jewish law (Galatians 1:13-14; Philippians 3:5-6). He had judged Christianity to be in conflict with the law, perhaps because Christians proclaimed as Messiah a crucified criminal whom the law declared accursed by God (see Deuteronomy 21:23, quoted in Galatians 3:13). Or perhaps he saw in Christianity the seeds of abandonment of the Jewish customs and openness to Gentiles (see Deuteronomy 27:26, quoted in Galatians 3:10). In any case, as a Pharisee, he was devoted to destroying the Christian church.

According to Acts, Paul's "conversion" came on the road to Damascus as he traveled there with the intention of continuing his persecution (Acts 9:3-22; retold in 22:4-16 and 26:9-18). Just before arriving in Damascus, he was struck down by a blinding light and the voice of Jesus speaking to him:

> "Saul, Saul, why do you persecute me?" . . . "I am Jesus, whom you are persecuting. But get up and enter the city, and you will be told what you are to do." (Acts 9:4-6)

Now convinced of the resurrection of Jesus, Paul was received by the Damascus church and baptized into the community of believers. In his letters, Paul describes his encounter with the risen Christ less as a "conversion" from one religion to another than as a "call" to be an apostle, comparable to the calling of the Old Testament prophets. The risen Christ had appeared to him, just as to the other apostles, and had made him an apostle as well (1 Corinthians 15:8-10; Galatians 1:15-17). Paul's conversion also gave him a new perspective on the Jewish law. He now believed that the death and resurrection of Christ provided the basis for a new kind of righteousness unavailable through the law and that it is equally open to Jews and Gentiles alike (Philippians 3:2-9). The persecutor of the church had become the "apostle to the Gentiles" (Romans 11:13).

2. Paul's Missionary Journeys. Following Paul's conversion, he drops out of our sources for more than a decade. We get only vague references to his presence in Arabia and in Syria and Cilicia (Galatians 1:17, 21). Likely, he was already engaged in evangelism, but we have no information about it. When the apostle comes to light again, it is in connection with the Hellenistic church in Antioch, to which he was brought by Barnabas. Paul and Barnabas spent a year teaching in that church, which had already begun a Gentile mission. Under Paul's leadership, the Antioch church then became a base of operation for an even greater missionary endeavor. Paul's missionary activity as reported in Acts can

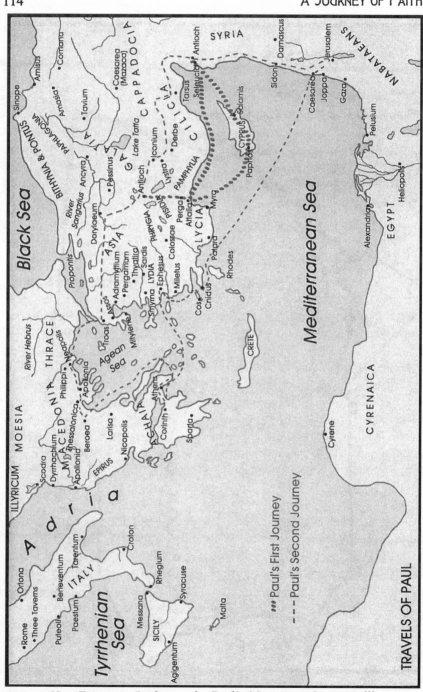

Artwork by Margaret Jordan Brown © Mercer University Press

New Testament Backgrounds: Paul's Missionary Journeys (1)

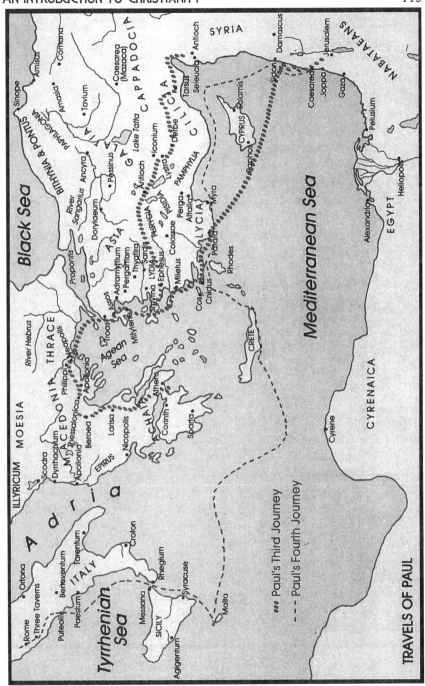

New Testament Backgrounds: Paul's Missionary Journeys (2)

Artwork by Margaret Jordan Brown © Mercer University Press

be conveniently arranged in three journeys, each beginning in Antioch, followed by a final journey to Rome.

The first journey (Acts 13–14) involved a brief tour of Paul and Barnabas through the island of Cypress and the relatively small cities of south-central Asia Minor. Along the way, a pattern emerged that would be repeated many times on the rest of Paul's journeys. In a given city, Paul typically begins in the synagogue with initial success, especially among the proselytes and God-fearing Gentiles. Then the unbelieving Jews in jealous anger drive them out, so that Paul turns to the Gentiles outside the synagogue, among whom he finds acceptance. Repeatedly, he meets rejection and hostility from the Jews. Among many other episodes, once he was stoned nearly to death, and five times he received the synagogue discipline of thirty-nine lashes (Acts 14:19-20; 2 Corinthians 11:24-25). The surprising, and shocking, result was that the churches Paul established were constituted mainly of Gentiles. When news of this "open door" to the Gentiles circulated, it touched off the greatest controversy in first-generation Christianity.

Conservative Jewish Christians from Jerusalem came to Antioch demanding that Gentile Christians be circumcised (Acts 15:1). Circumcision was the key ritual that distinguished Jews as belonging to the covenant people of God (Genesis 17:11) and obligated them to observe the rituals spelled out in the Jewish law. Male Jewish infants were circumcised on the eighth day. Gentiles who converted to Judaism were circumcised as adults. The implication of the demand, therefore, was that Gentiles can become Christians only by first converting to Judaism and subjecting themselves to all of the Jewish rituals and customs. Paul knew that such a requirement would not only hinder his mission but also send the wrong theological message, since he was convinced that salvation is found only by faith in Christ and not by works of the law (Galatians 2:16). As the issue proved too serious, and too contentious, to settle in Antioch, the church decided to send representatives to Jerusalem for a high-level conference.

The Apostolic Council in Jerusalem (Acts 15:1-35; Galatians 2:1-10) was a summit meeting of leaders from the Antioch church (Paul and Barnabas) and the Jerusalem church (Peter, John, and James the brother of Jesus) over the question of the circumcision of Gentile Christians. On the central issue, the Jerusalem apostles agreed with Paul that circumcision must not be imposed on the Gentiles. This decision, dated about 49 CE, is considered one of the most momentous events in earliest Christianity. It meant that the Gentile mission was free to go forward without opposition from the Jerusalem leadership. It also paved the way for the eventual separation of Christianity from Judaism, since, if the demand for circumcision had prevailed, Christianity would have remained a sect of Judaism. Nevertheless, tensions over the Gentile issue remained. At some point, the Jerusalem church, following a proposal of James the brother of Jesus, sought to impose on Gentile converts a compromise including certain dietary restrictions (Acts 15:19-21; 21:25), which Paul appears not to have accepted.[4] More seriously, a hardline faction continued to demand circumcision, and Paul had to battle this issue for years to come.

The second missionary journey (Acts 15:36–18:22) was much longer than the first. Paul, along with Silas and Timothy, traveled a vague route through Asia Minor to Troas on the northwest coast. From there, heeding the vision of a beckoning Macedonian man, he crossed into Macedonia, planting churches in Philippi and Thessalonica. Both of these churches— Paul's first in Europe[5]—later received letters from the apostle. Turning southward into Greece, Paul worked briefly in Athens, the city of philosophers and classical Greek culture. There, standing in the Areopagus ("Mars Hill," the city council or court), he preached a famous sermon, taking a text from an inscription, "To an unknown god," and weaving together themes from Stoic philosophy and biblical theology (Acts 17:16-34). Results in Athens were meager, and Paul soon left. He then settled in Corinth, where he spent eighteen months establishing a church, his longest stay on the second journey. There Paul met Priscilla (or Prisca) and Aquila, a Jewish Christian couple who, like Paul, were tentmakers. Priscilla is illustrative of Paul's openness to working with women. He later commends her warmly as one among "my fellow

---

[4]Acts 15:19-21 depicts this compromise as having been approved by all parties at the Apostolic Council. In Acts 21:25, however, James proposes the same compromise as if it is the first time Paul has heard it. In any case, Paul appears not to agree with it. His own account of the Apostolic Council (Galatians 2:1-10) leaves no room for such a compromise, and his position on idol meat in 1 Corinthians 8–10 differs with it.

[5]This is more significant from the perspective of Western history than from Paul's. Paul himself probably did not have a sense of a continental divide running between Asia Minor and Macedonia. In any case, this was not the first incursion of Christianity into Europe, as there were already Christians in Rome by this time.

workers in Christ Jesus" (Romans 16:3 RSV); she participates in giving theological instruction to the learned Christian missionary Apollos (Acts 18:26); four out of six biblical references to the couple list her name first.[6]

Near the end of his stay in Corinth, Paul was brought by Jewish opponents before the proconsul Gallio on charges of sedition, which were summarily dismissed. This appearance is significant because an inscription referring to Gallio allows us to date his term in Corinth. By extension, Paul's arrival in Corinth can be dated to approximately 50 CE. This gives a fixed date from which other Pauline events can be reckoned. Since 1 Thessalonians was written shortly after Paul's arrival in Corinth, Paul's earliest letter and the earliest book of the New Testament can with some confidence be dated about 50 as well.

After a brief return to Antioch, the third journey (Acts 18:23–20:38) took Paul back through Asia Minor to Ephesus, an important city on the southwest coast, which became a center of Paul's work for more than two years, his longest stay on any of the journeys. By now, Paul was surrounded by a team of coworkers—including Timothy, Titus, Priscilla and Aquila (now in Ephesus), and others—who shared Paul's ministry and were sent out on missions to establish new congregations and to stay in touch with existing churches. Most of the Corinthian correspondence was written from Ephesus and perhaps several other letters as well. Near the end of his Ephesian stay, Paul's team was the focus of a riot fomented by silversmiths who believed the Christian preaching was cutting into their business of selling miniature replicas of the great temple of Artemis in Ephesus. Based on references in the Corinthian letters, some scholars have theorized that Paul's stay in Ephesus may have involved a period of imprisonment, which could have been the occasion for some of his "prison letters." From Ephesus, Paul paid a final visit to his churches in Macedonia and Greece to complete a collection for the Jerusalem poor that he had been organizing among his churches (Romans 15:25-29). Besides relieving chronic poverty in Jerusalem, Paul hoped this collection, which symbolized the unity of Jewish and Gentile Christians, would help to ease the tensions between them. After delivering the collection to Jerusalem, he planned to go to Rome and from there to Spain.

---

[6]"Priscilla" in Acts, "Prisca" elsewhere: Acts 18:2, 18, and 26; Romans 16:3; 1 Corinthians 16:19; 2 Timothy 4:19.

The last main section of Acts describes Paul's final visit to Jerusalem, his arrest, and his journey to Rome (Acts 21:1–28:31). Here Luke recapitulates the overarching theme of the book: from Jerusalem to Rome. Paul's visit to Jerusalem did not go smoothly. His presence in the temple touched off a riot and he was arrested by Roman soldiers. He was jailed briefly in Jerusalem while the Romans tried to sort out what he might be guilty of. When it was discovered that his enemies were plotting to kill him, he was transferred to prison in Caesarea, Roman headquarters for Palestine. There, after languishing for two years without a verdict, he invoked his privilege as a Roman citizen to move the case to Rome for trial before the emperor. On a long, dramatic sea voyage, complete with shipwreck, Paul was taken as a prisoner to Rome. Under house arrest in Rome for two years while he awaited trial, he was free to receive visitors and preach the gospel.

Acts closes at this point without reporting the outcome of the trial or Paul's fate. Why? Some scholars believe Luke ends the story at this point because he wrote Acts before Paul's trial took place. More likely, Luke was writing later and knew that Paul had been executed by Nero (probably 60–65 CE), as later tradition maintains. In that case, Luke concludes his book as he does in order to end on a positive note. Acts, after all, is not a biography of Paul but a story of the triumphant march of the gospel of Christ from Jerusalem to Rome. With Paul in the capital city, "proclaiming the kingdom of God and teaching about the Lord Jesus Christ with all boldness and without hindrance" (Acts 28:31), that story is concluded.

Chapter 8

THE LETTERS AND REVELATION

Twenty-one of the twenty-seven New Testament books are classified as letters and two others (Acts and Revelation) contain letters—a reflection of the early Christians' desire to create and maintain community. The term "epistles," which is sometimes used for these books, really just means "letters" but connotes a more formal character which is more appropriate for some of the New Testament letters than for others. For convenience, the letters may be divided into the Pauline Letters (Romans through Philemon), which were written mostly between 50 and 65 CE, and the General Epistles (Hebrews through Jude), which belong to the post-Pauline period. Revelation, an apocalyptic writing with some letter-like features—it has an epistolary salutation and postscript (Revelation 1:4-5; 22:21) and contains seven letters to the churches of Asia (Revelation 2–3)—also belongs to the later period. This chapter will survey first the Pauline Letters, then the General Epistles and Revelation; it will close with a brief look at the formation of the New Testament canon.

THE PAULINE LETTERS

Paul's letters are the earliest Christian writings which have come down to us and, therefore, also the earliest books of the New Testament. They allow us to peer back into the lives of some of the earliest Christian communities as they were struggling to take shape. This section will discuss the character of Paul's letters and then briefly survey them in rough chronological order.

1. *The Character of Paul's Letters.* It is important to recognize that Paul's letters are "occasional" writings, written in response to real-life situations in his churches. Paul was not a systematic theologian attempting to provide comprehensive coverage of Christian doctrine for all time. Paul believed he was living in the last generation and shows no awareness of writing something that would become Scripture. He was, rather, a pastoral theologian whose thought was hammered out in dealing with real-life issues in his churches. Each letter typically addresses particular problems, questions, or issues that have arisen in one of Paul's young churches and often leaves unmentioned much of Paul's thought which is not at issue. Our understanding of a letter will be enhanced by trying to

formulate a picture of its occasion, that is, the situation in the church to which Paul is responding. The survey below will attempt to set the letters in the context of the occasions for which they were written and in selected cases to highlight some aspects of Paul's responses. Although Paul was writing to address particular situations in his first-century churches, his theological insights have proven so helpful to readers in every age that his letters have had a powerful, shaping influence on Christian theology.

Before turning to the letters, a word should be said about the issue of their authenticity. Many scholars believe that some of the Pauline Letters may have been written under Paul's name after his death. Pseudonymity (writing under an assumed name) was common in antiquity and was widely practiced by Christians from the second century on. Several of the New Testament letters attributed to Paul bear varying degrees of difference in style, thought, and setting from his undisputed letters and, therefore, may be pseudonymous. There is a strong consensus that 1 and 2 Timothy and Titus (collectively known as the "Pastoral Epistles") were written around the turn of the century by an admirer of Paul who wanted to speak in Paul's name to a new situation; they will be used in the following section to illustrate issues in the later period. There are similar concerns, although less consensus, about the authorship of 2 Thessalonians, Colossians, and Ephesians. The remaining seven letters— 1 Thessalonians, Galatians, 1 and 2 Corinthians, Philippians, Philemon, and Romans—are undisputed.

2. *1 and 2 Thessalonians: Questions about Eschatology.* Written from Corinth about 50 CE to the church in Thessalonica, the capital of Macedonia, shortly after its founding on Paul's second missionary journey, 1 Thessalonians is probably Paul's earliest letter. Having been driven out of town by Jewish hostility (Acts 17:1-10) and knowing that the Thessalonians were facing similar hostilities, Paul had sent his coworker Timothy back to check on them (1 Thessalonians 2:17–3:6). The letter is a response to Timothy's report. The church has so far remained faithful, but some critical questions about eschatology have arisen in response to the death of some church members. Paul's preaching had emphasized the nearness of the *Parousia*, when Christ would appear in glory to gather his own into the kingdom of God. Subsequently, the deaths that had occurred had raised questions about this hope. What is the fate of those who have died believing in Christ? Will they be left out? When will the *Parousia* come?

In a beautiful passage often read at funerals (1 Thessalonians 4:13-18), Paul instills Christian hope in the face of death by teaching the resurrection of believers. This hope is grounded in the resurrection of Christ: since Christ *was* raised, those who believe in him *will* be raised. When Christ returns, "the dead in Christ will rise first" (v. 16), so that they will not miss out on anything. "Then we who are alive, who are left, will be caught up in the clouds together with them to meet the Lord in the air; and so we will be with the Lord forever" (v. 17).

On the question of when the *Parousia* will come, however, Paul refuses to set a timetable or to speculate about the details of the end-time scenario (1 Thessalonians 5:1-11). It is enough to know that for believers the coming of Christ will be a day of salvation and that their task in the meantime is the business of faithful Christian living.

Second Thessalonians addresses further questions about the *Parousia*. If genuine, it was probably written soon after 1 Thessalonians to provide further clarification; if pseudonymous, it would have been written after Paul's death. In either case, it combats a false teaching, wrongly attributed to Paul, that the *Parousia* had already come (2 Thessalonians 2:1-2). This notion was shaking up the church and perhaps contributing to a problem of idleness. The letter insists that the *Parousia* has not yet come (2:3-12) and admonishes the idlers to return to work (3:6-13).

3. *Galatians: Questions about the Law.* Addressed to a group of churches located in north- or south-central Asia Minor, Galatians is Paul's feistiest letter. Depending on the exact location of the churches, Galatians could have been written as early as 49 CE or as late as 54 CE. In either case, it addresses a critical situation in which opponents of Paul were preaching "another gospel" and leading the churches astray (Galatians 1:6-9). Paul never says who these people were. Traditionally referred to as "Judaizers," they appear to have been conservative Jewish Christians who were insisting that Gentile Christians must be circumcised, in effect making them Jews subject to the Jewish law (5:2-3; 6:12-13). The situation is quite serious, with the heart of the gospel at stake, and Paul is very emotional, even angry, as he writes (1:8-9; 5:12).

Galatians is Paul's "manifesto of freedom" from the law. The main theme of the letter is justification by faith. The apostle argues "that a person is justified not by the works of the law but through faith in Jesus Christ" (Galatians 2:16). "Justification" depicts salvation under law-court imagery. To be "justified" means to be "declared righteous" before the judgment seat of God. Since the person being judged is actually a sinner, this verdict cannot be based on works of law but only on faith in the saving death of Christ. "Justification by faith," then, amounts to being acquitted, pardoned, or forgiven, and thereby being restored to a right relationship with God on the basis of faith in Christ.

Galatians 3–4 makes intricate arguments for this position. Paul uses Genesis 15:6 to show that Abraham was "reckoned righteous" on the basis of his faith *before* his circumcision and *before* the giving of the law. Abraham's heirs are not the circumcised but those who have faith. The law was never intended to be the basis for righteousness. Its function, rather, was to condemn sin and so to serve as a temporary disciplinarian until the coming of Christ. Now that Christ has come, he has redeemed us from the law. It is not necessary to receive circumcision and place oneself under the law. All who have faith in Christ, Jews and Gentiles alike, are children of God. Indeed, in Christ all human distinctions are erased: "There is no longer Jew or Greek, there is no longer slave or free, there is no longer male and female; for all of you are one in Christ Jesus" (Galatians 3:28).

In Galatians 5–6, Paul emphasizes that freedom from the law does not mean license to sin. Christian living is directed by the guidance of the Holy Spirit and by the commandment to "love your neighbor as yourself," which contains the "whole law" in itself (5:14).

Many interpreters have considered justification by faith to be the central theme in Paul's theology. Others have seen it not as the focal point of his thought as a whole but as an important argument which he uses primarily in combative situations where his law-free gospel to the Gentiles is under challenge. In either case, justification by faith has certainly been an influential theme in Christian theology, especially so in Protestant circles.

4. *1 and 2 Corinthians: Questions about Freedom.* Corinth was an industrialized, cosmopolitan, crossroads city in Greece. Famous even among pagans for its wide-open immorality, it was a place where many cultures and religions met and mingled, a phenomenon called "syncretism." Many of the problems which surface in the Corinthian church, established during Paul's long stay on the second journey, were products of this environment. Counting a "previous letter" mentioned in 1 Corinthians 5:9 and a "harsh letter" mentioned in 2 Corinthians 2:3-4 and 7:8 and 12, Paul wrote—mostly from Ephesus about 54–55 CE—at least four letters to this troubled church.

In 1 Corinthians, Paul tackles a laundry list of problems, many of which were reported to him on a visit by "Chloe's people" (1:11) and in a letter from Corinth (7:1). Among the many problems were quarreling factions with rival claims to superior wisdom, toleration of sexual immorality as a mark of spiritual liberation, issues related to marriage and divorce, claims to unrestricted freedom to eat meat sacrificed to idols, disorder in the Lord's Supper, overemphasis on ecstatic spiritual gifts, and misunderstanding of the resurrection of believers. In the letter, Paul takes up these problems one after another and deals with them.

First Corinthians graphically illustrates the risk involved in translating the gospel into a new culture. The Corinthians took Paul's emphasis on freedom from the law and misinterpreted it through Hellenistic presuppositions. Viewing Christianity as another of the mystery religions, they assumed that baptism and the Lord's Supper convey their benefits automatically, leaving one free to engage in immorality or to participate in the rituals of idol worship. The unbridled libertinism seems to be rooted also in Gnostic-like notions that the spirit is good and the body is evil. Through Christ, the Corinthians imagined, the good spirit has been resurrected, liberated from the evil body to enjoy the life of heaven already now. The evil body is then left free to do as it pleases. The Corinthians emphasized a purely "vertical" religion which consisted of one's individual spirit communing directly with God. Lacking was the "horizontal" dimension which involves ethical obligations and relationships with others.

Whereas in Galatians Paul fights for freedom from the law, in 1 Corinthians he seeks to rescue an unruly church from an irresponsible overemphasis on freedom. A key argument comes in chapter 15, where Paul treats a misunderstanding of the resurrection of believers. Against the Corinthians' notion of a purely spiritual resurrection which has already been fully achieved, Paul argues for a *future*, *bodily* resurrection of believers. This implies (1) that God lays claim to the whole person—including one's body and its conduct—and (2) that, until resurrection day, God is not yet finished with the believer, who must constantly be diligent to avoid evil.

First Corinthians also illustrates how Paul repeatedly cuts to the core of first-century issues and exposes principles that have enduring value. One of the best-loved passages in Paul's letters is nestled within his discussion of spiritual gifts (1 Corinthians 12–14). The Corinthians who practiced the gift of "speaking in tongues"—an ecstatic experience in which the worshiper loses control and speaks in a nonintelligible language—held it up as a sign of superiority and practiced it with relish, creating division in the church and disorder in worship. In chapter 12, Paul emphasizes that tongue speaking is not the only spiritual gift. There are many gifts, all given for the benefit of the whole church. Just as the human body consists of different members with different functions but all serving the whole, so the church is the body of Christ, made up of different members with different gifts, but each important to the whole. Then in chapter 14, Paul argues that tongue speaking is not the most important gift. Tongue speaking may be exhilarating for the individual, but prophecy (inspired preaching) is more beneficial, since, as *intelligible*

PAUL'S LOVE HYMN (1 CORINTHIANS 13:1-13)

If I speak in the tongues of mortals and of angels, but do not have love, I am a noisy gong or a clanging cymbal. And if I have prophetic powers, . . . but do not have love, I am nothing. . . .

Love is patient; love is kind; love is not envious or boastful or arrogant or rude. It does not insist on its own way; it is not irritable or resentful; it does not rejoice in wrongdoing, but rejoices in the truth. It bears all things, believes all things, hopes all things, endures all things.

Love never ends. . . . And now faith, hope, and love abide, these three; and the greatest of these is love. (NRSV)

---

speech, it serves to build up the church as a whole. The discussion closes with practical guidelines for the orderly practice of tongue speaking.

Sandwiched between the two chapters on "spiritual gifts" is Paul's famous "love hymn" (1 Corinthians 13), his ode to the most important spiritual gift of all. Love is the one gift for which all should strive, for if not accompanied by loving concern for others even the most spectacular spiritual experiences are pointless. Paul's word for "love" is *agape*, by which he means an unconditional, self-giving love that seeks the well-being of another without expecting anything in return. As the kind of love which believers have experienced in Christ, it is the supreme Christian virtue and should become the hallmark of every Christian's life. It was this, above all, that was missing in Corinth, and Paul's final word of advice in 1 Corinthians is, "Let all that you do be done in love" (16:14).

Second Corinthians reveals that 1 Corinthians did not solve the problems in the church. Things actually grew worse. Newly arrived opponents of Paul, whom he sarcastically calls "super-apostles" (2 Corinthians 11:5; 12:11), had turned the church against the apostle. Making a show of their Jewish credentials and of their signs, wonders, and lofty wisdom, they opposed Paul as weak and unimpressive. In the interval, Paul had paid a quick, "painful visit" (2:1) to Corinth to deal with the situation, but his efforts were rebuffed. Retreating to Ephesus, Paul wrote an emotional "harsh letter" (mentioned in 2 Corinthians 2:3-4 and 7:8, 12) in an effort to win back his church. Either this letter has been lost or, as many scholars surmise, has been partially preserved in 2 Corinthians 10–13. These chapters exhibit a severe tone not found in the preceding chapters and may represent a separate letter written at the height of the crisis. The stern, threatening tone of this letter seems designed to bring the crisis to a head, one way or the other.

As this "harsh letter" was being sent, Paul also dispatched his coworker Titus as a personal envoy to Corinth, with instructions to meet him afterwards in Troas with news of the outcome in Corinth. Once Paul got to Troas, however, Titus failed to appear as scheduled. So Paul anxiously crossed over into Macedonia and rendezvoused with him en route. Titus gave him the good news that the Corinthian church was ready to reconcile its relationship with Paul (2 Corinthians 2:12-13; 7:5-16). Overjoyed at this, Paul wrote a "conciliatory letter," found in 2 Corinthians 1–9, in which he breathes a sigh of relief and resumes the task of helping the church to work out its difficulties. A key theme in both sections of 2 Corinthians is Paul's defense of a ministry style of weakness and suffering as consistent with being an apostle of the crucified Christ.

5. *Philippians, Philemon, Colossians, and Ephesians: the Prison Letters.* Scholars are divided over the origin of these "prison letters." Traditionally, they are assumed to have come from Paul's imprisonment in Rome (Acts 28), which puts them late in his career (58–65 CE). Since Philippians and Philemon have close connections with Paul's work in the east, many scholars have argued that they were written during Paul's earlier imprisonment in Caesarea (56–58 CE; Acts 23–26) or during a hypothetical imprisonment in Ephesus (54–55 CE). The authorship of Colossians and Ephesians is often disputed because of peculiarities in style, vocabulary, and theology. Defenders of their authenticity typically date them to the Roman imprisonment, arguing that the later date helps account for the perceived differences in those letters. If they are in fact

pseudonymous, then the prison motif is a tribute to what the apostle was forced to endure for the sake of his ministry.

Philippians is a joyful letter to a friendly church with which Paul enjoyed a warm relationship. He writes to thank the church for sending a financial contribution (Philippians 4:15-18), to reassure them about his own well-being in prison (1:12-26), to settle a quarrel in the church (4:2-3), and to warn about a false teaching (3:2-21). A dominant theme in the letter is Paul's paradoxical joy even in prison, facing possible execution. He is confident that if he dies he will "be with Christ," and if he lives he will continue his ministry and see his friends again (1:21-26). He reassures his friends that, even in the midst of trying circumstances, "I can do all things through him who strengthens me" (4:13).

Philemon, Paul's shortest letter, accompanies the return to Philemon of his runaway slave Onesimus. After running away, Onesimus had come to be with Paul, had become a Christian, and had become "useful" in Paul's ministry (v. 11—a pun, since "Onesimus" means "useful"). As Paul is now returning him to his owner, he pleads for clemency on Onesimus's behalf—significant since Roman slave law gave the owner of a runaway a free hand for severe punishment. Paul asks Philemon to receive Onesimus back not as a slave but as a "beloved brother" in Christ (v. 16) and hints that he would like Philemon to release Onesimus and send him back to Paul. Although Paul's return of a runaway seems to give approval to the institution of slavery, it would be wrong to conclude that Paul's message is to commend the practice of slavery. Slavery was a fact of life in Paul's world—a world he thought was about to end with the return of Christ. Paul gives advice on Christian conduct within the existing structures. In asking that the slave be received as a brother, Paul establishes a Christian principle that ultimately is incompatible with slavery.

Colossians is addressed to a congregation established by Paul's coworker Epaphras (Colossians 1:7), probably as an extension of Paul's Ephesian ministry. Colossians opposes an esoteric Gnostic syncretism which advocated rigorous ascetic practices. Gnostics conceived of certain hostile angelic "principalities and powers" which separate the material world from God. The ascetic practices, apparently, were thought necessary to appease these powers, implying that faith in Christ was not sufficient for salvation. The letter argues that Christ is Lord of all the universe; he is the source, the sustainer, and the redeemer of "all things" (1:15-20). Whatever rebellious spiritual powers might be at large have been defeated through the cross of Christ (2:8-10, 15). Since the "fullness" of divine power dwells in Christ (1:19; 2:9), faith in him is sufficient for salvation, and the ascetic practices are unnecessary (2:16-23). Authentic Christian discipline is characterized not by ascetic rigor but by appropriate, loving conduct in all of one's relationships (Colossians 3–4).

It is difficult to recognize a concrete occasion behind Ephesians, and several early manuscripts even omit reference to a specific location in the salutation (Ephesians 1:1). Possibly, it was a circular letter intended to circulate among churches in a region. The emphasis on the unity of Jews and Gentiles in "one new humanity" (2:15) has suggested to some interpreters that the letter addresses a situation of tension between Jewish and Gentile Christians. Another theory is that it was written pseudonymously by the collector of Paul's letters to serve as an introduction to the published collection. This would account for Ephesians's marked distinctiveness in style, vocabulary, and theology, its lack of personal references, and its apparent heavy borrowing of phrases from the other letters, especially Colossians. In any case, Ephesians summarizes Paul's theology, including this memorable statement of his doctrine of salvation by grace, that is, by God's merciful, undeserved favor: "For by grace you have been saved through faith, and this is not your own doing; it is the gift of God—not the result of works, so that no one may boast" (2:8-9).

6. *Romans: "Paul's Testament."*[1] Romans is a letter of introduction to a church Paul did not establish but which he plans to visit. We do not know how Christianity came to Rome. Perhaps it was not by an organized mission but informally, as "all roads led to Rome." As Paul writes from Corinth about 55–56 CE near the end of his third journey, his plans are to take his poverty-relief collection to Jerusalem and then head west, first to Rome and ultimately to a new mission field in Spain (Romans 15:22-33). Paul is introducing himself to the Roman Christians and trying to enlist their support for his new work in Spain. Because his gospel of law-free inclusion of Gentiles was controversial, he outlines, explains, clarifies, and defends his theology in hopes that the Roman church will receive him and help send him to Spain. Paul may also have on his mind the defense of this gospel he will have to make on his impending visit to Jerusalem.

---

[1]See, e.g., "Romans as Paul's Testament," part 1, chap. 10 in Günther Bornkamm, *Paul*, trans. D. M. G. Stalker (New York: Harper & Row, 1971) 88-96.

Since the occasion of Romans has more to do with Paul's own agenda than with problems in the Roman church, the letter turns out to contain the most orderly, systematic presentation of Paul's thought. For that reason, it has also been the most influential letter in the history of Christian theology. Paul's theology in Romans is quite complex and interpretations of it differ at many points. What follows is an attempt to summarize the broad flow of Paul's argument.

In Romans 1:16-17, Paul states his overall theme. Through the power of the gospel, God seeks to save all people who respond in faith, Jews and Gentiles alike. God's own righteousness is demonstrated by making people righteous (that is, putting them in right relationship) on the basis of faith. Throughout Romans, Paul is concerned to show that Jews and Gentiles are on equal footing before God—both are saved only by a faith response to the gospel.

The first major section of the letter describes *the sinful human condition* (Romans 1:18–3:20). Sin means "missing the mark," rebelling against God's intention that created human beings should live in trusting obedience to the Creator. Paul's concern here is to show that Jews and Gentiles are equally guilty. Gentiles (1:18-32), without the law, committed the fundamental sin of idolatry, worshiping the creation instead of the Creator, and from that sprang all manner of immorality. Jews (2:1–3:8) sinned in spite of the law, since they did not keep it. Paul concludes that Jews and Gentiles alike are under the power of sin (3:9); none are righteous (3:10). All people, therefore, are sinners, rightfully subject to God's wrath. Works of the law cannot restore righteousness, for the law only creates knowledge of sin (3:20).

The next section turns to *God's solution—justification by faith in Christ* (Romans 3:21–4:25). In Christ, God has provided a new way of righteousness, apart from the law—"the righteousness of God through faith in Jesus Christ for all who believe" (3:22). The death of Christ is a "sacrifice of atonement" (3:25) which pays the penalty for sin. This benefit becomes effective when it is received in faith. For Paul, "faith" means not merely believing the gospel message but also trusting God for one's salvation and putting oneself at God's disposal in genuine obedience—just as Jesus did in accepting his fate on the cross. Such faith becomes the basis of a right relationship with God. God "justifies," or "declares righteous," those who have faith, acquitting them of sin and restoring them to a right standing. Since it is precisely undeserving sinners who are justified, justification is an act of God's grace, that is,

God's unmerited favor, his free gift of salvation. Righteousness, then, comes not by works of the law but through faith in Christ and is equally open to Jews and Gentiles alike. Chapter 4 uses the example of Abraham, as one whose faith was "reckoned as righteousness" apart from works, to show that this principle is consistent with Jewish scripture.

Paul now goes on to describe *the new life in Christ as a life of freedom* (Romans 5–8). Sinners justified by faith in Christ now have peace with God and *freedom from his wrath* at the final judgment (ch. 5). From this perspective Paul describes salvation as "reconciliation," the restoration of a broken relationship. Believers also have *freedom from sin* (ch. 6), *from the law* (ch. 7), and *from death* (ch. 8). Here "Sin" is depicted as a cosmic power that enslaves a person to a life of sin. Sin attacks the "flesh" (understood not as material stuff but as human weakness, frailty, and proneness toward sin) and even enlists God's law as an ally, misusing the commandments to incite their violation. The result is "Death," separation from God and the inability to do his will. Christ redeems believers from such bondage. "Redemption" depicts salvation as liberation from bondage to Sin, just as a slave could be set free by a benefactor who was willing to pay the purchase price. Here Paul makes it clear that justification should not be taken to imply that God pretends that sinners are righteous and leaves them free to go on sinning. Rather, the death and resurrection of Christ have broken the power of Sin and Death. Christ delivers sinners from the tyranny of Sin and gives them the power of the Holy Spirit to do God's will. At the same time, Paul acknowledges that Christians are not automatically zapped into sinless perfection. The new possibility must be actualized by rejecting sin and choosing righteousness, by living according to the Spirit and not according to the flesh. For Paul, salvation is a total transformation of one's life which is not yet complete. Salvation is a past accomplishment in the death and resurrection of Christ but also a continuing process and a future goal of being transformed into the likeness of Christ.

Romans 9–11 discusses *the place of Jews and Gentiles in God's plan of salvation.* Paul wants to make it clear that his successful mission to the Gentiles does not imply that God is being unfaithful to the covenant with Israel. God has not rejected Israel, but most Jews have rejected the righteousness of faith. Paul believes that the Jews' rejection of the gospel is being used by God to allow the Gentiles to be included in the people of God. He is hoping that the Gentiles' inclusion will make the Jews jealous enough to accept the gospel as well so that, in the end, "all Israel" will be saved (11:13-26).

The last major section of the letter is devoted to the *ethical application of the gospel* (Romans 12:1–15:13). Paul is concerned to show that his gospel of grace does not leave Christians free to do as they please but issues in ethical behavior. Paul's "therefore" (12:1) signals an ethic based on the preceding theology. Because of all the "mercies of God," Christians are under obligation to present themselves to God "as a living sacrifice." Christian living should no longer conform to the pattern of "this world," which is passing away, but should be transformed to fit the pattern of the coming age, to which by faith believers already belong (12:2). Paul goes on to give practical advice about Christian living in a variety of settings, including relationships with believers and nonbelievers. Above all, he again commends the practice of love, for in the end "the one who loves another has fulfilled the law" (13:8-10).

Depending on the origin of the prison letters, Romans may be the latest undisputed letter of Paul. It is surely his last letter as a free man. Written at a significant turning point in his ministry, it beautifully sums up his career as the "apostle to the Gentiles" and is a noble capstone to the development of Christianity in its formative period. Its influence in the history of Christian theology is unrivaled.

As mentioned earlier, Paul likely died under Nero, 60–65 CE. His most distinctive contribution was to have fought for the law-free inclusion of the Gentiles and in the course of that fight to have hammered out— mostly in Galatians and Romans—his theology of justification by grace through faith. His legacy is thirteen New Testament letters written by him or under the shadow of his influence and the stirring Acts account of his heroic efforts on behalf of the gospel.

THE GENERAL EPISTLES AND REVELATION

For the period after Paul we have no narrative account such as Acts provides for the earlier period. The literature of this period includes the Gospels, the General Epistles, Revelation, and any of the Pauline Letters that may be pseudonymous. By the end of the first century, Christianity had spread from Jerusalem and was well established in various places around the Mediterranean. The apostles and other first-generation Christians were beginning to die. The Gospels were written between 65 and 100 to preserve the Jesus traditions and to meet the needs of diverse Christian communities. The growing movement was becoming predominantly Gentile, was now in its second and third generations, and was beginning to settle down and take stock of itself. In this setting, a new set of issues began to confront the churches. This section will briefly examine a range of those issues as they are reflected in the General Epistles, the Pastoral Epistles, and Revelation. Because many of these issues were still unresolved in the New Testament period, this section also looks ahead to the period of early church history.

The General Epistles (Hebrews[2]–Jude) are so called because these letters are not addressed as specifically to particular churches as are Paul's letters. In most cases, the intended readers are either unnamed or very loosely defined. In fact, Hebrews and 1 John do not have a salutation at all. Although dating the General Epistles is very difficult and controversial, they appear to belong mostly to the later New Testament period (late first century to early second century). The Pastoral Epistles (1 and 2 Timothy and Titus) are widely believed to have been written pseudonymously in Paul's name around the turn of the century. They differ markedly from the undisputed letters in style, vocabulary, and theology; they are difficult to fit into the circumstances of Paul's career; and they presuppose an advanced level of false teaching and church structure. They will be considered here as illustrating concerns of the post-Pauline period.

1. *Christian Complacency: Hebrews and James.* As Christianity moved into its second and third generations, there was a natural tendency, at least in times of peace, for complacency and apathy to set in. The Spirit-filled enthusiasm of the earlier period gradually gave way to a more staid emphasis on doctrine. "Faith," understood as a dynamic quality of trusting obedience, yielded to "the faith," understood as sound doctrine. Christians whose parents and grandparents had been Christians before them tended to take the faith for granted. They were Christians but it seemed not to matter much to them. This problem in the church has never gone away; church history has been punctuated by the need for periodic revival and renewal movements. Two of the General Epistles, Hebrews and James, can be viewed as calls to wake up from such lethargy.

The anonymous "letter" to the Hebrews has no epistolary address. It reads much like a sermon designed for a church that has grown cold and complacent. That church is drifting and is in danger of falling away. At

---

[2]Although Hebrews was for a long time grouped with Paul's letters, it is actually anonymous; today, very few believe it was written by Paul.

some time in the past the church had faced persecution and had remained faithful (Hebrews 10:32-34). But what if persecution should come again? Would these complacent Christians stand the test? The author tries to rouse them from their apathy by demonstrating that Christianity is a "superior" faith worth being excited about. Christ is superior to Moses (3:1-6), to the Israelite priests (7:23-28), and to the sacrifices (10:11-12). Christ offered himself as the perfect sacrifice which takes away sin "once for all" (7:27; 9:25-26) and does not need to be repeated. Surely this is worth holding onto. But the author exhorts the readers to do more. He encourages them neither to go backward, nor to stand still, but to move forward on the journey of faith (12:1-2, 12-13).

The Letter of James is a collection of moral exhortations concerned to emphasize the importance of moral action in the Christian life. Lip service and profession of faith are not enough; words must be translated into action: "be doers of the word, and not hearers only" (James 1:22). True religion is defined not in terms of correct doctrine but of moral action: "to care for orphans and widows in their distress, and to keep oneself unstained by the world" (1:27). James is protesting a trend toward resting content with adherence to sound doctrine as if that were all that matters. His insistence that "a person is justified by works and not by faith alone" (2:24) sounds as if he might be taking issue with Paul's doctrine of justification by faith. But the two are actually not so far apart. For Paul, the "faith" that justifies is an attitude of trusting obedience which issues in deeds of love (Galatians 5:6). For James, the "faith alone" which does not justify is a mere intellectual assent to doctrine which does not result in good works. A religion concerned only about doctrine and not about caring for the poor and needy is a dead religion (James 2:14-17).

2. *"Delay" of the Parousia: 2 Peter.* Closely related to the problem of complacency, and probably contributing to it, is the "delay" of the *Parousia*. First-generation Christians believed the coming of Christ in glory was imminent. Paul writes about it as if he fully expects to see it soon, which gave a sense of urgency to his mission. As decades passed and new generations arose, that sense of imminence and urgency began to fade. Slowly the realization dawned that the end was not as near as once believed. This does not appear to have created a crisis for the church, but the church did have to adjust to the new reality. It had to find ways of settling down and learning to live in the midst of this world for a more extended period. Of course, in times of intense crisis more imminent expectations could be revived.

This issue is most directly addressed by 2 Peter, which refutes false teachers who are scoffing at the *Parousia* expectation and denying that it will ever come (2 Peter 3:3-4). The author insists that "the day of the Lord" *will* come, although not necessarily "soon" from our perspective (3:8-10). God, who has eternity as a frame of reference, measures time a bit differently than we do. The so-called "delay" should be viewed, rather, as an opportunity to repent before the day of judgment. Second Peter, incidentally, is widely regarded as a pseudonymous work written in Peter's name in the first half of the second century and may be the latest book in the New Testament.

3. *Development of Organizational Structures: the Pastoral Epistles.* In the earlier period, church structure appears to have been relatively free, charismatic, and spontaneous. As time passed and the churches grew and settled into the reality of an indefinite life in this world, it is natural that more definitive organizational structures would emerge. Probably there was not a uniform development throughout all the churches, but different patterns appeared at various times and places. It is possible to see here the beginnings of the hierarchical structure which came to characterize the later patristic church (see chapter 9). The noncanonical letters of Ignatius of Antioch (died about 110 CE) describe three church offices arranged in a graded hierarchy. At the top stood the *bishop* (literally, "overseer"), who supervised the many congregations in and around a given city. Under his authority, the *presbyters* (literally, "elders")[3] served as pastors of individual congregations. Below the presbyters came the *deacons* (literally, "servants"), who ministered to the sick and needy.

Not many years earlier, the Pastoral Epistles mention the same three offices and state qualifications for holding them (1 Timothy 3:1-13; 5:17-19; Titus 1:5-9), although here they do not seem to stand in a hierarchy. It is not even clear that bishops and presbyters are totally separate offices at this point. There are hints that women may have been included among the deacons (1 Timothy 3:11; cf. Romans 16:1). There may also have been an "order" of widows which played some role in the churches (1 Timothy 5:3-16). Unfortunately, we do not have any job descriptions for these offices. One important function of the bishop is teaching the church and safeguarding "sound doctrine" against the threat of heresy (1 Timothy 3:2; Titus 1:9), a role that will become increasingly important

---

[3]Greek *presbyter* became *priest* in English.

in the centuries ahead. Presbyters also are said to be involved in teaching and preaching (1 Timothy 5:17).

4. The Problem of Heresy: 1, 2, and 3 John and Jude. Internally, the greatest challenge the churches faced was heresy, that is, false teaching. Certainly this was not entirely new in the later period. Many, if not most, of Paul's letters confront some sort of false teaching. But by the turn of the century heresy was beginning to reach new proportions. Gnosticism (see chapter 5) in particular was maturing into fully developed systems of thought. Soon it would have teachers, schools, literature, and organizational structure. By the late second century it would threaten to become the dominant form of Christianity.

The anonymous author of the letters of John confronts a Gnostic heresy which has already provoked a division in his church. Two characteristic Gnostic features are evident in the false teaching—docetism and libertinism. Both are rooted in the Gnostic contempt for the evil fleshly body. Docetism (from Greek *dokeo*, "to seem") taught that the spiritual Christ could not really have come in the flesh but only appeared to do so, thus denying Jesus' true humanity (1 John 4:2-3). Libertinism, the absence of moral restraint, was justified by the assumption that, since only the spirit is to be saved, the deeds of the body are of no consequence. The opponents seem to have claimed the freedom to live deliberately in an immoral way and still profess to be without sin (1 John 1:6-10). The author argues that claiming to know God without obeying God's commandments, especially the commandment to love one another, is living a lie (1 John 2:3-11). Knowing God cannot be purely a matter of private piety having no implications for living. Rather, a true relationship with God will turn us in love toward our brothers and sisters, for "God is love" (1 John 4:8).

The little Letter of Jude also denounces some sort of heresy with tendencies toward libertinism. The heretics may have been of Gnostic type, although it is difficult to be sure, since the author does not discuss their theology but only condemns their lifestyle.

The Pastoral Epistles confront a Gnostic heresy which advocated ascetic practices such as celibacy and abstinence from certain foods. In countering this teaching, their author appeals to scripture (2 Timothy 3:16-17) and in particular to the Old Testament doctrine of the goodness of God's creation (1 Timothy 4:1-5). He also advocates the standard of Paul's teaching as it has been handed down through Timothy in a living chain of tradition (2 Timothy 2:1-2). A third safeguard of sound doctrine is church office. The Pastorals' emphasis on church structure and qualifications for office, mentioned above, is largely motivated by the need to have good people in office in order to fight heresy. All three of these safeguards—scripture, apostolic tradition, and church office—were developed further in the later patristic church (see chapter 9).

5. *The Growing Hostility of the Roman Empire: 1 Peter and Revelation.* Externally, the Christians' greatest threat was the growing hostility of the Roman Empire. The earliest period had generally been characterized by benign neglect. Through the time of Paul, hostility was more likely to come from Jewish authorities than Roman. As long as the Christian movement was small and could still be viewed as a sect of Judaism, it was easily ignored. Judaism was an officially "legal religion" and was exempt from the expectation of worshiping the Roman gods and the emperor. In the early period, Christians enjoyed the same privilege. However, in the latter part of the century, as Christianity grew and became more distinct from Judaism, it faced a rising tide of suspicion. There was constantly the danger that local rulers could use acknowledgement of the gods and the "divine" emperor as tests of loyalty and punish severely those unwilling to comply.

In the New Testament period, persecution is associated with three emperors. The first major conflict occurred under Emperor Nero in 64 CE. In that year, a major fire devastated the city of Rome, and rumors abounded that Nero himself was responsible. Looking for a place to shift the blame, he found a convenient target in the unpopular Christians. He organized a horrible persecution in which many Christians in Rome were tortured and put to death. Relatively early traditions maintain that the apostles Peter and Paul were executed by Nero. By some accounts, persecution broke out again in the mid-90s under Domitian (reigned 81–96 CE) when Christians refused to give the emperor the divine honors he demanded. This is the traditional setting for the Book of Revelation. By the time of Trajan (reigned 98–117 CE), it was possible to punish Christians simply for being Christians. When Christians were accused, they were given a chance to renounce the faith and to prove it by offering worship to images of the emperor or of the gods. Otherwise, they were punished. Roman persecution was a continuing threat for Christians until the fourth century and will be discussed in more detail in chapter 9.

Two New Testament books, 1 Peter and Revelation, are set against the background of persecution. Scholars are divided over whether 1 Peter was written by Peter himself or is pseudonymous, as well as over whether it was written during the reign of Nero, Domitian, or Trajan. In any case, it addresses Christians in Asia Minor who are facing persecution for the faith. The letter encourages the readers to honor and obey the civil authorities in spite of the persecution (1 Peter 2:13-17); to live above reproach and to be ready to defend the faith so that persecution will serve as an opportunity for witness (3:13-17); and not to consider suffering "as a Christian" to be disgraceful, since Christ himself suffered (4:12-19).

Revelation is usually dated about 95 CE near the end of Domitian's reign. The author, a Christian prophet named John—probably not to be identified either with the apostle John or with the author of the Fourth Gospel—is in exile on the little island of Patmos (Revelation 1:9), just off the coast of Asia Minor near Ephesus. There John received the visions on the basis of which he writes to strengthen and encourage persecuted churches in western Asia Minor. He gives them assurance that "soon" Christ will return to destroy the evil powers oppressing the church.

Revelation is an apocalyptic writing and shares many features of that type of literature. Apocalypses were typically written in times of persecution or crisis and described in fantastic images and symbols an end-time cosmic battle between Good and Evil which results in God's victory. It is the symbolic language of Revelation that has made it seem so impenetrable and given rise to such diverse interpretations. Some Christians avoid Revelation because it is so hard to understand; others are obsessed with it and try to interpret its imagery as predictions of historical events down to their own time and beyond.

Modern readers of Revelation should recall that the book was originally addressed to persecuted first-century Christians as a word of encouragement to them. It calls them to "endurance" in the midst of trial (Revelation 13:10; 14:12) and promises God's deliverance "soon" (1:1, 3; 22:6, 7, 10, 12). Its apocalyptic symbols, then, were a way of interpreting their circumstances and giving hope in a hopeless situation. To interpret those symbols as referring to events of our day would be to impose on them a meaning from which the first readers would have been excluded, yet the book is addressed to them! This is not to say that Revelation does not have a message for us. It certainly does, but to hear it we must first set it in its original context and try to see how the first readers would have understood it.

The churches addressed in Revelation seem to be facing a persecution related to the issue of emperor worship. In Revelation 13, two beasts appear, one from the sea and one from the earth. The first beast (13:1-

10)—with ten horns, seven heads, and ten crowns—represents the Roman Empire with its emperors. The beast receives power from the dragon (Satan) and rules the whole earth without rival, just as Rome did. The "blasphemous words" uttered by the beast and his being worshiped by the whole earth reflect the practice of worshiping the emperors as divine. (Three of the seven cities addressed in Revelation 2–3 had temples to the emperor.) The beast's war on "the saints" (a term for Christians) suggests persecution. The second beast (13:11-18), which compels the whole earth to worship the first beast, represents the imperial cult which enforces emperor worship. Those who refuse to worship the image of the beast are killed. Those who refuse to bear the mark of the beast are denied the right to buy and sell. The mysterious number of the beast, 666, is a *gematria*, a kind of numerical symbolism in which the numerical value of the letters in a word or name was totaled up. Of the countless possibilities, the most likely reference here is to "Neron Caesar" (Nero) who was popularly believed to have returned to life in Domitian.

The context, then, is a crisis in which the mighty Roman Empire is making war on the tiny Christian church—overwhelming odds. Already there have been martyrs (Revelation 2:13; 6:9-11) and John the prophet is under banishment. Of course it did not take a "revelation" to see this much; it was all too evident. What the visions allow John and his readers to "see" is that this conflict is but an earthly manifestation of a larger cosmic battle. Behind Rome stands Satan; behind the church stands God—the timeless conflict of Good and Evil. Revelation takes an extremely harsh view of Rome. It is the embodiment of satanic power. It is "Babylon the great" (17:5), a reincarnation of the wicked city that had conquered God's people and destroyed the temple in Old Testament times. It is the "great whore" (17:1) and is "drunk with the blood of the saints and of the martyrs" (17:6).

The visions also show that God in Christ is in the process of defeating Satan and his human agents. Already the decisive battle has been won by the death and resurrection of Christ (Revelation 12:5, 11), and "soon" Christ will return to consummate the victory. The readers are assured in advance that "Fallen, fallen is Babylon the great" (14:8; 18:2) and the wreckage of the once-great city is surveyed (chaps. 17–18). John then depicts the final victory over Satan (chap. 20) and the coming of "a new heaven and a new earth" (chaps. 21–22). Punctuating the visions are choruses of praise celebrating God's victories: "Hallelujah! For the Lord our God the Almighty reigns" (19:6; cf. 11:15; 19:1-5).

On this basis, John calls the churches to faithful endurance, assuring them that, in spite of appearances, God has things under control and ultimately will be victorious. That message can reassure Christians in all ages, especially in times of crisis. Although Revelation probably is not the latest book of the New Testament, it appropriately stands last in the canon, pointing forward to the day when we can finally rejoice, "The kingdom of the world has become the kingdom of our Lord and of his Messiah, and he will reign forever and ever" (Revelation 11:15).

FORMATION OF THE NEW TESTAMENT CANON

Within a century after the death of Jesus, all of the New Testament books had been written, yet even then there was not a "New Testament." First the books had to be sifted out of the many Christian writings which would soon be in circulation and had to be gathered into a recognized collection, a "canon." The word "canon" originally meant "reed" or "measuring stick." The New Testament canon came to be a "standard" by which orthodoxy was measured. The process of gathering and sorting the New Testament books is referred to as "canonization." For the most part, each of the writings was originally intended for a particular church or region and was read only there. Gradually, churches began to share writings, and eventually collections began to form. The formation of the canon was a long, slow, and messy process. The following glance at four stages along the way will give a sense of its course.

By 100 CE, Paul's letters were being collected. Originally addressed to individual communities in scattered places, they were now being read in collected form in places far from their original destinations. Ignatius of Antioch (died about 110 CE) quotes them freely. The author of 2 Peter 3:15-16 is familiar with "all the letters" of Paul and laments that false teachers are able to twist them "as they do the other scriptures" (that is, the Old Testament).

The earliest New Testament canon on record is one created about 140 CE by Marcion on the basis of views that the church in Rome found to be heretical. Marcion believed that the God of the Old Testament was a God of law and punishment, while the God of Jesus Christ was a God of love and grace. For Marcion, these were two different Gods. He further maintained that, of all the apostles, only Paul had properly grasped the gospel of grace which does away with Jewish legalism. On these grounds, Marcion rejected the Old Testament and established a Christian canon which consisted of Luke's Gospel and ten letters of Paul (the Pastorals were not included). He was excommunicated but founded his own network of churches which flourished for several centuries. Marcion's canon stimulated the mainline church to develop its own canon.

During the last half of the second century, the four Gospels were collected out of what was by then a growing body of gospel literature. By 200 CE, these had been added to the Pauline letters to produce the core of an emerging canon. The lists of New Testament books from this period regularly include the four Gospels along with Acts, thirteen letters of Paul, plus additional writings. It is that third category which was still fluid at this stage. No list from this period includes all of our General Epistles; and writings not in our present New Testament were sometimes included.[4]

It took nearly two more centuries for the third division of the New Testament to stabilize. Not until 367 CE did a canon list appear which exactly agrees with the canon we have inherited. In that year, Bishop Athanasius of Alexandria circulated among his churches a list of twenty-seven books corresponding exactly to our own and declared that they alone should be read as New Testament. His declaration did not settle the issue for the whole church, but by 400 CE his list, for all practical purposes, had prevailed. There is a touch of irony in the fact that, by the time the New Testament canon had taken shape, the persecution of Christians had ended and the Roman government was officially sponsoring the production of biblical manuscripts.

---

[4]Of the books eventually canonized, the ones most frequently missing at this stage are 2 Peter, 3 John, Jude, and to a lesser extent Hebrews and James. Examples of books ultimately excluded from the canon but sometimes included at this stage are the *Apocalypse of Peter*, the *Epistle of Barnabas*, and the *Shepherd of Hermas*.

Part Three

CHURCH HISTORY

Chapter 9

EARLY CHRISTIANITY (100-500 CE)

By the close of the first century, the apostles and other eyewitnesses to the life and ministry of Jesus were gone. The Christian religion was about to undergo a significant transition in the second century of its existence.[1]

EARLY CHRISTIANITY (100-312)

SEPARATION FROM JUDAISM

As we learned in part two above, Christianity began as a sect within Judaism. Relatively soon there was a mission to the Gentiles and the issue was raised whether or not to admit them without requiring circumcision. The decision of the Apostolic Council not to impose that requirement meant that in the long run Christianity was destined to become a separate religion. Yet that separation did not take place immediately. For quite some time Christianity remained in close relationship with the Jewish synagogue. Jewish Christians continued to practice their traditions and to participate in synagogue life. Even Gentile Christians considered themselves to have been incorporated into "Israel" and adopted the Jewish scriptures as their own.

In the period following the fall of Jerusalem and the destruction of the temple (70 CE), however, tensions began to increase. Christians saw that catastrophe as retribution for the Jews' rejection of Christ. Jews tended to blame the Christians. The survival of Judaism after the disaster was secured largely by a newly established academy of Jewish scholars at Jamnia, near the Palestinian coast, which took the lead in restructuring the Jewish faith. The reorganization was chiefly along Pharisaic lines, and the Judaism that emerged was much more uniform and less tolerant of

---

[1]I am indebted to several works for this unit on the history of Christianity. Much of the basic structure of these chapters was taken from Justo Gonzalez, *Church History: An Essential Guide* (Nashville: Abingdon Press, 1996). Material was gleaned from this source as well as from Justo Gonzalez, *The Story of Christianity*, vols. 1 and 2 (San Francisco: HarperSanFrancisco, 1984 and 1985) and R. Dean Peterson, *A Concise History of Christianity*, 2nd ed. (Boston: Wadsworth, 2000).

diversity than earlier. Christians felt less and less welcome in the synagogues. Near the end of the century, the rabbis added to the synagogue liturgy a "benediction against the heretics" which effectively made it impossible for Christians to participate and sealed the break between Judaism and Christianity. In spite of this break, the Jewish roots of Christianity are still evident in a number of Christian practices which were carried over from Judaism.

The Old Testament. To this day, Christians and Jews share the Old Testament scriptures and both regard these writings as sacred and authoritative. The term "Old Testament" by definition is Christian in origin. Christians believe that the Old Testament contains important theological concepts and provides the important context for understanding the life and ministry of Jesus the Messiah.

Worship. Earliest Christian worship was modeled after the style of worship in the Jewish synagogue. Reading of scripture, singing, praying, and exhortation were all standard synagogue practices. These practices were brought into Christian worship, although with a different focus. Christian worship centered on the person and work of Christ.

Baptism. Many people think baptism originated with John the Baptist. But, in early Judaism, whenever a Gentile wanted to convert to Judaism a ceremony was involved which included circumcision and a ceremonial washing. This washing was considered the entrance into the Jewish fellowship. In the same way, the early Christians used baptism as a rite of initiation into the Christian fellowship.

IMPERIAL PERSECUTION

Almost from its inception, Christianity encountered opposition. The Acts of the Apostles indicates that the first to persecute Christians were Jewish religious leaders who refused to accept that Jesus of Nazareth was the Messiah. In the earliest days of Christianity, Rome considered the religion to be another sect of Judaism. Judaism was a legally acceptable religion in the Roman Empire; therefore, Christians were free to practice their faith. While they encountered opposition from Jews, the Romans paid them little attention. That changed in the latter half of the first century.

Nero. The first Roman emperor to persecute Christians was Nero, who ruled from 54 to 68 CE. Early Christian tradition indicates that both Peter and Paul were martyred in Rome during Nero's reign. Although Nero's persecution was confined to the city of Rome itself, it was nevertheless a severe persecution as described by the Roman historian Tacitus. Writing in the early part of the second century, Tacitus describes the horrible treatment Christians received from Nero as he blamed them for a fire that swept through the city in the summer of 64.

But all the endeavors of men, all the emperor's largesse and the propitiations of the gods, did not suffice to allay the scandal or banish the belief that the fire had been ordered. And so, to get rid of this rumour, Nero set up as the culprits and punished with the utmost refinement of cruelty a class hated for their abominations, who are commonly called Christians. Christus, from whom their name is derived, was executed at the hands of the procurator Pontius Pilate in the reign of Tiberius. Checked for the moment, this pernicious superstition again broke out, not only in Judaea, the source of the evil, but even in Rome, that receptacle for everything that is sordid and degrading from every quarter of the globe, which there finds a following. Accordingly, arrest was first made of those who confessed [to being Christians]; then, on their evidence, an immense multitude was convicted, not so much on the charge of arson as because of hatred of the human race. Besides being put to death they were made to serve as objects of amusement; they were clad in the hides of beasts and torn to death by dogs; others were crucified, others set on fire to serve to illuminate the night when daylight failed. Nero had thrown open his grounds for the display, and was putting on a show in the circus, where he mingled with the people in the dress of a charioteer or drove about in his chariot. All this gave rise to a feeling of pity, even towards men whose guilt merited the most exemplary punishment; for it was felt that they were being destroyed not for the public good but to gratify the cruelty of an individual.[2]

Two important items should be noted here. First, Tacitus suggests that Nero was to blame for the fire but used the Christians in Rome as the scapegoats in order to escape the blame himself. Second, he indicates that Christians were a "class hated for their abominations." This can only be interpreted as misunderstandings Romans had about Christian religious practices and indicates that Christians were hated by many of the people in the city of Rome.

Domitian. After the death of Nero in 68, Christians enjoyed a relatively quiet period in which there was little or no persecution. But that changed with the reign of Domitian, who ruled Rome from 81 to 96. Toward the end of his reign, Domitian started to demand that he be

---

[2]Henry Bettenson, ed., *Documents of the Christian Church*, 2nd ed. (London: Oxford University Press, 1963) 1-2.

worshipped as a god. Because Christians believed in only one God and that their worship should be exclusive of other gods, many refused to comply. It should be added that Jews were in the same dilemma under Domitian. Because they were unwilling to worship the emperor, Domitian called for a widespread persecution of both Jews and Christians. According to tradition, the Book of Revelation was written during this time by the apostle John who had been exiled to the island of Patmos.

Trajan. Trajan was the emperor of Rome from 98 to 117. He was the first of the Roman emperors to formulate an imperial policy for dealing with Christians. Trajan's policy said that Christians were to be punished only if they were brought before the authorities and charged with practicing Christianity. They were to be examined and asked to recant. If they refused to do so, they were then to be punished. The important thing to recognize about his policy, which was followed for the next two centuries, was that Trajan specified that the resources of Rome were not to be used in hunting down Christians. Therefore there were periods of persecution of Christians over the next several centuries, but the next 200 years were not years of continuous persecution.

Diocletian. It is a frequent misunderstanding to assume that the early Christians were persecuted continually during the first three centuries. Persecution of Christians at the hands of the Romans was frequently brutal, but sporadic. According to many interpreters, the most severe persecution of all came during the reign of Diocletian, who ruled Rome from 284 to 305. During this period, Christians were expelled from the Roman legions out of fear that they were disloyal to Rome because of their refusal to participate in emperor worship. Diocletian also ordered that Christian buildings be seized and that copies of Christian scriptures be destroyed. Eventually, Christians were subject to torture and death.

Martyrs and Apologists. Christianity continued to grow despite periods of persecution. Because Christianity differed from the pagan religions practiced in Greco-Roman society, Christians were misunderstood. They tended to be withdrawn from society, refusing to involve themselves in the normal social intercourse in their respective communities. Therefore, to non-Christians, they appeared to be reclusive and suspicious. Furthermore, many in Roman society misunderstood the practices of Christianity. There are several examples that serve to illustrate how non-Christians misunderstood various practices within Christianity. One charge made against Christians was that they were "atheists." To the modern mindset it seems odd that such a charge would be leveled against Christians. But since Christians refused to believe in the gods of the Greek and Roman pantheons and were unwilling to participate in the state cult of emperor worship, they were believed to be "atheists." A second charge made about Christians concerned their observance of the Lord's Supper. Christians talked of the bread and wine being the body and blood of Christ. Many nonbelievers hearing this began to think that Christians practiced cannibalism in their worship services. Christians were also perceived to be disloyal to Rome and even subsequently a threat to the very well-being of the Empire itself. This charge came from their worship of Jesus of Nazareth, considered an insurrectionist by the Romans. Christians holding an insurrectionist in such high regard would naturally be viewed with suspicion. Along with these charges came other sensationalized charges such as incest, infanticide, and various practices of immorality. Since much of the Roman animosity against Christians grew out of a misunderstanding of their religious practices (admittedly very different from Roman paganism), some early Christian theologians began to produce writings defending the religion against these false charges. These writers are called "Apologists." The writings of the Apologists provide an important source of information for helping to understand early Christianity and the social and political forces that were working against it. Typically, the Apologists would describe the various misunderstandings about Christians and then respond to those charges attempting to explain the traditions and beliefs of Christians. This was done to defend the Christian religion and to show that when properly understood, it posed no threat to the Roman Empire's well-being. It is interesting to read the writings that have survived from some of these Apologists. They provide a fascinating glimpse into the first few centuries of Christianity when Christians were struggling to survive during various periods of persecution and continuous ostracism. The Apologists provide a very different portrait of the Christian religion than that of later centuries when Christianity became entrenched within the power structure of Europe and other parts of the world.

Justin the Martyr, frequently called simply "Justin Martyr," was the principal apologist of the second century. He was martyred for his faith in 165. Justin is famous for several significant writings. His essays titled *First Apology* and *Second Apology* are concerned with rebutting various charges against Christians. They argued that Christians were innocent of the kinds of charges being brought against them. The *Second Apology* was addressed specifically to the Roman Senate. In *Dialogue with Trypho the Jew* Justin defended Christianity against attacks from Judaism, especially attacks on the person and work of Christ. An interesting characteristic of Justin's thought is that he argued that there were points of contact between pagan philosophy and Christianity. He believed the pagan philosophers of his day had received truth but that Christianity was the ultimate and fullest expression of that truth.

Another important martyr, though not usually considered an Apologist, was Ignatius of Antioch. Ignatius was born around 35 CE, making him one of the so-called Apostolic Fathers, a group of early Christian writers traditionally regarded as having some contact with the apostles. Ignatius was arrested in Antioch in the early part of the second century and transported to Rome for execution. During the journey, he wrote seven letters, which have survived the centuries and provide an important glimpse into his thoughts about his faith and his impending martyrdom. These letters are an important early witness to developing ideas concerning the function of the office of bishop in the church. Ignatius's letters also provided encouragement and strength to other Christians who were called upon to suffer for their beliefs throughout the successive centuries of Christian history.

HERESY

In addition to the problem of persecution encountered by the church, there was also a problem within the fellowship associated with incorrect doctrine or false belief. Theologians traditionally refer to false doctrine as "heresy." "Orthodoxy" is the term for what most Christians have traditionally understood to be correct doctrine. During the period from 100 to 313 there were several important heresies that created problems for the early Christians.

Gnosticism. One of the biggest threats to orthodox Christianity in its early centuries came in the form of a movement called Gnosticism. Because there were so many variations of this movement, it is really hard to define it in a simple way. Some New Testament scholars argue that the roots of Gnosticism were present in the first century and that some of the New Testament writings were aimed at countering this movement, which may have already been a threat to orthodox belief. However, it is generally believed that Gnosticism did not exist in a mature form until well into the second century.

While Gnosticism took many different forms, the form that presented a challenge to orthodox Christianity blended together a variety of ideas gleaned from many different sources. There were traces of Greek philosophy, Eastern religion, and Greco-Roman mystery religions, mixed together with some of the teachings of Christianity. It takes its name from the Greek word *gnosis*, which means "knowledge." Gnosticism taught that a special kind of secret knowledge was necessary before one could acquire salvation or spiritual enlightenment. Gnostics made a clear distinction between the flesh and the spirit. The physical universe was created by a lesser god and was totally evil. The Gnostics taught that each human being has a divine spark which is entombed in an evil body of flesh. The flesh is evil, incapable of doing anything good. The spirit is represented by this divine spark. Salvation consisted of freeing this divine spark from its fleshly prison.

Since the flesh was considered evil, the Gnostics had two different approaches toward ethics. Some Gnostics taught that since the flesh was evil, the person needed to do whatever necessary to keep the flesh in check. These Gnostics devoted themselves to extreme asceticism, attempting to deny the body its natural cravings. Other Gnostics had the opposite idea. They taught that since the body was evil, there was no way the flesh could ever be tamed. Therefore, they lived a life of libertinism, indulging in whatever their flesh craved.

Gnosticism's understanding of the person of Christ made it a serious challenge to orthodox Christology. They taught that the Son of God could not possibly be a real human being since the flesh is inherently evil. They believed that Jesus just appeared to be human, a concept referred to as *Docetism*, from a Greek word meaning "seem" or "appear." What appeared to be a human body was simply an illusion. This belief challenged the very essence of the atonement, indicating that Jesus did not really suffer and die on the cross, a serious challenge to early Christian understandings about salvation.

Marcionism. Another threat to orthodox Christian belief in the second century was Marcionism. Marcion (d. ca. 154), the son of a bishop, went to Rome around 140 and was active in the church there. He eventually came under the influence of a Gnostic teacher and developed ideas similar to Gnosticism. Consequently, he was expelled from the Roman church, prompting him to begin his own church. His movement gained in popularity and his ideas were spread all over the Roman Empire in the middle of the second century. He was so popular that Marcionism was still an active movement and threat to orthodox belief almost a century after his death.

Although he was influenced by Gnosticism, Marcion was not really a Gnostic. He believed that there were two competing Gods in the world. The creator of this world, the God of the Old Testament, was an evil, inferior, incompetent God. The God of the New Testament and of Jesus was a benevolent, superior God. Therefore, Marcion rejected Judaism, the religion of the Old Testament, and taught his followers to disregard anything Jewish. Regarding the New Testament, Marcion taught that only Paul was the correct interpreter of Jesus' life and teachings. Furthermore, from Galatians 1:8-9, Marcion surmised that there was only one true Gospel, which he believed was the Gospel of Luke. Marcion was one of the first to propose a "canon" of scripture for his followers to read as the true interpretation of the Christian faith. His canon consisted of ten of the Pauline Epistles (he did not include the Pastoral Epistles) and an abridgment of the Gospel of Luke. Many scholars believe that the "Muratorian Canon" usually dated in the last half of the second century, was an orthodox response to Marcion's canon and teachings.[3]

Safeguarding Orthodoxy. Because heresy became such a threat to the existence of orthodox Christianity, the church needed to develop ways to safeguard orthodoxy. At least three responses to heresy gradually emerged over time. The first means for protecting orthodoxy was to develop a "canon" of scripture. As we have seen in the previous chapter, it took several hundred years for the writings of the New Testament to be accepted universally by all Christians. As heretics produced writings that challenged orthodox Christian beliefs, Christians began to collect writings that had apostolic connections to protect the orthodox faith. The fact that the canonized books of the New Testament had traditions that connected them directly to the apostles and were eventually accepted universally by the churches provided Christianity with a method for judging the soundness of doctrine.

A second method for safeguarding orthodoxy was to develop "creeds." A creed is a short statement of belief which was used for teaching doctrine in the churches. When a new convert to the faith became a member of the church, he/she went through a period of instruction called "catechism." Creeds were used for the pedagogical purpose of teaching the catechumens. One of the first to appear and be used by Christians was a confession of faith called the "Roman Symbol."

---

[3]Hendrik F. Stander, "Marcion," in *The Encyclopedia of Early Christianity*, ed. Everett C. Ferguson (New York: Garland Publishers, 1990).

The use of the term "symbol" has its derivation in a Latin word which related to the concept of a "password" used for security reasons in a military camp. Therefore, the "creed" became a test of membership in the church. Acceptance of the creed was necessary for full membership.[4] The old Roman Symbol, which probably originated in the fourth century but was based on earlier traditions, eventually evolved into what has come to be called the Apostles' Creed. The name that this confession of faith gradually developed was no coincidence. Early Christians believed that the theology of the Apostles' Creed was indeed the theology of the apostles. One version of the Apostles' Creed reads as follows.

> I believe in God Almighty,
> And in Christ Jesus, his son, our Lord
> Who was born of the Holy Spirit
> and the Virgin Mary,
> Who was crucified under Pontius Pilate
> and was buried
> And the third day he rose from the dead
> Who ascended into heaven
> And sits on the right hand of the Father
> Whence he comes to judge the living and the dead
> And in the Holy Spirit
> The holy church
> The remission of sins
> The resurrection of the flesh
> The life everlasting.[5]

A third safeguard to orthodoxy developed by early Christians was an episcopacy. The word "episcopacy" refers to an authoritarian hierarchy in the church. Very early in the history of Christianity local churches began to be grouped together and put under the authority of a bishop. The earliest bishops were either apostles or persons who had a direct tie to one of the apostles. Bishops also tended to be well schooled in theology either by studying with an apostle, or in an area where an apostle had lived. Gradually, five bishoprics rose to prominence: Rome, Constantinople, Jerusalem, Antioch, and Alexandria. The reasons these bishoprics

---

[4]*The Encyclopedia of Early Christianity*, 135.

[5]An early version of the Apostles' Creed taken from Peterson, *A Concise History of Christianity*, 80; for historic variations of the Apostles' Creed, see Bettenson, *Documents of the Christian Church*, 23-24.

developed such power is obvious. The emperor and the power base of the Roman Empire were located in Rome. In the fourth century, the capital was moved to Constantinople, thereby making it the major center of power for the empire. Jerusalem was the city where Christianity began. Antioch was the city from which Paul departed for his missionary journeys and an important city for early Christians. Finally, Alexandria was an important city because of its reputation for scholarship and learning. Gradually, the bishops of Rome and Constantinople gained prominence over the other bishops.

Bishops gained power because of their connection with an apostle. As the apostles died, they appointed bishops to succeed them. Those bishops in turn passed down that apostolic authority to those succeeding them, and so on. This procedure is called "apostolic succession." A bishop could therefore claim authority because that authority had been handed down to him from the apostles. The second-century bishop of Lyons named Irenaeus wrote a treatise, titled *Against Heresies*, in which he claimed that as a youth he had seen Polycarp, bishop of Smyrna, who had been taught by the apostles and had numerous contacts with those who had been with Jesus. Irenaeus was concerned about heresy and in order to combat it, he argued that the bishops transferred their apostolic authority down to their successors. He said that there was an unbroken line of succession among the bishops that extended back to the apostles. He said that Peter and Paul established the church at Rome and that they transferred their authority to Linus who was followed by others in an unbroken line of succession to the twelfth in the line, who was bishop of Rome when Irenaeus wrote his treatise.[6] The bishop was therefore more than an administrator. The bishop served as the spiritual authority over the churches and the bishop's word was the final word on theology. They had, and often exercised, the authority to dismiss priests who taught doctrines not in accord with the bishop's interpretation of orthodox, apostolic Christianity.

EARLY CHRISTIANITY (313-476)

The fourth century brought significant changes to the Christian religion. Christianity entered the century as a persecuted religion. But by the end

---

[6]Kenneth Scott Latourette, *A History of Christianity*, 2 vols., rev. ed. (New York: Harper & Row, 1975) 1:131-32.

of the century it had become the favored religion of the Roman Empire. This major development was the result of events which began with the ascension of Constantine (306–337) as emperor of the empire.

CONSTANTINE AND THE EDICT OF MILAN

The story of how Constantine came to embrace Christianity is an interesting one. Beginning his reign in 306 with the death of his father Constantius, Constantine embarked on a series of political and military maneuvers which ultimately led to his ascension as sole ruler of the Roman Empire in 324. The most important event during that period was the Battle of Milvian Bridge in 312. Tradition has it that before the battle, Constantine had a dream or vision in which a voice spoke to him saying that he was to go forth and conquer under the sign of the cross. Reportedly, Constantine ordered that crosses be painted on his soldiers' shields and other equipment. His victory in the battle gave him sole control of the western portion of the empire.

The following year, Constantine and Licinius, the ruler in the East issued the Edict of Milan, which called for an end to the persecution of Christians and a return of all property seized in earlier persecutions. In 324, when Constantine gained complete control of the empire, he gave to Christianity an official sanction that made it equal with the other religions of the empire.

CHRISTIANITY AND IMPERIAL SUPPORT

Constantine's attitude toward Christianity created an entirely new environment for the religion, now more than three centuries old. In those three centuries Christianity encountered and overcame tremendous obstacles. But the most startling changes were about to take place.

Although Christianity was never made the official state religion of Rome during Constantine's reign, he did show favoritism to the religion and it was during his reign that the most significant changes began to occur.[7] Large amounts of wealth and power began to make their way into the church. Church buildings began to be constructed which were much more ornate and lavish than had ever been built before. With many important politicians and other dignitaries joining the churches, the simple worship style began to give way to a more organized liturgy. The empire

---

[7]Christianity became the official state religion of the Roman Empire during the reign of Emperor Theodosious I who ruled from 379 to 395 CE.

began to do favors for the church and the church reciprocated. Things were definitely different!

Christians reacted to these new dynamics in two different ways. Some accommodated themselves to Christianity's new position in the empire. One of the chief spokespersons for this position was Eusebius of Caesarea. Eusebius was an important theologian and church leader in the fourth century. He is best remembered as the author of the first history of Christianity. But Eusebius's history of the church is not objective history like that which most twenty-first century students are used to reading. Eusebius's history serves as an apology for Constantine's administration. He lavished praise on the emperor and indicated his belief that Constantine became emperor by divine decree from none other than God. In short, Eusebius believed Constantine was a part of God's grand purpose for the church and a positive influence.

On the other hand, there were many Christians who were slow to accept these changes to Christianity and even sought to resist them. They believed that wealth, power, and prestige served only to hurt the witness of the Church and damage the purity of the faith. Many of these Christians believed that the pursuit of pure Christianity could no longer be possible in society. Their withdrawal to the remote regions of the empire (usually the desert areas) marks the beginning of the monastic movement.

As the monastic movement developed, it took two different forms. The earliest type of monasticism to develop is called *eremetical* monasticism. Eremetical monasticism refers to individuals who left society and went to the mountains or deserts by themselves to live solitary lives devoting themselves to the pursuit of holiness. These people were called "monks," from a Latin word which means "alone." Monks usually practiced asceticism, denying the desires of the flesh out of their belief that only the spiritual appetite should be fed. While it is impossible to know for sure who was the first monk, the father of monasticism is usually considered to be Anthony of Egypt (ca. 251–356).

Cenobitic monasticism developed later as monks began to live and work together in monasteries. Pachomius (ca. 290–346) built the first monastery at Tabenisi. He is also remembered for developing a *Rule* or guide for practicing monasticism.

THEOLOGICAL DEVELOPMENT

During the early centuries of Christianity significant discussions about theology occurred. This was due in part to the rise of certain heretical groups discussed earlier. As Christians encountered heresy they were forced to think about theological issues.

Arianism and the Council of Nicea. The fourth century in particular was a century of theological development. One of the most important theological events to occur during that century was the Council of Nicea (325), the first "ecumenical" council in Christian history. It is called an "ecumenical" council because it brought together bishops from all over the empire.

The Council of Nicea was the result of a dispute that arose in the city of Alexandria between Arius, a priest, and Alexander, his bishop. Arius taught that Christ had not existed coeternally with the Father but instead had been created by God as the "firstborn of all creation." Arius's famous phrase to describe his belief was "there was a time when he was not." The technical term used to describe this position is *heterousious*, meaning that Christ was of a "different substance" than the Father. Arius was a popular priest, young and well educated. His ideas developed a large following and caught the attention of Alexander, who ordered Arius to stop his teaching. Alexander believed that Christ had existed coeternally with the Father and was of the "same substance," or *homoousious*. Alexander, and others that opposed Arius, believed that Arius's teaching dangerously de-emphasized the divinity of Christ, hence making him less than fully God.

When Arius refused to stop teaching his ideas, the controversy spilled out into other parts of the empire. It became such a threat to the unity of Christianity and hence of the empire, that it eventually came to the attention of Emperor Constantine. Constantine decided that the best way to resolve the issue was to bring together all the bishops into a council and let the issue be discussed. The council's decision would then be definitive.

Meeting in Nicea in 325, several hundred bishops, mostly from the eastern part of the Empire, came together to discuss the issue. During the course of the discussions three positions developed. Representing Arius's position was Eusebius of Nicomedia. The most important leader of the opposing party was Athanasius, who became bishop of Alexandria three years later when Alexander died. A compromising position was held by Eusebius of Caesarea (discussed earlier) who argued that Christ was of "similar or like" substance with the Father (*homoiousious*). After hearing the arguments and discussions for days, Constantine finally grew impatient and took the initiative to rule in favor of Athanasius and the *homoousious* party. The council issued a creed referred to today as the

Nicene Creed. It is repeated regularly in many Christian churches today, almost 1700 years after the council met.

The Council of Nicea did not destroy Arianism, which remained a strong presence well into the Middle Ages. For the rest of the fourth century disputes arose between the two parties. Further doctrinal disputes would divide Christians for centuries to come. Six more ecumenical councils met over the next five centuries.

Important Theologians. The early centuries of Christianity produced a number of brilliant theologians whose work shaped the future of Christian theology. Irenaeus, Tertullian, Clement of Alexandria, Origen, and Cyprian were important theologians in the second and third centuries.

Irenaeus, mentioned earlier, was bishop of Lyon in Gaul (modern-day France) and was greatly concerned about combating heresy. He was not an original thinker but attempted to teach his parishioners the theological concepts passed on to him. He believed that by teaching the theological tradition passed on to him, he would strengthen his flock against heresy. Tertullian was an important theologian in Carthage, North Africa. Much of his writing was also concerned with defending orthodox Christian theology against heresy. Clement of Alexandria, like Justin Martyr mentioned earlier in this chapter, attempted to explore Greek philosophy and its possible connections with Christian theology. His successor, Origen carried that tradition even further. Many of Origen's writings are philosophical. Although many of his more extreme doctrines were later rejected by orthodox Christianity, he remained an important influence on later theologians, especially in the East. Cyprian was bishop of Carthage when persecution broke out under the emperor Decius in 249. Rather than face persecution, he escaped and hid with the hope that he could continue in his leadership role as bishop. Although he was martyred in a later persecution period (258), he was criticized for having fled. As a result, much of his writing concerns the issue of the "lapsed," or those Christians who desert the faith during periods of persecution but later desire to return to the church.

Several theologians in the fourth century also deserve mention. Athanasius of Alexandria became bishop upon the death of Bishop Alexander. He became the great champion of Nicene orthodoxy throughout North Africa. One of Athanasius's Easter letters to the churches in his charge—"Festal Letter" number 39, for the year 367—includes the earliest listing of the twenty-seven New Testament books as we now have them. During the last half of the fourth century the champions of Nicene orthodox theology were three theologians referred to as the "Cappadocian Fathers": Basil of Caesarea, his brother Gregory of Nazianzus and Gregory of Nyssa. Sometimes forgotten by historians, but nevertheless an important contributor to theology of the fourth century, was Macrina, the sister of Basil of Caesarea and Gregory of Nyssa. The work of the Cappadocians built upon the contributions of Athanasius, particularly concerning the doctrine of the Trinity. Their work greatly influenced the conclusions of the second ecumenical council, the Council of Constantinople which met in 381.

Ambrose was an influential figure in Western Christianity. He was a Roman public official who became bishop of Milan. He was known for his preaching ability and for his defense of Nicene orthodoxy against Arianism. Ambrose may best be remembered for his influence on Augustine, arguably the most influential theologian in the first millennium of Christian history.

Augustine's journey to Christian commitment was an interesting one. He was born in Tagaste in North Africa. His father was a devotee of the pagan religions of his day; his mother, Monica, was a Christian. In his famous *Confessions* he describes how he came to accept the claims of Christianity. Educated in his youth as a Christian, Augustine eventually abandoned those teachings as he moved to Carthage to continue his education. There he took a mistress who gave birth to an illegitimate son. His intention was to study rhetoric (public speaking) in order to become a lawyer. He also began to study philosophy.

Augustine soon became attracted to Manicheism, a heresy based on the teachings of Mani, who taught a radical dualism between the world of the spirit (light) and the material world (darkness). In many ways Manicheism was similar to Gnosticism. After nine years as a Manichean, Augustine became disillusioned with its teachings.

After a move to Rome for a short period of time and then to Milan, Augustine became attracted to Neoplatonism, a popular philosophy in the Roman Empire at the time. Neoplatonism taught that by discipline, study, and meditation one could achieve unity with God, the ultimate source of all things. Evil consists of moving away from God and is not identified with the material world. Neoplatonism helped Augustine with some of his questions, but he eventually rejected its teachings.

It was during this time that Augustine began to attend church in Milan to hear the preaching of Ambrose. He also began to study the New Testament. According to his *Confessions*, he was in a garden one day contemplating his spiritual questions when he heard a child's voice say, "Take up and read." He saw a scroll of the New Testament on a nearby bench and he picked it up and read from Romans 13 where it said, "Not in reveling and drunkenness, not in debauchery and licentiousness, not in quarreling and jealousy. But put on the Lord Jesus Christ and make no provision for the flesh to gratify its desires." This led to Augustine's conversion experience and not long thereafter he and his son were baptized.

Desiring to start a life of monasticism, Augustine sent his mistress back to her home, took his son and some friends and moved back to North Africa to the city of Hippo where they entered a monastery. It was not long before he was ordained as a priest and eventually elevated to the office of bishop of Hippo.

Augustine was a prolific writer and an original thinker. His *City of God* was written during the time when the Roman Empire was beginning to crumble, and served as his explanation for its demise. His theology, perhaps more than that of any other theologian, set the stage for later theologians in Western Christianity.

Two other significant contributors to early Christian theology were Jerome and Chrysostom. Jerome was a monk in Palestine who produced the *Latin Vulgate*, the translation of the Bible into Latin that became the official Bible of Roman Catholicism. John Chrysostom was a native of Antioch. The name Chrysostom means "golden mouth" and brings to mind the fact that Chrysostom is best remembered for his preaching ability. He served as bishop of Antioch but eventually became bishop of Constantinople. Many of his sermons were preserved and still survive today. They reveal his courage in refusing to accede to everything the emperor wanted. They also reveal a champion of the common people in the city of Constantinople and his concern for their well-being.

By the beginning of the fifth century Christianity had become a major force in the Roman Empire. But an ominous future lay ahead for Rome. The story of Christianity's survival as the Roman Empire collapsed and the church's subsequent rise to power in Europe is told in the second major phase in the history of the church, the Middle Ages.

THE EXPLOSIVE DECADES

PERCENTAGE OF CHRISTIANS IN THE ROMAN EMPIRE

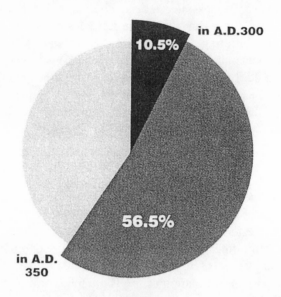

Year	Number of Christians	Percentage of Empire's Population
100	7,500	0.0126
150	41,000	0.07
200	220,000	0.36
250	1,170,000	1.9
300	6,300,000	10.5
350	34,000,000	56.5

These estimates are based on 40 percent growth per decade, and roughly correspond with figures found in early church documents. For more details, see Rodney Stark, *The Rise of Christianity: A Sociologist Reconsiders History* (Princeton NJ: Princeton University Press, 1996). Chart adapted from *Christian History* issue 57 (vol. 17, no. 1): 26.

Chapter 10

MEDIEVAL CHRISTIANITY (500-1500 CE)

The demise of the Roman Empire is a convenient place to mark the transition of Christianity from its earliest centuries into the Middle Ages. The next era of Christian history would last for a millennium.

THE EARLY MIDDLE AGES (500-1000 CE)

Barbarian Invasions. The fall of the Roman Empire was a complicated event with a variety of causes. One of the most important factors contributing to its final dissolution was the invasion of various Germanic tribes from regions beyond the Danube and Rhine Rivers in modern-day Germany. The Romans called these Germanic tribes "barbarian" after the Latin word *barbarus* which means "foreign," "strange," or "ignorant." These tribes invaded the western portion of the Empire in two different ways. Many of the invasions were the result of violent clashes between the Roman legions and these warlike tribes. In other instances, they simply migrated peacefully into the regions of the Empire.

As these people made their way into the western edge of the Empire, their powerful kings began to settle in certain regions and claim the territory for themselves. Several of these groups became well known for their influence on the later history of Western Europe. For example, the Vandals settled in the region now called Spain. Arian missionaries had earlier evangelized them, so they had a tendency to persecute orthodox Christians. They established a settlement in North Africa and from there invaded Rome, sacking the city in 455. Another group settling in the Toledo area of Spain was the Visigoths, also Arian in their theology.

The Franks settled in Gaul and gave that region its modern name of France. Originally pagan, they eventually converted to orthodox Christianity largely due to the influence of their king, Clovis. What led Clovis to convert to the Christian faith is not fully known. He was surrounded by a large number of Christians. But his conversion was much more than simply good politics. Clovis's wife Clothilda was a Christian and according to Clovis's biographer, she pleaded with him to forsake his pagan gods and accept the God of Christianity. He refused but allowed her to have their firstborn son baptized. The child tragically died shortly after its baptism and Clovis blamed the baptism for the child's death.

Later, another child was born and surprisingly, Clovis consented to its baptism. Again, after the baptism the child became gravely ill and Clovis thought baptism would kill it as well. But this time the child recovered. The turning point for Clovis (like Constantine) came on the eve of a battle in which he was outnumbered and sure to lose. Reportedly, he prayed, "Jesus Christ, Clothilda says thou art the son of the living God, and thou canst give victory to those who hope in thee. Give me victory and I will be baptized. I have tried my gods and they have deserted me. I call on thee. Only save me."[1] Clovis won the battle and on Christmas Day in the year 496 he was baptized into the Christian faith. That same day, three thousand men in his army were also baptized.

The invasions of the Germanic "barbarian" tribes brought about the end of the Roman Empire. The final blow came in 476 when the last emperor, Romulus Augustulus, was deposed. Although it may sound as if this era were bad for the church, there were some positive factors in spite of the challenges. First, the Germanic tribes brought new subjects for the church to proselytize, although many of these tribes had already been converted to Arianism and were familiar with Christianity. Western Christianity eventually gained converts from many of the Arian tribes.

Second, the turmoil created in Roman society by the barbarian invasions forced the hierarchy of the church to evolve even further. This gave greater structure to what became the Roman Catholic Church and laid the foundation for Christianity in the Middle Ages. Furthermore, as the hierarchy developed, many people in society began to look to the leaders of the church for stability. The bishop of Rome, called *papa* in Latin by the people, began to acquire more prestige and power as the empire began to collapse. The "Pope" brought a sense of stability to the minds of the people in Roman society who were fearful in such a time of turmoil and social upheaval.

Third, the barbarian invasions divided Eastern and Western Christianity. The imperial capital had been in Constantinople (formerly Byzantium) since Constantine had moved it there in the fourth century. The barbarian invasions blocked the western portion of the Empire from the influence of the emperor in Constantinople. This gave Western Christianity (centered in Rome and thus eventually called "Roman Catholicism") the

---

[1]Quoted in Roland H. Bainton, *Christendom: A Short History of Christianity and Its Impact on Western Civilization*, vol. 1 (New York: Harper & Row, 1966) 145. Clovis's biographer was Gregory of Tours (538–593/594).

ability to develop its own distinctive characteristics. Eastern Christianity (eventually called "Eastern Orthodoxy"), now blocked from Western influence, developed characteristics of its own as well.

Eastern versus Western Christianity. As Christianity progressed through the Middle Ages, distinct differences began to develop between Christianity in the East and West. As seen above, the Germanic invasions into the empire created a rift in communications between East and West. Furthermore, the cultural differences served to create theological differences.

In the West, Latin became the dominant spoken language and a culture developed which emphasized precision in theology. When councils met to discuss theological issues, Western theologians saw the council decrees as settling issues rather than prompting more discussion and speculation as they were viewed in the East. In the East, the Greek language was predominant, and Eastern theologians tended to be more philosophical and speculative in their writings. They placed great emphasis on art and the mystery of God. Furthermore, Eastern theologians thought that the basic problem of humanity was that people had lost their divinity as a result of sin. The work of Christ was to restore that lost divinity to humans. Western theologians believed that the human problem was sin itself. The work of Christ was to pay the penalty for sin. Therefore, the most important aspect of Christ's work for the East was the resurrection, which they viewed as providing a restoration of lost divinity, whereas the West placed great value on the cross, which verified that sin's price had been paid.[2]

Finally, there were differences in church and state relations in the two regions. The emperor continued to reside in the East in Constantinople until the Moslems conquered the city in 1453. The state dominated the church there. In the West, the church stepped in to fill the vacuum in Rome created in the fourth century when Constantine moved the imperial capital. Therefore, the church dominated the state in the West.

The differences between the two regions became more acute at some times than others. The most important crisis came in 1054. That date marks the formal break between Eastern and Western Christianity. One of the issues leading to the division involved an addition to the Nicene

---

[2]See Peterson, *A Concise History of Christianity*, 110, for this discussion of the differences between East and West.

Creed called the *Filoque Clause*. The word *filioque* in Latin means "and from the Son." The West inserted it into the Nicene Creed after the statement which says that the Spirit proceeds from the Father. Aside from the theological changes that this created, the East refused to accept the *Filioque Clause* because it had not been voted on in an "ecumenical council" composed of all bishops. Their refusal to accept the addition forced the pope in 1054 to excommunicate the patriarch of Constantinople, who then proceeded to do the same to the pope. The sacking of

A sixth-century paten depicting Christ giving communion simultaneously to his disciples in the East and the West.

Constantinople in 1204 by the Western crusaders during the Fourth Crusade forever sealed the division between East and West.

Conflicts with Islam. In Arabia, in the early seventh century, a new religion began to develop under the leadership of Mohammed, an Arab merchant. Inquisitive about religious issues, Mohammed had been in contact with Christianity, Judaism, and Zoroastrianism, three religions that were prevalent in that part of the world in the seventh century. These three religions shared several things in common, bringing them into sharp contrast with the native polytheistic religions of Arabia: (1) belief in one God; (2) belief in a collection of scriptures considered to be divinely inspired; and (3) belief in an afterlife in which the righteous will be rewarded and the unrighteous punished.

Mohammed began a quest for the "true" religion. This search led him into the wilderness for periods of time in which he claimed that the one true God named "Allah" revealed truth to him in a series of ecstatic visitations. Mohammed began to identify himself as a "Muslim," meaning "one who submits to Allah" and began to teach others about his revelations. He resisted the claim that he was starting a new religion. Instead, he contended that he was preaching the completion of the truth revealed first to the Hebrew prophets and then to the person of Jesus, who was a great prophet, but not divine.

At first Mohammed's message fell on deaf ears with the people of his native Mecca. Polytheism was prevalent among their religious traditions. So Mohammed moved in 622 to Medina, a nearby city that became receptive to his preaching. Very shortly thereafter, Mohammed and his followers led a military campaign back to Mecca where he captured control of the city. Soon the city converted to the Moslem faith. Mohammed forgave his former enemies but outlawed all idols in the city. By the time of his death in 632, most of Arabia was in Moslem hands.

Following Mohammed's death, the Moslem religion began to spread beyond Arabia under the leadership of the "caliphs" or successors of Mohammed. By the middle of the seventh century, all of Arabia, Syria, Palestine, and Egypt were in Moslem hands. During the second half of the seventh century Moslem armies continued along the northern part of Africa. Carthage fell in 695 and in 711 a group of Moslem armies crossed into Spain. Charles Martel successfully halted the Moslem advance in 732 at the Battle of Tours in France.

The Moslem conquest of what had previously been Christian strongholds was significant for Christianity. First, the spread of Islam hastened the division between Eastern and Western Christianity. The Moslems, though relatively tolerant of Christians in many quarters, effectively isolated Constantinople from the West and kept the emperor from having any contact or influence there. Second, the conquest by the Moslems of many areas that had once been important Christian territories (such as Jerusalem) set the stage for the Crusades, which began several centuries later. Third, the Moslem invasions forced Christianity to turn its attention north. It is no coincidence that within two hundred years, Christianity would be accepted formally in Russia, and following the fall of Constantinople in the fifteenth century Moscow would proclaim itself the "Third Rome."

THE LATE MIDDLE AGES (1000-1500 CE)

Development of the Papacy. The story of the papacy during the late Middle Ages is a tale of both a rise to power as well as a fall into decadence. The tenth century represents one of the most corrupt eras in the history of the papacy. During the first part of the century a rapid succession of popes occurred (seventeen from 897 to 955) with numerous assassinations and political intrigue. The papacy had become a political prize for the ruling families in Italy. It was not uncommon for a pope to have his rivals executed.

One of the most bizarre examples of the decadence of the period came in 897. The "Cadaveric Council," as it came to be called, was presided over by Stephen VI. Formosus, one of Stephen's rival predecessors and already dead, was exhumed. His remains were then dressed in papal robes and his body was paraded through the streets of Rome. He was then placed on trial, and posthumously condemned for a variety of crimes, followed by the mutilation of his body. His remains were then thrown into the Tiber River.[3]

The so-called "Pornocracy" of the church occurred from 904 to 964. During these years the papacy was controlled by three women, who provided sexual favors to a number of weak-willed popes in exchange for wealth, titles, and land. One of the women bore an illegitimate son who was fathered by Pope Sergius III. The child later became Pope John XI.[4]

During this dark era in Roman Catholicism, an effort at reform was underway in the monasteries. Duke William III of Aquitaine began a monastery at Cluny in France. He appointed as abbot a monk named Berno, who had a reputation for reform and strict discipline in monastic circles. Through the leadership of Berno and his successors, Cluny

---

[3]See Gonzalez, *The Story of Christianity* 1:275.
[4]William Ragsdale Cannon, *History of Christianity in the Middle Ages: From the Fall of Rome to the Fall of Constantinople* (Grand Rapids: Baker Book House, 1960) 133.

spawned numerous other monasteries and this revival of monasticism eventually led to greater stability in the church.

As the late Middle Ages progressed, three popes should be recognized for their contributions. They represent the height of papal power in the Middle Ages. Gregory VII (1073–1085), known as a reformer, is perhaps best remembered for his clash with Henry IV, emperor of the Holy Roman Empire. The controversy generated between these two men concerned the issue of "investiture." By the eleventh century, the tradition had developed whereby the emperor "invested" or selected individuals to serve in high-church offices such as that of bishop or abbot. In return, the emperor expected homage from the person appointed, thereby solidifying his power against potential enemies. The system worked well for the emperor. Gregory VII disagreed with the practice, however. He believed the appointment of ecclesiastical offices was the prerogative of the church. He reasoned that when the emperor chose a bishop the person filling that office had more of a political obligation than spiritual, thereby compromising the spiritual integrity of the office.

The matter came to a head in the winter of 1077. Gregory forbade Henry to appoint any more ecclesiastical offices. Henry, however, convened synods on two different occasions calling for Gregory to be deposed as pope. With support in other quarters, Gregory then excommunicated Henry and placed him under the "ban." This meant that all those who were Henry's subjects were released from their oaths of allegiance to him. Henry eventually became desperate with the loss of support. He made his way across the Alps to the papal palace in Canossa, Italy, seeking forgiveness from Gregory. The pope made Henry stand in the snow for three days in sackcloth and ashes begging forgiveness before finally allowing him inside and granting him absolution. Through a political twist of fate several years later, Henry succeeded in having Gregory removed from power where shortly thereafter he died in exile. But the episode stands as a remarkable illustration of papal power in the Middle Ages.

Innocent III (1198–1216) might be regarded as the most powerful pope in history. Certainly, he represents the height of papal power in the Middle Ages. He was the most powerful man in Europe during his reign. He was the first to use the phrase "Vicar of Christ" to describe the papal office. Innocent III also called the Fourth Lateran Council into session in 1215. Though the belief had been around for centuries, this council officially confirmed transubstantiation as the theological definition of the

Mass. Transubstantiation is the doctrine that when the priest elevates the "host" (the bread) during the Mass and pronounces the words of institution, "This is my body," the bread and wine are transformed into the body and blood of Christ in their substance while the "accidents" (or appearance) remain bread and wine.

Boniface VIII (1294–1303) was a third Middle Ages pope who believed in the absolute power of the papacy. He is best remembered for a papal bull (official papal opinion) called *Unam Sanctam* (1302). It formally declared that outside of the church there is no salvation or forgiveness of sins. Therefore, when persons are excommunicated from the church they are severed from their spiritual salvation. Consequently, the salvation of every human depends upon his or her submission to the pope's authority. Boniface further declared that in the world there are two "swords," the sword of temporal authority and the sword of spiritual authority. The clergy wields the sword of spiritual authority while the sword of temporal authority is in the hands of the secular rulers to be used for the church and under its direction. *Unam Sanctam* declares that the pope is the supreme head of the church and all on earth are subject to him.

The Crusades. The Crusades were a series of military campaigns from 1095 to 1291 to recover the Holy Land from the Moslems. The motives of the Crusades were mixed—partly religious, but also economic and political. Pope Urban II proclaimed the First Crusade in 1095. He promised forgiveness of sin and eternal life to those who died in the endeavor. On the journey toward Jerusalem, the crusaders raped and pillaged throughout the countryside. Innocent villagers were killed for no reason as the bloodthirsty army pressed forward. Four years later, Jerusalem fell to the crusaders and remained in Latin hands for approximately one hundred years.

The Fourth Crusade was notable. Instead of attacking the Moslems the crusaders detoured into Constantinople and sacked the city in 1204, attempting to establish Latin Christianity there. This disastrous episode further eroded relations between Greek-speaking Christians in the East and Latin–speaking Christians in the West and weakened the empire in the East.

After the Seventh Crusade, the crusading spirit in Europe died. Generally, the Crusades were a tragic failure because the Holy Land remained in Moslem hands except for a brief period following the First Crusade. Still, there were some important—if not always positive—results of the Crusades. First, they served to further ill feelings between

Christians and Moslems. Second, they created a further division—which has never been overcome—between Eastern and Western Christianity. Third, the power of the papacy grew. The popes called the Crusades into being, appointed the leaders and promised spiritual favors to those who volunteered. Fourth, the Crusades created a renewed interest in Christian piety. The veneration of relics became popular in Europe with crusaders claiming to bring back such things from the Holy Land as bones and other remains of martyrs and biblical characters and pieces of the cross. Fifth, new monastic military orders blending monasticism and warfare developed with names such as the Order of Saint John of Jerusalem and the Knights Templar. Some of these new orders continued to be active in Europe long after the Crusades ended. Sixth, the attention to the Moslems and the rhetoric used to describe them as "infidels" created a renewed interest in heresy in Europe which was ultimately addressed with the organization of the Inquisition. Seventh, contact with the Moslem world opened the eyes of many in Europe to new ideas, especially in the areas of theology and philosophy. The writings of the Jewish philosopher Maimonides and the Moslem philosopher Averroes had an important impact on the theological and philosophical development in Europe in the thirteenth century. Eighth, the Crusades introduced new economic and social reforms in Europe. Commerce and trade routes were opened and a "middle class" began to rise in Europe.[5]

Early Reformation Movements. Although the Protestant Reformation did not begin until the sixteenth century, several early reform movements deserve attention. Two of these movements are most notable.

John Wycliffe was an English Catholic priest and professor at Oxford. Wycliffe lived in the fourteenth century during a time when there was a tremendous amount of corruption in the papacy and the church's hierarchy. He became critical of the pope and began to disagree with the church on a number of issues. First, he disagreed with the church about the Bible. He believed the Bible was the possession of all Christians and that any Christian should be able to read and interpret the Bible for oneself. The church taught that the Bible belonged to the clergy because they were the only ones with the proper training to allow its interpretation. The church hierarchy believed it would be dangerous for the laity

---

[5]The results of the Crusades were gleaned from Gonzalez, *The Story of Christianity* 1:298-300.

to read and interpret the Bible for themselves because that would possibly encourage heresy and would create anarchy within the church.

Wycliffe's ideas about the Bible led him to the conclusion that the Bible should be translated into English. Although he probably did not do any of the translating himself, he inspired the translation of the Latin Vulgate into English by his followers, later called "Lollards," who completed the project just after his death in 1384.

Wycliffe also disagreed with the doctrine of transubstantiation. He believed Christ was present only spiritually during the Lord's Supper and not physically as the doctrine of transubstantiation taught. Furthermore, he believed that immoral or incompetent clergy, including the pope, should be replaced if they failed to carry out their offices properly; if the church would not replace them, then the secular rulers should.

Needless to say, Wycliffe raised the eyebrows of many of those in positions of power in the Roman Catholic Church. Although he died of natural causes in 1384, the Lollards continued to preach his ideas throughout the English countryside. Eventually, their preaching became so controversial that their movement was forced underground. Wycliffe's ideas became so threatening to the power structure of the church that the Council of Constance, which met from 1414 to 1418, declared him, posthumously, him to be a heretic. They ordered his body to be exhumed, and his bones burned to ashes and the ashes scattered. Wycliffe's ideas and the work of the Lollards made them true forerunners of the Reformation a century later.

John Hus (1374–1415) was contemporary with Wycliffe and was greatly influenced by his thought. Hus was from Bohemia in Eastern Europe. A professor at the University of Prague, and every bit as outspoken as Wycliffe, Hus believed that Scripture is the final authority for the Christian life and that both the church and the clergy should be reformed based on Scripture. He also rejected the doctrine of transubstantiation and became a vocal opponent of it. He preached sermons in which he vehemently opposed the corrupt morals of the clergy and frequently made the pope the chief target of his sermons.

Hus became a folk hero in Bohemia and soon had a large following of the people and the monarch in his region. This eventually came to the attention of the Roman Catholic Church. In 1414 he was invited to appear before the Council of Constance to defend his views. He was given a safe conduct to the Council. But when he arrived the safe conduct was rescinded and he was arrested. He was tried and condemned as a heretic.

In 1415 he was burned at the stake. When Hus's followers in Bohemia heard of his death they rebelled. The Catholics finally quelled the rebellion but not without first making some concessions. The Bohemian Brethren (which became the Moravian Brethren or Moravian Church) in Bohemia, along with the Lollards in England became important voices advocating reform of the church almost a century before the Protestant Reformation of the sixteenth century.

During the thousand years called the Middle Ages, the Church gained great wealth and power and became entrenched as a political force in Western Europe. In the East, the orthodox expression of Christianity achieved the same status until 1453 when the Moslems gained control of Constantinople. Christianity in the East never recovered its power. In the West, the sixteenth century brought about a wave of reform creating a new expression of Christianity called "Protestantism," the focus of our next chapter.

Chapter 11

THE REFORMATION

As we saw in the previous chapter, the movement of reform in Western Christianity began many years before the sixteenth century. It could be said that early reformers like Wycliffe and Hus planted the seeds of reform that sprouted and blossomed in the sixteenth century with Martin Luther in Germany. The Reformation of the sixteenth century was not a monolithic movement. There were several independent movements in Western Europe, working simultaneously toward reform in the sixteenth century. They shared a common foe in the Roman Catholic Church, but these different movements also experienced turmoil and conflict between themselves at times.

The varied movements that taken together constitute the Protestant Reformation can be divided into two categories. Magisterial reformers, like Martin Luther, Ulrich Zwingli, John Calvin, and Henry VIII in England, used the power of secular governments and rulers to accomplish their reform goals. Radical reformers, such as the Anabaptists, represent the second category. They were opposed to any kind of government efforts to carry out the spiritual reform goals for which they worked.

MAGISTERIAL REFORMERS

Martin Luther. The story of Martin Luther is one of the most interesting in the history of Christianity. He was born in 1483 in Eisleben, Germany to parents of very humble means. A precocious child, Luther excelled in his schooling in spite of a schoolmaster who would be considered cruel by today's standards. It was not unusual for the children in Luther's class to receive severe beatings for unprepared lessons or for misbehavior. After completing his early schooling, Luther entered Erfurt University in 1501. He earned his B.A. degree in 1502 and his M.A. in 1505.

Throughout his childhood Luther's harsh treatment by his father coupled with a stern schoolmaster gave him a fear of authority figures. Gradually, this fear began to impact the way Luther viewed God. He began to see God as a vengeful, wrathful God rather than loving and benevolent. As Luther increasingly became aware of his sinfulness, he became even more frightened of God, and his fear of God grew more acute during his years at the university.

Upon completion of his university education, Luther intended to pursue a career in law. That changed suddenly. One night, while walking in the midst of a thunderstorm, Luther was struck by lightening. Already made aware of the transience of life by the death of a friend, this experience terrified Luther and made him fearful of his own mortality in ways he had not experienced before. Picking himself up from the ground he cried out, "Save me Saint Anne [the patron saint of his hometown]; I will become a monk." Luther began to see this experience as a divine sign and because of his fear of God, he responded immediately by entering an Augustinian monastery in Erfurt in 1505.

As a monk, Luther began preparation for the priesthood, which included studying theology. But the more he studied, the more his view of a vengeful God terrified him. He became obsessed about his own sinfulness and inability to find a sense of forgiveness. He would go into the confessional and confess sometimes for hours at a time and then come out saying that he felt worse than he did before entering. He even began to torture his body by self-flagellation, beating himself until he passed out. Still, he could not find any peace in his soul.

In 1508 Luther left Erfurt for Wittenberg where he became a lecturer in Theology and began to study for his doctorate. This became a turning point in his life. One evening, while preparing a lecture on the Pauline Epistle of Romans, Luther was struck by the phrase in Romans 1:17: "The just shall live by faith." This discovery became the key for which he had been looking. For the first time he understood that justification before God did not depend on his own righteousness. In fact, Luther began to believe that a human being could never be righteous in his or her own strength. Rather, by placing faith in Christ alone, Luther believed that God pronounced the sinner righteous. Suddenly, Luther had an entirely new understanding of God. No longer seeing God as cruel and vengeful, Luther now saw God as loving, benevolent, and willing to provide forgiveness of sin and the means by which that forgiveness could be attained, namely, the sacrifice of Christ on the cross.

After completing his doctorate, Luther remained at Wittenberg. Focussing his attention on theology, Luther increasingly came to believe that the Roman Catholic system of the sacraments was inadequate for dealing with human sin because it was based more on human works than faith. With his new understanding of salvation by faith alone, Luther began to attack the church and the sacramental system. He became so vocal in his attack that he eventually captured the attention of the church's hierarchy.

Luther's new ideas about justification by faith eventually brought him into direct conflict with the Roman Catholic Church. The first episode involved a man named Tetzel, who came to Wittenberg to raise funds for the renovation of St. Peter's Cathedral in Rome by selling indulgences. During the Middle Ages, the church developed the practice of selling indulgences in order to raise extra income. The theory behind the practice was based on lives of the saints. The church believed the saints had built up more merit than they actually needed to cover their own sins. Therefore, the extra merit was stored in the "Treasury of Merit" in heaven. The church believed the pope had the authority to tap into this Treasury of Merit and assign various amounts of forgiveness to those who bought indulgences.

Luther's personal struggle with sin and his view of the inadequacy of the Roman Catholic system for providing him the peace he sought, led him into a public confrontation with Tetzel. On October 31, 1517 (All Saints' Eve), Luther posted on the church door at Wittenberg a formal challenge for debate. This document contained ninety-five theses on the topic of indulgences that Luther wanted to debate with a representative from the Roman Catholic Church. Within a matter of weeks copies of Luther's ninety-five theses were published all over Europe. The Protestant Reformation had begun!

At first, the church sought to silence Luther through his monastic order. But that proved ineffective. Many of Luther's faculty colleagues began to adopt his new theological ideas. In a more concerted attempt to silence Luther, the church sent one of its champion debaters, John Eck, a revered Catholic theologian, to engage him in a public debate. To the surprise of the Catholic authorities, Luther won the debate. When the pope, Leo X, became the focus of Luther's attacks and when the German people began following him, the resulting upheaval led to Luther's excommunication in June 1520. By the next year, the entire matter came to the attention of Emperor Charles V of the Holy Roman Empire.

In the sixteenth century, the seven most powerful nobles in Germany had the authority to elect the emperor. In 1521, Luther was called to appear at the emperor's annual meeting with his electors in the city of Worms. At this yearly meeting, in a moment of high drama with all the emperor's electors present, Luther was called upon to recant his writings and attacks on the pope. In response Luther exclaimed,

Unless I am convicted by Scripture and plain reason—I do not accept
the authority of popes and councils, for they have contradicted each
other—my conscience is captive to the Word of God. I cannot and I
will not recant anything, for to go against conscience is neither right nor
safe. God help me, Amen.

Supposedly, Luther added the famous words,

Here I stand, I cannot do otherwise.[1]

The Edict of Worms, issued on 26 May 1521, formally condemned
Luther's teachings. He was now at odds with both the pope and the
emperor.

Luther probably would have been arrested and executed had it not
been for his popularity with the German people and with the elector from
his home region of Saxony, Frederick III. Frederick was a supporter and
friend to Luther. He was instrumental in the founding of the University
of Wittenberg and in the invitation to Luther to teach there. When Luther
was excommunicated in 1520 Frederick refused to support the order.
After the Diet of Worms Frederick had Luther kidnapped and hidden for
protection in a castle in Wartburg. These years in hiding proved to be
some of Luther's most productive. A most significant publication from
this period was a complete translation of the Bible into German.

Luther's reform efforts in Germany continued for another twenty-five
years until his death in 1546. By that time, a thriving Protestant
movement was in place and Germany would never again be completely
in the hands of Roman Catholicism. Historians note that in the last years
of Luther's life his personality became very different from that of his
early years. He became somewhat irascible, crude, and stubborn with his
ideas. This may have been due partly to his declining health and partly
due also to the political pressure under which he found himself at times.

There remained another side to Luther's work and life. As his reform
work was beginning in Germany, he began encouraging priests to marry.
The monasteries emptied and Luther began matching priests with nuns
from the convents. Luther himself married Katherine von Bora and
together they had six children. They bought an old monastery building for
a home and, along with their children, raised four orphaned children. In

---

[1]Roland H. Bainton, *Here I Stand: A Life of Martin Luther* (Nashville:
Abingdon Press, 1950) 185.

addition, they rented rooms to some of Luther's students. Altogether, the household numbered twenty-five at its peak. His family was one of the great joys of his life.

How should Luther be evaluated? First, he can be credited with igniting the spark that flamed the Protestant Reformation of the sixteenth century. Other movements paralleled Luther's, but his reform movement in Germany paved the way in Europe for other reform movements to take hold. Second, Luther developed a fresh understanding of the doctrine of salvation with his understanding of justification by faith alone. It could be argued that he returned to Pauline theology, which the Roman Catholicism of the Middle Ages had modified to such an extent that it was no longer recognizable as Pauline. Third, Luther effectively became the founder of the Lutheran denomination, one of the major denominations in Protestantism today.

Ulrich Zwingli. While Germany was occupied with the Lutheran reform movement, Switzerland was engaged in its own reform. The Swiss Reformation began in Zurich with Ulrich Zwingli (1484–1531). A contemporary of Luther, Zwingli developed his disagreements with the Roman Catholic Church in a different way. Zwingli did not have the emotional and spiritual struggle that was present in Luther's journey to reform. Born in Wildhaus, Switzerland, Zwingli's father was mayor of the town. After studying with an uncle who was a priest, Zwingli furthered his education at the universities of Basel, Bern, and Vienna. He was greatly influenced by the Renaissance humanist scholars who sought to study the best of ancient Greek and Roman culture.

Zwingli completed his M.A. in Classics (Humanism) in 1506 and became priest at Glarus. He taught himself Greek and began to study the New Testament closely. At Glarus, Zwingli volunteered as chaplain to mercenary troops provided by the Swiss to other countries. His first experience in war was with an army that was victorious in battle and that subsequently looted and pillaged the defeated enemy. A few years later he saw war from the perspective of a defeated, demoralized army. These experiences prompted Zwingli to begin speaking out against Switzerland's practice of providing mercenary soldiers to other nations.

In 1516 Zwingli became a priest in Einsiedeln where his Protestant views continued to develop. Einsiedeln was famous for its shrine to the Virgin Mary, which attracted large numbers of religious pilgrims. Zwingli observed the way many of the pilgrims were treated, especially by indulgence sellers who were active in the city. He began to oppose the idea that pilgrimages and indulgences were efficacious for salvation and began preaching to the pilgrims who came to visit the shrine.

Two years later, in 1518, Zwingli was appointed as priest to the largest church in Zurich. By that time, he had thoroughly embraced Protestant theology. Zwingli arrived at his Protestant faith through careful study of the Greek New Testament in the style of the humanists of his day. He eventually gained the support of the city council in Zurich which supported his Protestant ideas and he began to reform the city by purging it of any trace of Roman Catholic practices or traditions.

Though Zwingli and Luther were contemporaries, a word should be said here about the difference between them concerning their views of the Lord's Supper. In 1529, supporters of both movements brought the two reformers together in Marburg, Germany. The goal was for the two men to reach an accord, thereby presenting a united front against the Roman Catholic Church. They were able to agree on almost every point except their respective views of the Lord's Supper. Both men rejected transubstantiation. But Luther believed that the body of Christ was present in the bread and wine while Zwingli believed that the Lord's Supper was symbolic of Christ's body. This difference, and the inability to resolve it, forced the two movements to go their separate ways.

The city council of Zurich continued to embrace Zwingli's reforms. In 1531 the five Catholic cantons in Switzerland launched an attack on Zurich. Zwingli joined the efforts to defend his city and was tragically killed in battle in a town called Koppel. Within a month the Peace of Koppel was signed. The result was that each canton in Switzerland would have the freedom to choose between Catholicism and Protestantism.[2]

John Calvin. Following the death of Zwingli, John Calvin became the most important name associated with the Reformation in Switzerland. Calvin was born in 1509 in Noyon, France. His father had an important job as secretary to the bishop of Noyon, a position that paid well, thereby providing the necessary funds for Calvin's schooling. He studied for a career in law at the universities of Paris, Orleans, and Bourges. During his schooling, like Zwingli before him, he became thoroughly influenced by the spirit of humanism and its attention to ancient culture.

---

[2]For a good discussion of Zwingli's Swiss reform movement see Gonzalez, *The Story of Christianity* 2:46-52; and Peterson, *A Concise History of Christianity*, 207-10.

Very different from Luther, Calvin wrote little about any kind of inner struggle with sin or a spiritual crisis. It is not known when Calvin made his formal break with the Roman Catholic Church. It is clear that he was Protestant by 1534 because in that year he fled from France's persecution of Protestants. He finally settled in Basel, Switzerland.

In 1536, Calvin wrote the first edition of the *Institutes of the Christian Religion*. One of the most important theological works in Christian history, the *Institutes* brought immediate attention and fame to Calvin. Originally published as a manual that could be easily concealed in one's pocket, it went through a number of revisions. The final edition, which occupied four volumes, was published in 1559. Reading the different editions of the *Institutes* provides an interesting picture of how Calvin's theology grew and developed from 1536 until 1559.

A significant turning point in Calvin's life came in 1536 when he visited Geneva. There he met William Farel who had initiated a Protestant reform in the city. Farel, needing help, requested that Calvin stay in Geneva and join the reform movement. Calvin agreed to stay and remained there for two years; but it was a turbulent period. Almost immediately, Calvin began writing laws which he expected the city council to endorse. He sought to establish a "theocracy" in Geneva which would be governed by the same laws as the ancient Hebrews in the Old Testament. His vision included such things as "blue laws" (which forbid any business dealings on Sundays), forced church attendance, a confession of faith to which all citizens of Geneva were expected to assent, training of children in Protestant ideas, and a system of lay inspectors who would observe the conduct of the citizens and report any moral problems to Calvin. The laws proved so unpopular that the people initiated a riot against the city government. Although the annual election of 1537 favored Calvin and his supporters, a year later the opposition won and took over the council. Calvin and Farel fled to nearby Strasbourg.

Calvin spent three years in Strasbourg which proved to be his happiest and most peaceful. Though he turned his attention to writing, he always yearned to return to Geneva to complete the experiment with theocracy he started there. That opportunity came in 1541. The political situation with the city government changed once again and Calvin was invited to return. This time he was assured that there would be support for his reform efforts. He remained in Geneva until his death in 1564. During those years, his dream of creating a "theocracy" was realized although by modern democratic standards it was an oppressive, restrictive place to live. Nevertheless, Calvin should be regarded as one of the greatest reformers of the Reformation era, especially because of his keen theological insights and writing.

Calvin's theology as found in the *Institutes* was systematized by his followers years after his death. Students of Calvinism have used the acrostic "TULIP" as a mnemonic device to remember the salient points of his theological system. The first letter stands for "total depravity," the belief that all humans are totally depraved by original sin, meaning that there is nothing good that humans can do for salvation under their own power. Second, "unconditional election" represents one of the most controversial points in Calvinism. This is the concept that before the world and human beings were ever created God predestined or "elected" certain people to salvation and others to eternal damnation. Third, "limited atonement," is the idea that the death of Christ (or the Atonement) is only for the elect. That follows logically. If only the elect can be saved, then Christ's death could only be applicable to them. Fourth, "irresistible grace" is the notion that if a person is one of God's elect, God's grace will be irresistible when that person is confronted with it. Fifth, "perseverance of the saints" indicates that the elect will persevere in their salvation until the end of their lives, making loss of salvation impossible.

John Calvin ranks as one of the greatest figures in the history of Christianity. Many have disagreed with his theology but all acknowledge the importance of his influence. The English Puritans were influenced by his theology. They brought that influence across the Atlantic Ocean to the Massachusetts Bay Colony. John Knox was a student of Calvin and took Calvin's theology back to Scotland where his reforms of the Church of Scotland led to the rise of Presbyterianism. One segment of the early Baptists of the seventeenth century was thoroughgoing Calvinistic in its theology. Calvin has certainly left his mark on Christianity since the sixteenth century.

The English Reformation. Although it was magisterial in nature, the English Reformation was very different from both the German and Swiss reform movements. One could argue that the German and Swiss reforms were religiously motivated with political effects. The English reform, on the other hand, was a politically motivated movement that had religious consequences. Protestant reform in England began with the king, Henry VIII. The story of how he reformed the church in England is most interesting indeed.

Henry VIII was happy as a Roman Catholic. In fact, when Luther's reform began in Germany, Henry was initially critical of it. His support of the Roman Catholic Church earned him the title "Defender of the Faith" from Pope Leo X in 1521. Henry certainly never intended to break away from the Roman Catholic Church. But events began to take place which eventually made separation a necessity. Henry VIII became obsessed with having a male heir to his throne.

Henry's older brother Arthur, the heir to the throne, married Catherine of Aragon (daughter of Ferdinand and Isabella of Spain) as a political arrangement between England and Spain. But Arthur died four months after the marriage. At this point Henry assumed the throne and it was determined that he would marry Catherine to keep the alliance between Spain and England intact. Church law prohibited marriage to a brother's widow. Therefore, a special dispensation from the pope was needed for the marriage. The pope willingly granted the dispensation. However, of six children born to Catherine and Henry, five died leaving only a daughter Mary to survive infancy. Henry became convinced that the failure to have a male heir from Catherine was because of God's judgment on what he now became convinced was an illegitimate marriage. Therefore, Henry began to seek an annulment from the pope, claiming that the marriage was illegal in the first place. To make matters worse, by this time Henry was involved in a romance with Anne Boleyn whom he wished to maarry.

The pope probably would have granted the annulment except for a political problem. Catherine was the aunt of Charles V, the emperor of the Holy Roman Empire whose armies were present in Italy and were protecting the pope. The pope simply could not risk angering Charles V. Granting the annulment would have been an embarrassment to the Spanish in general, and to Catherine and Charles V in particular. Therefore, the pope refused to comply.

Henry then decided to take matters into his own hands. In 1533 he married Anne Boleyn in spite of the pope's objection. The following year he asked Parliament to pass the Act of Supremacy which severed the Church of England from Rome and made the monarch of England the sole head of the English church. The Reformation had arrived in England! Henry VIII eventually married four other women and finally got a male heir, Edward VI. Henry died in 1547 leaving Edward, his nine-year-old son, as king.

Henry had not been a theologian and for his part the church in England remained essentially the same as the Roman Catholic Church. However, he was surrounded by those who were already influenced by the Reformation that was in full force on the Continent. The major theologian of this English Reformation was Thomas Cranmer. Through Cranmer's influence and guidance the English church began to develop its own distinctiveness. Cranmer became a major advisor to Edward VI and, because Edward was so young and impressionable, a significant amount of reforms were generated. Worship services in English churches began to be in English rather than Latin. Cranmer also wrote a *Book of Common Prayer* which was decidedly Protestant. The reform movement was in full force in England until Edward VI died suddenly only five years into his reign. His successor brought a screeching halt to the Protestant reformation in England.

Edward's successor was his half-sister Mary, the daughter born to Catherine of Aragon and Henry. She had grown up with an intense hatred for her father because of the embarrassment he had caused her mother and her mother's family in Spain. Mary also grew into adulthood with a strong commitment to the Roman Catholic Church. When she acceded to the throne in 1553 she was determined to return the Church of England to the Roman Catholic fold. She married Philip, who later became king of Spain forming an alliance that gave her the political strength to carry out her aggressive efforts in England. She officially returned the Church of England to the papal fold in 1554. To make matters worse for Protestants, Mary began a systematic persecution throughout England of those who resisted her efforts. Many Protestants were imprisoned. A large number of Protestants fled to Geneva and became thoroughly immersed in the reform of John Calvin. These "Marian exiles" would later return to England as the beginning of the Puritan movement.

More than three hundred Protestants were martyred during Mary's reign, the most famous of which was Thomas Cranmer. Cranmer had been the leader of the Protestant movement in England during the reigns of Henry and Edward. Mary had him arrested and forced him to recant his Protestant views. She then had him condemned to be burned at the stake. He was taken to the platform and before the fire was started given a chance to speak. It was expected that he would affirm his recantation and ask for forgiveness for his sins. Instead, he withdrew his recantation and called the pope the Antichrist. He became one of the most important

Protestant martyrs in England. Mary's persecution of Protestants was so severe that she earned the nickname "Bloody Mary."

England would probably be Roman Catholic today if Mary had lived longer. She died in 1558, however, after only five years as queen. Her successor was her half-sister Elizabeth I, the daughter of Henry and Anne Boleyn. Elizabeth came to the throne realizing that there was much political and religious instability in England. She was politically wise and understood that in order to survive she needed to forge a compromise. Her *via media* came in the form of the *Thirty-nine Articles*, passed by Parliament in 1563. Elizabeth sought to steer a middle course between extreme Protestantism and Roman Catholicism. The Church of England today owes much of its distinction to Elizabeth I. She issued a new *Book of Common Prayer* and her "middle way" brought stability to England for the rest of the sixteenth century. She died in 1603 after forty-five years on the throne. Because of her, the Church of England (called the Anglican Church in England and the Episcopal Church in the United States) became Protestant, but not in the more aggressive style of the Protestantism in Germany and Switzerland.[3]

Radical Reformers

The Radical Reformation, embodied primarily in a group known throughout Europe as "Anabaptists," was different from the Magisterial Reformation. The Anabaptists were not as interested in "reform" of the church as they were in "restoration" of "New Testament Christianity." Therefore, they did not rely upon the magistrates to aid them in carrying out their reform movement. In fact, one of the distinguishing characteristics of the Anabaptists was their insistence on complete separation of the institution of the church from the institution of the state.

The Anabaptist movement began in Zurich, Switzerland. Several of Ulrich Zwingli's students to whom he had taught Greek began studying the New Testament closely, especially on the topic of baptism and discovered that infant baptism is never mentioned in the New Testament. What they found was that the New Testament model of baptism was "believer's baptism," the idea that a person should make a personal faith commitment to Christ and then be baptized as a symbol of that commitment. Infant baptism as a practice developed in the early centuries of

---

[3]See Peterson, *A Concise History of Christianity*, 219-24.

Christian history and represented a diversion from the New Testament pattern. Convinced that the proper understanding of baptism must be recovered, about a dozen men came to the home of Felix Manz on the evening of January 21, 1525. According to an eyewitness account, Conrad Grebel baptized George Blaurock who in turn baptized Grebel and the others present. This marks the birth of the Anabaptist movement.[4] The name "Anabaptist" was assigned to this group by its enemies as a term of derision. The name is formed from the Greek prefix *ana* meaning "again" (thus "re-") and *baptizo*, "to immerse [in water]" (Hence "baptize"). Therefore, the Anabaptists were "*re*baptizers."

As the message of Anabaptism spread, the movement grew in number. As the numbers increased, both Protestant and Catholic leaders became concerned. From the perspective of both Roman Catholicism and other Protestant leaders, Anabaptism was a radical movement and a dangerous threat to a well-ordered society. Because there was complete union between church and state in Europe in the sixteenth century, when a child was baptized shortly after birth, the record of that baptism in the parish church served as the record of that child's citizenship in the state. Therefore, a rejection of one's infant baptism was tantamount to rejecting citizenship. Their enemies believed that the order of society could be disrupted if such a movement were allowed to continue. Consequently, Anabaptists became targets for persecution from Catholics, Lutherans, and the followers of the Swiss Reformers alike. Some historians estimate that tens of thousands lost their lives holding to their Anabaptist convictions. Interestingly, the more the movement was persecuted, the more it grew in Europe.

The Anabaptist vision of the church was very different from that of the Magisterial Reformers in several areas. In addition to different views of baptism (Luther, Zwingli, and Calvin retained the practice of infant baptism), the Anabaptists had an entirely new concept of the nature of the church. The Magisterial Reformers (and Roman Catholicism for that matter) considered every member of society to be a member of the church. Infant baptism tied it all together. But the Anabaptists believed that only those who have had a personal faith experience with Christ can

---

[4]For a good discussion of the beginnings of the Anabaptists, see William R. Estep, *The Anabaptist Story*, 3rd ed. rev. and enl. (Grand Rapids MI: Eerdmans, 1996) 10-11.

be members of the church. Baptism served as the outward symbol of a person's Christian rebirth and their becoming a part of the church.

Discipleship was another area where Anabaptists differed from the Magisterial Reformers. Anabaptists believed persons have a free will to follow Christ. They placed a great emphasis on Jesus' teachings in the so-called Sermon on the Mount and the importance of following the commands of Jesus literally. Luther and other Magisterial Reformers placed most of their emphasis on the conversion experience and forgiveness of sin. The emphasis on discipleship and following the teachings of Jesus literally led the Anabaptists to such views as pacifism (Jesus was arrested in the Garden of Gethsemane and refused to fight) and refusal to swear oaths in court (in the Sermon on the Mount, Jesus commanded against swearing oaths). This in turn led to more persecution and suspicion for their rejection of military service and swearing oaths.

The Anabaptists also believed that the church should be entirely separate from the state. In fact, they were one of the first groups in history to argue for separation of church and state. So extreme were they in this position that they refused to allow their members to serve in secular governmental positions. Furthermore, the Anabaptists tended to live in communities separate from society in general. Some of this may have been due to the persecution they received. Nevertheless, a strong sense of community existed among the Anabaptists who valued their fellowship with one another. This sense of community provided comfort and strength during times of persecution.

In 1533, a group of Anabaptist extremists in the German city of Münster forever tarnished the reputation of the Anabaptists in Europe. Led by Jan Matthys, these fanatics believed they could establish the Kingdom of God in the city. They captured control of the city and held it for two years. They also introduced the practice of polygamy and other sordid practices. Finally, their grasp on the city was broken and the leaders of the group were arrested and executed. But the memory of Münster would taint the name "Anabaptist" for centuries to come. It has only been in the last century that historians have begun to see the movement for its value as a legitimate part of the sixteenth-century Reformation. Today, the descendants of the Anabaptists are found in groups such as the Mennonites, Amish, and Hutterites. Although these groups are different from one another, they owe their heritage to the Anabaptists of the sixteenth century.

THE ROMAN CATHOLIC REFORM

A frequently forgotten aspect of the Reformation of the sixteenth century is the fact that the Roman Catholic Church, though staunchly opposed to Protestantism, did in fact undergo a spiritual reform. The Roman Catholic Reform of the sixteenth century can be seen in a variety of movements within the church. There were spiritual renewal movements led by groups such as the Oratory of Divine Love, founded in 1517 in Rome. Spiritual

Balthasar Hubmaier (1485–1528)

renewal also came through mystics such as Saint Teresa of Avila (1515–1582) and Saint John of the Cross (1542–1591) both of whom wrote of their mystical experiences with God.

One of the most important events to bring about reform in the Roman Catholic Church of the sixteenth century was the founding of a new monastic order called the Society of Jesus or Jesuits. The founder of the Jesuits was Ignatius of Loyola (1491–1556). Born in Spain to a wealthy family, he became involved in the military and was wounded in battle with the French. During his long recovery he began reading certain types of devotional literature. He reported that one night he had a vision of the Virgin Mary and the Christ Child. This experience led to a profound conversion in which he vowed to serve Christ for the rest of his life. Loyola eventually gathered a group of followers and formed a new religious order which would be intensely loyal to the pope and at his disposal anywhere in the world. The pope granted his blessing to the new order in 1540 and the Society of Jesus was born. Loyola was the author of a famous devotional book called simply *Spiritual Exercises* which still serves as a guide to spirituality for the Jesuits.

The Jesuits became famous throughout the world for two things. First, they were devoted to education. Many Jesuits serve as teachers, and Jesuit schools are some of the best in the world. Second, Jesuits are famous for their missionary activity. They heroically carried the Gospel to other parts of the world where many from Europe dared not go. The Society of Jesus remains an active, important monastic order in the Roman Catholic Church almost five centuries after it's founding.

A second major event that brought reform to the Roman Catholic Church was the Council of Trent which met sporadically from 1545 to 1563. The council met for the purpose of addressing questions raised by Protestants. Had moderates in the church been stronger, the Council might have made it possible to win back many of the Protestants. But the Council of Trent was dominated by conservatives and any hope of reunion between Catholics and Protestants was lost forever.

Doctrinally, the Council of Trent rejected almost all of the important Protestant developments and ideas. While it did affirm the doctrine of justification by faith, so important to Luther's thought, it said that faith must always be accompanied by good works. It also established the "twin towers" of authority making the Bible and tradition equal in their authority over Christians. It declared that the Latin Vulgate was the official Bible of the Church. The council upheld papal authority and declared the seven sacraments as administered by the Church to be the means by which the grace of God comes to humans. The Council also reaffirmed the doctrine of transubstantiation and that Latin was to be the language of the Mass.

THE AFTERMATH OF THE REFORMATION

The Council of Trent made any hope of reunion between Catholics and Protestants impossible. For thirty years, from 1618 to 1648 Europe was torn apart by wars between Catholic and Protestant factions. Finally, the Peace of Westphalia (1648) ended this bitter period of warfare.

Protestantism continued to grow in many places throughout Europe. Following the sixteenth century there were now three major divisions in Christianity: Roman Catholicism, Protestantism, and Eastern Orthodoxy. Protestantism established itself around three major ideas. First, all Protestants agreed that Scripture alone, (*sola scriptura*) was the only source of spiritual authority. This made it distinct from both Catholicism and Orthodoxy both of which taught that tradition was equal to Scripture in authority. Second, Protestants taught that faith alone (*sola fide*) produces salvation and does not come through any kind of human works. Third, Protestants introduced a new doctrine into Christianity, the doctrine of the "priesthood of the believer." This doctrine involved three things: the believer has a direct relationship with God and does not need an intermediary such as a priest; the believer has the ability through the guidance of the Holy Spirit to interpret Scripture for herself or himself; and believers are ministers to one another, thereby somewhat blurring the lines of distinction between clergy and laity.

After fifteen hundred years, Christianity had grown from the simple faith of the disciples of Jesus to being a major world religion. For the next five hundred years Christians would continue to create diverse ways to practice Christian religion. The story of Christianity in the modern era is the topic to which we now turn.

Chapter 12

MODERN CHRISTIANITY

The birth of "Protestantism" during the Reformation era established an entirely new branch of Christianity with new ways to live out the Christian life. During the modern era, Protestantism continued to evolve into diverse denominations and groupings of Christians.

THE SEVENTEENTH CENTURY

The seventeenth century began with war between Catholics and Protestants in Germany. The two sides battled one another sporadically for three decades. The Peace of Westphalia in 1648 formally marked the end of the war with a treaty guaranteeing religious freedom for Catholics, Lutherans, and Calvinists. One might say that the Peace of Westphalia brought an end to the Reformation Era and the beginning of the Modern Era. Unfortunately, freedom was not granted to the Anabaptists. They continued to be harassed and persecuted by both Protestants and Catholics for years to come.

The Enlightenment. One of the most significant movements to impact Christianity in the seventeenth century was the Enlightenment. Enlightenment thinkers began to stress the importance of human reason and autonomy, which eventually led to challenges to the church's authority and new ways of interpreting Christianity. Enlightenment thinkers generally had two presuppositions. First, they believed the world was created like a machine which functions according to "natural laws," such as the law of gravity. Isaac Newton, whose experiments demonstrated the law of gravity, believed that the order of the universe proved the existence of God. Second, Enlightenment thinkers believed in the importance of human reason. They held that through reason, along with observation of the universe and experimentation, ultimate truth could be discovered. Truth is not so much "revealed" by God but is discovered through the power of human reason.

Lord Herbert of Cherbury attempted to blend together religion and Enlightenment rationalism. He is usually considered the father of Deism, which could be regarded as the religion of Enlightenment thinkers. In his famous book, *On the Truth* (1624), Cherbury held that there were five natural laws of religion that can be discovered through reason: (1) there is a God; (2) God should be worshipped; (3) the primary expression of worship should be a virtuous life; (4) humans have a duty to repent from sin; and (5) there is an afterlife where deeds will be judged.[1]

Influenced by Herbert of Cherbury, Deists developed a way of viewing Christianity that placed complete emphasis on human reason. The only expression of Christianity that had any value was a Christianity that could be proven to be rational. They affirmed that God created the universe and that it was a perfect creation, but the universe was created to operate on natural laws. They believed that God never intervened in the universe through "miracles" which requires a suspension of the laws of nature. For God to interfere in the universe would be tantamount to admitting that the world was not perfect, and it was unreasonable to assume that a perfect God would create an imperfect universe. Deists also denied the Trinity and regarded Jesus as a human being only, against the Christian understanding of Jesus as both God and man. They placed great emphasis on the moral teachings of Jesus. Finally, Deists rejected the divine inspiration of the Bible.

Puritanism. Another important movement that developed in the seventeenth century was Puritanism. In some ways, Puritanism was the seventeenth-century continuation of the English Reformation from the previous century. As we saw in the preceding chapter, following the death of Henry VIII's son Edward VI, Henry's daughter Mary came to the throne and sought to return the Church of England to the Roman Catholic fold. She persecuted Protestants, causing many to flee from England to Europe where they could worship unhindered. Many of these "Marian exiles" ended up in Geneva and were greatly influenced by John Calvin's teachings and his ideas of a theocratic society.

When Elizabeth I came to the throne of England, many English Protestants returned from Europe, expecting Elizabeth to hasten a return of the Church of England to more thoroughgoing Protestantism. Unfortunately for them, she crafted a *via media* between Catholicism and Protestantism. These returning Protestants, now thoroughly imbued with Calvin's reforming ideas, became frustrated that Elizabeth was not "purifying" the church enough. This desire to purge the church of anything that resembled Roman Catholic practices gave them the name "Puritan."

---

[1]See "Herbert, Edward," in *Oxford Dictionary of the Christian Church*, ed. F. L. Cross, 3rd. ed., ed. E. A. Livingstone (Oxford: Oxford University Press, 1997) 756-57.

Many Puritans stayed within the Church of England hoping that gradually the Church would be further reformed. But, in the early decades of the seventeenth century following the death of Elizabeth I, the Puritans found themselves to be the targets of persecution. Many journeyed to America where they established a colony in Massachusetts Bay. This became one of the most productive colonies in the New World. From the influence of John Calvin they sought to implement a theocracy in Massachusetts Bay calling the colony a "city set on a hill." But, by the beginning of the eighteenth century, the colony had lost much of its spiritual vitality and Puritanism was relatively dead in Massachusetts Bay.

Some Puritans became so frustrated by the lack of significant reform that they began to separate and establish their own autonomous churches. These "Separatists" were much more radical in their reform goals and less patient in their ability to work within the Church of England. One group of Separatists led by John Smyth left England for Holland where they could worship in freedom. When they arrived in Holland they were befriended by a group of Mennonites. Eventually, Smyth became convinced of the importance of "believer's baptism." He proceeded to baptize himself and then the members of his congregation in 1609, thereby becoming the first "Baptist" church. Three years later in 1612 the congregation split and a group led by Thomas Helwys returned to England establishing in London the first Baptist church on English soil.

Arminianism. The seventeenth century also saw the birth of "Arminianism" as a response in opposition to the theology of John Calvin. During the last half of the sixteenth century, following his death, Calvin's theology became highly systematized by his successors. This rigid Calvinism eventually drew a response from Jacob Arminius of Holland, who disagreed with the way Calvin's theology was being portrayed. Favoring a significant role of human free will, Arminius began to lecture against Calvin's concept of predestination. The lectures led to a national controversy in Holland. Arminius died in 1609 and following his death his followers issued a document called the *Remonstrance* (1610). It stated the Arminian position in five articles, each disagreeing with the major points of Calvinism.

The controversy became so heated that the Calvinists met together in the city of Dort. The Synod of Dort, as the meeting came to be called, met from 1618 to 1619. The Calvinists condemned the theology of Arminius and issued five statements in response to the Arminian points.

This gave rise to "five-point Calvinism," mentioned in the previous chapter with the mnenomic acrostic "TULIP."

From the seventeenth century until the present, the Calvinism/ Arminianism debate has raged among Protestant Christians. Several Protestant denominations have their roots in these two theological viewpoints. Presbyterianism is rooted in the theology of Calvinism and is based on the "Westminster Confession," which was written by English Calvinists in 1646. John Wesley, on the other hand, a thoroughgoing Arminian and critic of Calvinism, founded the Methodist denomination with a strong Arminian focus theologically.

THE EIGHTEENTH CENTURY

There were three important movements in the eighteenth century, all related to one another, and all evangelical in nature. By "evangelical" is understood that all three of these movements emphasized a personal faith experience in Christ. These three movements were responses to the rationalism that developed in Protestant circles during the sixteenth and seventeenth centuries and all three tended to emphasize the importance of emotion in the Christian experience.

Pietism. The first of the eighteenth-century evangelical movements is Pietism. It began in Germany toward the end of the seventeenth century with the preaching and writing of Philip Jacob Spener (1635–1705). Spener was a Lutheran pastor who underwent a personal conversion experience and eventually came to the conclusion that all the Lutheran churches in Germany were in need of an evangelical awakening. He organized the *Collegia Pietatis* which met in his home twice each week for prayer and Bible study. He also wrote a book called entitled *Pia Desideria*, which explained his Pietist ideas and became immensely popular. Because of its popularity, *Pia Desideria* became a major primary source for Pietism in Germany.

Another important advocate of Pietism was August Hermann Francke (1663–1727). Influenced by Spener, he became an advocate of Pietism. In 1695 he became a professor at the University of Halle which, because of his presence on the faculty, became a center for Pietism in Germany. He also served as pastor of a congregation in Halle where he devoted himself to the practice and promotion of Pietism. The University of Halle also developed a commitment to missions during the eighteenth century.

From Halle came sixty missionaries sent to foreign countries to spread the Christian faith.[2]

One student educated at Halle was Count Nicolaus von Zinzendorf (1700–1760). Zinzendorf was from a wealthy, pietistic family. In 1722 he began to use one part of his land as a shelter for a group of refugees from Bohemia who were escaping persecution. He organized these refugees into a community, which attempted to live according to the ideas of Pietism which Zinzendorf had learned at Halle. The community eventually called itself "Moravian Brethren." They developed an intense missionary zeal and began sending missionaries to other countries.

Methodism. The principles of Pietism eventually came to the British Isles through the influence of the Moravians on John Wesley (1703–1791). Wesley was the fifteenth child of a very large family. He enrolled at Oxford and became involved with several student colleagues in a group they called the "Holy Club." Their desire was to devote themselves to prayer, Bible study, and Christian service. Soon their friends gave them the nickname "Methodists" because of their discipline and methodical attention to various devotional practices such as prayer and Bible study.

Wesley graduated from Oxford and in 1735, along with his brother Charles, set sail for the colony of Georgia to do mission work. On the ocean voyage from England to Georgia, the ship was caught in a ferocious storm. Wesley feared for his life, but noticed that a group of Moravians on board was peaceful and content in the midst of such impending peril. Seeing the calmness of the Moravians and recognizing his own terror during this storm intrigued Wesley who began a process of spiritual introspection. His central concern was whether or not there was more to the Christian experience than simply practicing the disciplines of the faith such as prayer, Bible Study, and caring for the poor.

Wesley's work in Georgia did not progress very well. Following a failed romance which impacted his work in the church he served, Wesley decided to return to England. Upon his return, his mission failure, coupled with his inward spiritual struggle, led him to seek out the Moravians in England. On 24 May 1738 while attending a Moravian worship service on Aldersgate Street in London, Wesley had a faith

---

[2]Peterson, *A Concise History of Christianity*, 261.

experience like nothing he had ever experienced before. In his journal he wrote: "I felt my heart strangely warmed."[3]

Sussana Wesley, mother of John Wesley,
who may have had more impact on his life than anyone else.

With a new outlook toward his faith, Wesley began to preach—in Church of England churches—the importance of a personal conversion experience. Gradually, however, churches began to close their doors to him so he took to preaching in the fields. He rode thousands of miles on horseback to preach all over England. He organized a system of lay

---

[3]Wesley' journal, 24 May 1738, as cited in Gonzalez, *The Story of Christianity* 1:212.

ministers to do follow-up for his evangelism. Although Wesley wanted the movement to remain within the Church of England, it eventually became separated and took the name Methodism. Methodism also made its way to the American Colonies where it achieved great success largely due to the efforts of Francis Asbury (1745–1816) who had been sent to America by Wesley for the purpose of organizing the movement there. Asbury eventually became one of the first Methodist bishops in America.

The First Great Awakening. The American Colonies served as the setting for the third eighteenth-century evangelical movement. The First Great Awakening, as it is frequently called, was a series of revivals of religion, which occurred in the American Colonies during the middle decades of the eighteenth century.[4] By the beginning of the eighteenth century, religion was at low ebb in the Colonies. Puritanism, so prevalent in New England during the early seventeenth century, was essentially dead as a movement. A Dutch Reformed pastor in New York, Theodore Jacobus Frelinghuysen (1691–1747), who was influenced by German Pietism, began to preach about the lack of piety in his congregation. He began to emphasize the importance of personal, heartfelt faith. This emphasis on Pietism and personal conversion led to an outbreak of revival in his church which spread to the other Middle Colonies. Frelinghuysen thus is usually regarded as the initiator of the First Great Awakening in the American Colonies and provides the connection between this movement and Pietism in Germany.

One of the most important figures of the First Great Awakening was Jonathan Edwards (1703–1758). Edwards was educated at Yale College and served as pastor of a Congregational church in Northampton, Massachusetts. He began to preach of the importance of personal piety much as Frelinghuysen had done earlier in New York. This led to a tremendous awakening in his congregation from 1734 to 1735. Edwards's writings about the revivals, especially his *A Faithful Narrative of a Surprising Work of God* (1737), serve as a theological explanation and justification of the revivals. He remains a most significant theologian from early America and is considered by many to be the major theological interpreter of the First Great Awakening. Edwards is probably best remembered

---

[4]Many scholars of American religion prefer the term "First Great Awakening" because another spiritual awakening occurred in the early decades of the nineteenth century, commonly called the "Second Great Awakening." Some scholars, however, still refer to the first as simply the "Great Awakening."

for his famous sermon "Sinners in the Hands of an Angry God," first preached in 1741. Edwards's preaching was intellectually challenging with use of carefully worded manuscripts that he read to the congregation from the pulpit.

By contrast, George Whitefield (1714–1770) brought a completely different style from England to the American Colonies. Educated at Oxford and a member of the Holy Club (later known as the first "Methodists") with John Wesley, Whitefield made a total of seven

George Whitefield preaching in an open field. His voice was so strong— it was reported—that he could preach to 30,000 with no amplification.

preaching tours of the American Colonies, the most important of which occurred in 1740. Whitefield was a powerful preacher and his preaching attracted large numbers of people. Unlike Edwards, Whitefield routinely preached simple, extemporaneous sermons. Emotional excesses at some of the revivals eventually caused many of the churches to reject Whitefield's preaching. Like Wesley before him, he was thereby forced to preach in open fields, where it was estimated that Whitefield preached to crowds as large as 30,000 with no voice amplification. Nicknamed the "Grand Itinerant," Whitefield was the first evangelist to capture the American public's attention and was the most important preacher of the First Great Awakening.

The First Great Awakening left a variety of permanent results on the American religious landscape.

1. The Awakening brought in large numbers of new converts to the churches in America. The major Protestant denominations in the colonies at that time, Congregationalists, Baptists, and Presbyterians, experienced unprecedented growth as a result of the revivals.

2. The Awakening produced divisions in those same denominations. The controversial nature of the revivals with frequent emotional outbursts turned many away from supporting them.

3. The First Great Awakening underlined the importance of "voluntary" religion in America. America has never had a state church. Membership in a church is not automatic; it is voluntary. The Awakening helped create such an environment.

4. As a result of the First Great Awakening, revivalism became an important characteristic of American religion.

5. The revivals produced new converts to the Christian faith and also many who decided to prepare for careers in ministry. This caused the birth and growth of educational institutions in the eighteenth century. Along with the spiritual awakening came many new candidates who expressed a desire to train for the ministry. Institutions such as Princeton, Brown, Rutgers, and Dartmouth were all formed in the eighteenth century due in large part to the influence of the revivals and the need to train new ministers.

6. The revivals left a legacy of humanitarian concern in American religion and promoted mission work among slaves as well as among the Native Americans.

7. Finally, the First Great Awakening contributed to the growing "democratization" of American religion, creating an atmosphere whereby those who were dissatisfied with their current denominations simply left to join dissenting groups.[5]

---

[5]For a more detailed discussion of the results of the First Great Awakening, see Sydney A. Ahlstrom, *A Religious History of the American People* (New Haven CT: Yale University Press, 1972) 280-329; Mark A. Noll, *A History of Christianity in the United States and Canada* (Grand Rapids MI: Eerdmans,

THE NINETEENTH CENTURY

In his classic seven-volume series, *A History of the Expansion of Christianity*, church historian Kenneth Scott Latourette referred to the nineteenth century as "The Great Century" and devoted three of his seven volumes to that period.[6] Indeed, there was a remarkable amount of activity and energy within the Christian religion during that century, particularly in the American context. While it would be impossible here to describe all of the important Christian movements during that century, several deserve mention.

The Second Great Awakening. One of the most important religious events in America during the early decades of the nineteenth century was the Second Great Awakening. Like the Awakening of the eighteenth century, the Second Great Awakening was a series of revivals that emphasized personal piety and heartfelt devotion to God. The most important evangelist of the Second Great Awakening was Charles G. Finney. Highly educated for a career in law, Finney was converted to Christianity and felt a calling to preach. His crusades, particularly on the frontier in early nineteenth-century America, were attended by large, emotional crowds. Unlike Jonathan Edwards, who believed a revival was "a surprising work of God," Finney believed a revival was "the result of the *right* use of the appropriate means."[7]

In other words, Finney believed that it was possible to *make* a revival happen by doing certain things. His "new measures," included such things as praying for the unconverted by name in his services; the "anxious bench," where all of the unconverted were segregated from the other worshippers; and massive advertising before he ever came to town. Finney's "new measures" became the prototype for how evangelists would conduct revival meetings in the nineteenth and twentieth centuries.

The Second Great Awakening provided some lasting results for American Christianity, such as numerical growth for certain denomina-

---

1992) 110-13; and Winthrop S. Hudson and John Corrigan, *Religion in America*, 6th ed. (Upper Saddle River NJ: Prentice-Hall, 1999) 97-101.

[6]Kenneth Scott Latourette, *A History of the Expansion of Christianity*, 7 vols. (repr.: New York: Harper & Row, 1970; orig., 1937–1945) vols. 4-6.

[7]Charles G. Finney, *Lectures on Revivals of Religion* (New York: Fleming H. Revell Co., 1868) 13.

tions, particularly Baptists, Methodists, and Presbyterians. But, the most important lasting impact of this movement was its legacy of attention to the social evils of American society. Emphasis on temperance in alcohol use, poverty, and especially the abolition of slavery can be traced to the enduring effects of the Second Great Awakening.

The emphasis on personal piety in the Second Great Awakening and the success of the revivals also led many American Christians to begin looking beyond the borders of America to those in other parts of the world. The result was the birth of the modern missions movement. Two of the pioneers in the early missions movement were Adoniram and Ann Hasseltine Judson. Originally appointed by the Congregationalist denomination as missionaries to India, they became Baptists and subsequently moved their missions emphasis to Burma. By the end of the nineteenth century, American Christians were serving as missionaries not only in Burma, but also in Africa, Asia, and Central and South America.

Liberalism and Fundamentalism. As the nineteenth century progressed, theologians began to look for ways that Christianity could meet the challenges of modernity. This was due to the popularity of Charles Darwin's *Origin of the Species* (1859) and *The Descent of Man* (1871). The response came in the form of "Liberalism," a movement which sought to reassess Christianity through the lens of modernity. One of the first theologians to reinterpret the Christian religion in light of modern ways of looking at the world was the German theologian Freidrich Schleiermacher (1768–1834). Schleiermacher believed the essence of Christianity was not to be found in doctrine or morals. Instead, he believed Christianity, at its very foundation, is rooted in the feeling of absolute dependence upon God and that all Christian beliefs could ultimately be traced to that root source.

Liberalism had an impact on other concerns of Christianity as well. For example, the modern study of the Bible known as "higher criticism" was a result of Liberalism's influence as scholars began to use the same tools to study the biblical materials as were used to study other kinds of literature. One result of this new Bible-study methodolology was the Documentary Hypothesis, made famous by Julius Wellhausen (1844–1918). Wellhausen studied the Pentateuch carefully and questioned the traditional Mosaic authorship theory. He believed the Pentateuch evolved over several centuries, and was the work of numerous authors and editors from different historical periods in Hebrew history.

As might be expected, this new approach to scripture and theology was met with opposition by many Christians. Fundamentalism was the movement which arose to counter Liberalism. Named after the publication of a series of articles called *The Fundamentals*, Fundamentalists argued that there were five important Christian beliefs which could not be compromised: (1) the virgin birth of Jesus; (2) the verbal/plenary inspiration of the Bible; (3) the bodily resurrection of Jesus; (4) the visible second coming of Christ; and (5) the satisfaction theory of the Atonement.[8] Fundamentalism has remained a powerful movement in Christianity to the present day. Its effects can be seen in several of the major denominations in America such as Baptists, Presbyterians, and Methodists. Its influence is also seen in a growing number of nondenominational churches.

THE TWENTIETH CENTURY

The Social Gospel Movement. Several important movements during the twentieth century should also be highlighted. At the beginning of the century, some Christians (especially in America) became highly sensitive to the poor in society. The Industrial Revolution had created a large class of poor people, particularly immigrants in large cities, who had to endure terrible living conditions in tenement housing or unsafe, unhealthy working conditions in their employment. Walter Rauschenbusch (1861–1918) was a German Baptist pastor who served as pastor of a congregation in one of the slums of New York City called "Hell's Kitchen." There he saw poverty in some of its worst forms. It made such an impression upon him that he began writing and lecturing about ways the Christian Gospel implies that believers must work to alleviate the suffering of the poor. For Rauschenbusch, simply converting everyone to the Christian faith by evangelism would not take care of all of the social ills in society. He called for a more radical remedy, a transformation of the social structures of society. Rauschenbusch referred to himself as a "Christian socialist." He wanted to see a systematic redistribution of wealth in society so that the differentiation between the haves and have-nots would

---

[8]Gleaned from R. A. Torrey, A. C. Dixon, et al., *The Fundamentals: A Testimony to the Truth* (repr.: Grand Rapids MI: Baker Book House, 1988). The "satisfaction theory of the atonement" is the belief that the death of Christ *satisfies* the wrath of God which is aimed at humans for their sinfulness.

no longer exist. Further, he thought government should create and enforce laws that would oblige large corporations to pay better wages and provide safer working conditions. He lobbied for laws that would make cities create better housing situations for the underprivileged. Rauschenbusch was a pioneer in what came to be known as the Social Gospel Movement. This movement remained popular for the first two or three decades of the twentieth century and to a great extent was successful in bringing about many reforms of the political and economic sectors of society.

Neoorthodoxy. Liberalism provided an optimistic outlook toward the world and humanity and was a popular movement in the closing decades of the nineteenth century and the early decades of the twentieth century. However, the horrors of World War I shattered this optimism and led theologians to reconsider Christianity once again and how it impacts the world.

One of the most notable theologians of the twentieth century was Karl Barth (1886–1968). Barth precipitated a theological innovation called "Neoorthodoxy," as a reaction against Liberalism. Neoorthodoxy attempted to combine the critical study of the Bible and modern ways of viewing the Christian faith, with a strong doctrine of the reality of human sinfulness and need for salvation. Barth left an enormous impact with his thought. He was an organizer of the Confessing Church which produced the Barmen Declaration (1934) that formally opposed the Liberalism of the German Lutheran Church. Later, the Confessing Church provided a voice of dissent as other German churches capitulated to Nazism. Neoorthodoxy became the most innovative theological force in Protestantism during the middle of the twentieth century. Several other Neoorthodox voices also became important shapers of Christian thought and the reality of sin. They include Dietrich Bonhoeffer (who was executed by the Nazis as a result of his opposition to Hitler) and the Niebuhr brothers, H. Richard and Reinhold, who were important Neoorthodox voices in America.

Vatican Council II. The most important event in Roman Catholicism during the twentieth century was the convening of Vatican Council II (1962–1965), called into session by Pope John XXIII, the most progressive pope of the century. Convinced of the need for the Roman Catholic Church to open itself up to the modern world, John XXIII presided at the formal opening of the council but died before its completion. Vatican II brought several important reforms to the Roman Catholic Church, including the celebration of Mass in the vernacular of the people instead of Latin, and openness to dialogue with Protestants as well as religious traditions outside of Christianity.

Pentecostalism. At the end of the twentieth century one of the strongest expressions of Christianity was found in the Pentecostal movement. Participants in Pentecostalism claim to experience the presence of the Holy Spirit in the same way as the early Christians described in Acts 2. They claim that in addition to the salvation experience of God's grace, there is a "baptism of the Spirit" which is evidenced by sign gifts such as speaking in tongues (or *glossolalia*). Other signs which accompany the presence of the Holy Spirit include healing and prophecy.

While it shares similarities with the earlier Holiness Movement, such as its emphasis on the baptism of the Spirit, Pentecostalism's roots can be traced to the Azusa Street Revival in Los Angeles in 1906. Since then, the movement has grown steadily during the twentieth century with an explosion of growth in the last quarter of the century. For most of the century it tended to be a movement among the poor and lower classes (particularly in America); but during the last several decades it has experienced growth among both middle and upper classes.

Several features of the movement make it attractive to new converts. First, from its inception, Pentecostalism has had a tradition of racially integrated worship services and churches. While many Protestant denominations fought integration, Pentecostalism welcomed it. Second, Pentecostalism is open to women in positions of leadership within the church, including preaching and pastoral ministry, while some Protestant denominations are still reticent or even hostile toward women leaders. Third, Pentecostal worship services are very emotional and exciting, a feature that attracts many people.

At the end of the twentieth century Christianity was one of the largest religions in the world with almost two billion adherents. We have seen how over two millennia Christianity has grown, been shaped by culture, and diversified to respond to its environment. As the twenty-first century begins there are three main branches of Christianity: Roman Catholicism, Eastern Orthodoxy, and Protestantism, with varieties of expressions within those broad categories. Yet there are some basic beliefs that all Christians share in common. We now turn to examine those beliefs.

Part Four

CHRISTIAN THEOLOGY

Chapter 13

THE NATURE OF THEOLOGY

THEOLOGY AS LOGIC[1]

The aim of this unit is to give a brief description of the central elements of the Christian faith. That is the task of Christian Theology: to describe the contents of the Christian faith. If it is the "Christian" faith that is the object of interest, then our description must not be narrowly restrictive. While the perspective offered here is clearly Protestant in orientation, it is intended to be ecumenical in spirit, so as not to rule out the other two major branches of Christianity, namely, Roman Catholicism and Eastern Orthodoxy. On the other hand, if the study focuses on "Christian" faith, then the beliefs described naturally will be incompatible with many ruling components in, say, Muslim or Buddhist thought. In short, not just any religious or philosophical way of thinking about "God" or "creation" or "salvation" can count as "Christian." When all is said and done, there is a definable shape to the Christian faith which it is theology's task to describe.

But that brings us to that big word "theology." There are all kinds of misunderstandings about what theology is and does, most of them attributing to theology a highly inflated role. It is true that those who share the Christian faith make striking claims about such imposing topics as God, history, nature, and humankind. For this reason, theology as a discipline takes up these matters for discussion. But the theologian is not one who has privileged access to the truth about these topics by comparison to other "ordinary" believers. On the contrary, as the truth revealed in Jesus Christ is available to one, so it is available to all alike. But this is not to say that every believer is a budding theologian any more than everyone who has thoughts about the laws of the land or knows about the human anatomy is a budding lawyer or physician. Just as one must prepare to practice law and medicine, so also there is requisite training for

---

[1]In this chapter and much that follows, there is a longstanding debt to Ludwig Wittgenstein, notably his *Philosophical Investigations*, trans. G. E. M. Anscombe (New York: Macmillan, 1953) and to the writings of the Danish theologian/philosopher Søren Kierkegaard.

the theologian. Preeminent in that training are certain logical skills in making distinctions and unfolding consequences of thoughts, along with deep familiarity with the Bible, Christian creeds, and an assortment of other things. So a theologian is one who, by virtue of natural talent and training, takes up the task of describing the "logic" or lineaments of the Christian faith.

It is assumed that the Christian theologian is one who shares the faith which is being described. In that sense, the theologian is not neutral; like other believers, the theologian is one who passionately trusts in and gives allegiance to the God revealed in Jesus of Nazareth. In worship and prayer, in hymn and confession of faith, in life and in deed, the theologian speaks the language "of" faith right alongside others in the Christian community, the strong and the weak, the haves and the have nots. But as a theologian, one also performs the very different task of writing or talking "about" the faith, describing it with accuracy and acumen.[2] In executing this role, the theologian (who is also a believer) must exercise logical skill, maintain objectivity, and isolate what cannot (and thus what can) be said within the Christian faith. Indeed, one might liken the work of the theologian here to that of a logician. If the logician talks about the rules governing our speech in a wide variety of ordinary contexts, the theologian discusses the ruled ways of making sense with reference to God in the religious life. One could say that the theologian helps us see the logic of our language about God, Jesus Christ, faith, redemption, and a host of other concepts. The comparison between logic and theology might be further explored in the following way.

No one learns for the first time how to make sense in their speech when they take a university course in Logic. Perhaps some will sharpen their wits so they may better organize their thoughts or may avoid various fallacies in reasoning. But in general, people learn to make sense in their talking and thinking long before and often even without any formal instruction; indeed they learn how to reason as they learn to speak. In much the same way, people do not first learn how to make sense with reference to God when they take a course in Theology. Typically, most ways of speaking intelligibly with regard to God's will, Jesus, sin, and a large range of other matters have already been learned. They are laid

---

[2]The extremely helpful distinction between the language "of" faith and the language "about" faith is one made by Paul L. Holmer at various points in his *The Grammar of Faith* (San Francisco: Harper & Row, 1978); see, e.g., 25ff.

down in the language of the faith, in what one has learned from mothers and fathers, parsons and priests, and by means of engaging in such activities as prayer and praise, preaching and sacrament. But even then it is not so much the rules themselves—in abstraction—that one learns as it is the actual skill in *using* the words intelligibly in accordance with the rules. Certainly, it is the logician upon whom we depend to isolate and explicitly state the logical rules that govern our language generally. Likewise, we depend upon the theologian to formulate and state those "theo-logical" rules of faith which dictate what can and cannot be said in a Christian context. At the same time, however, those who are most faithful and adept at exercising themselves in the language and life "of" faith are not always, or even typically, those most skilled theologically in describing the rules of that language and life, the language "about" faith.

None of this is intended to give the impression that theology is some kind of theory behind the practice of the Christian life and speech; nor, for that matter, is logic theoretical by comparison to our ordinary ways of speaking and understanding one another. The Christian life is a life of faith in which the language "of" faith is put to work in very strenuous ways—in confessing Christ, ministering to others, singing hymns, preaching, praying, giving alms, and a host of other ways. Herein the words of faith are typically used in the first person and with a certain ardor; they are woven into a way of living which is inseparable from the central tenets of belief. It is here in the stream of life, in the lives of the faithful, that the language has its home. The task of theology is one step removed: theology's job is to talk "about" the faith, to describe the logic of that language and life of faith. No one should ever get the impression that theology somehow comes first, like a theory, and then, later, the practice of faith. Rather, the priority is the other way around and it is of a logical sort. The life of faith has primacy. By comparison, theology is derivative and secondary; it is a "second level" kind of description of the Christian faith. Put it another way: were it not for a faith already shared within the church there would be no object for the theologian's attention and descriptive account.

With this, attention is drawn to another feature of the Christian faith: it is a faith that is shared by those making up the body of the faithful. Indeed, it is a faith and language that is held in common with all who have come before us in the church—apostles and prophets, saints and martyrs, lofty rulers and humble servants. Or, put another way, it is because they hold this faith in common that we call all of these individuals "Christians," as over against Muslims or Buddhists, humanists or behaviorists. Therefore, theology is not so much interested in what makes us Baptists or Methodists, or even Catholic or Protestant, as much as it is committed to describing the faith that unites Christian believers. This does not mean that theology now is a sociological study in which polls are taken; nor does theology become a merely historical study in which former ways of thinking, worshipping and speaking are annotated. No, theology once more is a discipline more like logic whose purpose it is to offer a description of the shared Christian faith.

But that means that theology is both analytical and critical in its purpose. Theology is analytical in the sense that it would objectively and positively provide us with an analysis or description of the lineaments of the faith. Theology is critical in the sense that it rules out those elements, those ways of speaking and thinking, that are out of harmony with the faith. The Christian faith is supple and rich enough to include the very different Gospels of Mark and John, the likes of fishermen and emperors, the ways of monks and martyrs, the prayers of Lutherans and Quakers, preaching on street corners and in elevated pulpits. But there are ways of living and thinking that cut across or even against the grain of Christian faith. In his or her critical role, the theologian has the task of identifying and purging such elements, be they unabashedly pagan (as with atheistic humanism) or within the Christian fellowship (as became clear during the Protestant Reformation) or on its fringes (as with the Mormons)and whether they are philosophical concepts (for example, God as a First Cause or Pure Actuality) or concepts associated with popular religion (for instance, God as a "good buddy").

Since the emphasis has been on likening theology to logic, perhaps a final note will be surprising. Can theology as a rigorous discipline be helpful to a person in the religious life? Can the logical distinctions and clarifications made in the name of Christian theology have any import for a life of passionate faith in God? Strange as it may seem, the answer is Yes. If we recall that theology describes the logic, the shape, of the language and life of faith, we will not be far from seeing this point clearly. To have the Christian concept of 'God' distinguished from "the man upstairs" or from an abstract notion of a 'First Cause,' to discern the difference between Christian 'love' as self-sacrificing and other types, to have a grasp of what it means to live a 'new life' in Jesus Christ—these and many more theological elucidations can help a Christian straighten his or her thinking and living as a believer. Or again, the creeds of the

Christian Church provide much grist for the theological mill. What does it mean to believe in God the Father, Maker of Heaven and Earth? Is this not more than an intellectual belief that is espoused? Does it not logically (and not merely psychologically) imply that a believer will actually look at the world as God's handiwork and demonstrate a corresponding heartfelt gratitude for it. What does it mean to claim that Jesus Christ is God incarnate who brings forgiveness of sin and a resurrected life ever-lasting? Surely this is something more and different than a claim we give our mental assent. Among other things, does not this belief entail (logically) that Christians are people who, despite the way the world is, live always with hope in their hearts? What does it mean to be judged by God unless it means to live one's life from start to finish before One who knows us through and through? And the list could go on. The point is that the elements of the Christian faith give shape and tone to the life as well as the words of those who share it. When theology brings clarity to the contours of that faith then a believer gains a more perspicuous view of the kind of life that one is to live along with and as an integral part of that faith.

THEOLOGY AND THE WORD OF GOD

We have already noticed that the Christian faith which theology describes is a shared faith. Furthermore, it is a faith in which the theologian participates. So theological reflection is not done in a vacuum. The theologian is not some kind of "loner" who is isolated from community and historical context. No, the Christian community of fellow believers is the matrix in which the theologian performs the task described above. That means that, like those others, he or she is not neutral but utterly committed in singular faith to Jesus Christ. Of course, in the specific task of describing the content of the faith, the theologian exercises just as much painstaking attention and logical restraint as a logician would expend on, say, a problem in the language of mathematics. But the theologian is not dispassionate about the shared faith which is at once the object of investigation and the bond that unites him or her to other believers around the globe and through all ages.

The central claim that Christian believers dare to confess is this: God, the Almighty, has disclosed God's divine nature with completeness and finality in the life, ministry, death, and resurrection of Jesus of Nazareth. It is this bold confession that binds together the members of the body of Christ. If Christians differ in how they construe the means of inspiration for the Bible or the importance they bestow upon a virgin birth or their views on the sacraments—the one thing that is at the heart of the faith is like Peter's confession at Caesarea Philippi: "You are the Christ, the Messiah." Jesus Christ has been confessed to be the very Word (Logos) of God from the earliest days of the Church (see John 1:1ff). Indeed, even before there was a written Word of God, there was the living Word of God by whom every other word is measured. Insofar as God is disclosed elsewhere—in nature, in a person, or in a book—that revelation must be tested against this singular event of God's act in Jesus Christ. For this reason we say that the Christian faith is Christ-centered; it is Christocentric. This is a fundamental element in what we have called the "logic" of the faith.

Of course, the Christian faith is also theocentric, that is, God-centered. This does not mean, however, that there are *two* points that comprise the center of the faith. There is only one center: God revealed in Jesus Christ. Jesus Christ is of crucial importance to believers not in and of himself but because even Christ points beyond himself to the God who, apart from Christ, remains unfathomable, mysterious. What we can come to know about God we know first and always in and through the "Christ event" in which God "became flesh and dwelled among us." We cannot be diverted from that central event. Still, what gives that event its importance, its irrevocable centrality is this: that it is *God*—the God of majesty who is otherwise hidden from us—who is disclosed therein. It is in this God that we place our ultimate trust because we confess that we have found this God active in what took place in the life as well as the cross and empty tomb of Jesus.

Perhaps we could put it this way: the logic of the Christian faith is *Christocentric* because its center is in the God who is revealed in *Jesus Christ*; that same faith—without addition or subtraction—is *theocentric* because its center is in *God* as God is revealed in Jesus Christ. Christ is the living Word of God.

At the same time, God's Word—that is, God's will and purpose—is given derivative and authoritative expression in other forms too. For example, Christians confess that the Bible is the Word of God. For the most part, they say that because it is the Bible that bears witness to the central manifestation of God in Jesus Christ. Even when the Old Testament is the text, the Christian reads it—cannot help but read it—in light of what God has done in Christ Jesus. The stories of the beginning of things, the Exodus event, the Psalms, the prophets—all these are gathered

up and read through the eyes of one who already shares a faith of a
Christian sort. Indeed, some elements of the Old Testament must be dis-
counted or at least reinterpreted precisely because Jesus himself taught his
listeners to do so. Thus Jesus often disregarded the Jewish ceremonial law
and was infamous for his reinterpretation of the Ten Commandments. In
so doing, Jesus—himself Jewish through and through—naturally aroused
the opposition of those who were leaders in the Jewish religion of his
own day. But even more radical was the divergence from the faith and
expectation of the Jews when, as their Messiah, Jesus suffered as a
derelict on the cross. But this is precisely the folly of the Gospel to which
Christians bear witness—that in the utterly scandalous death of an
itinerant Jewish rabbi is to be found God's salvation for anyone in the
world who dares to believe. It is no wonder that Christians and Jews read
the same texts differently. Yet for several decades this Jewish book, our
"Old Testament," was the only sacred literature Christians possessed.

In making this observation, we are reminded that for many years
early Christian believers had no "New Testament." Both the writing of
the New Testament materials (extending from the early 50s CE into the
early second century) as well as the subsequent endorsing of them as
sacred (by mid to late fourth century) came only in due time. Not one of
the authors imagined his letter or "Gospel" as eventually being included
in a body of sacred literature of the Christian movement. But when the
Christian community began to see the need for such a "canon" there were
some criteria that had to be met. Above all, if any piece of literature was
to be considered "sacred" it had to bear clear testimony to Jesus Christ
as did the early apostolic preaching and teaching which served as the
paradigm. Reputed apostolic authorship bestowed considerable authority
on a writing; but, it should be noted carefully, it did not guarantee entry
into the canon. For any writing also had to pass another test: it must
square with the already established faith of the Christian church which
was rooted in the apostolic witness. Not all the writings to which the
name of an apostle was attached met that criterion, notably the *Gospel of
Thomas*. The point in all this is that before there was a New Testament,
there was a shared Christian faith and the central feature of that faith was
its testimony to Jesus Christ—its Christocentric foundation. The Old
Testament was read in light of what Christ had done; the New Testament
writings were chosen as "holy" on the basis of that consideration.

The Christian church, then, eventually reached unanimity about a
Holy Scripture—the written Word—which had its center in Jesus Christ,

the living Word. The theologian works as a member of that Christian community with a common set of sacred writings. Accordingly, the Bible—with its center in Christ—should be regarded as the norm for Christian theology. The shape, the logic, of the Christian faith is given instance in the commands of the Law, the oracles of prophets, the verses of the Psalter, the narrative of the Gospels, the preaching of Peter and the letters of Paul. Thus, all theological reflection is to be traced back to the fundamental themes in Scripture while the center of written Scripture is the living Christ himself. Theology is Christocentric because the faith of the Church (and thus the Scripture) is centered in Christ. Every theme in the Christian faith can be traced directly or indirectly back to that central hub—that God has revealed the divine nature in Christ as testified in the Bible. There is, after all, one God, one Savior, one baptism, one faith. Perhaps one could say that is why theology is "systematic." Or, if that seems a bit strong, one might say that there is a clearly discernible pattern that comes into the foreground as one considers the logical tapestry of the Church's faith.

If we have said that the center of Christian faith is Christ himself, his life, ministry, death, and resurrection—if this is the logical center—then surely this must give a clue to the remaining themes, or "doctrines," of the faith. Indeed it does in not one, but many, ways. Consider this. By all accounts, Jesus was a Jewish rabbi who spent his career in the regions of Palestine. His ministry began with a baptism by John the Baptist in the Jordan River and ended with a final trip to Jerusalem. There the Jewish leadership conspired to do him in and he was finally crucified under the auspices of the Roman government. None of this is very contentious; it is regarded as a factual profile of Jesus' career. But how can one move from these facts to the scandalous confession that this carpenter apprentice is God incarnate reconciling the world unto God's self? Yet, that is the warp and woof of the Christian faith—that while it is Jesus of Nazareth, it is also the invisible God in the flesh. Or, from the other side, the Christian confession is that the very Son of God is none other than the cursed man on the cross outside Jerusalem. However that may strain the believer, it is also the source of his/her life. That is the strange logic of the faith.

Or, take a closely connected example which is a mirror image of the same kind of logic derived from the central event of Christ. It is clear to all alike that the Bible is comprised of human documents written by human beings in human language. They are marked by diversity of genre:

some are prehistorical tradition while some are historical narrative, some are poetry, some are laws, some are letters. The authors are marked by their own varying talents and styles. Different purposes drove the writing and/or collecting of the sermons by the prophets, the lore of Israel, the laws of old, the sayings of Jesus, the letters of Peter and Paul. All of this is largely agreed. But to come to confess with the Jews regarding their Scripture or with other Christians with reference to the New Testament that God's presence and will accounts for these writings—well, that is to go way beyond what the facts dictate. It is to claim that these collected materials comprise "Holy Scripture"—that these words of human beings are also the "Word of God." Alternatively, it is to confess that the divine and authoritative Word is concealed in the humble words of men and women. Once more there is an odd sort of "logic" to the faith that Christians dare to affirm.

In sum, the revelation of God in Christ—this incongruous, even paradoxical, center of the Christian faith—determines the shape of everything else that is said—about God, about creation, about human beings, about the church, about salvation, about the sacraments. While at its deepest level, faith is absolutely simple repose in the God who is disclosed in Christ, there is also a profound mystery at the foundation of that revelation—so that faith always sees only in part, only through a glass darkly. So in this life at least, there always remains a wide assortment of tensions in the faith of the Christian Church. God is both revealed and concealed in Christ; Christ is both a human being and God; the Bible is a human word and the Word of God; creation is at once the product of natural forces and the handiwork of God; human beings both belong alongside the animals and are created in the image of God; sin is both inevitable and voluntary; faith is both a divine gift and a human act; the believer is both justified and sinner; the church is a human institution and the Body of Christ; the Kingdom is at work now in the church but it is yet to come. While there are different dynamics at work in these various paradoxical tensions of the faith, there is a certain common thread or logic that pervades. It is this: there is a fundamental tension between the divine and the human, that which has its source in God as over against creation. However one twists and turns, this tension will not go away, cannot be reconciled. That is one among several reasons why the Christian faith is not for the weak-willed or the fainthearted.

HISTORY, REVELATION, AND FAITH

One thing seems plain: God can use almost any means to reveal the divine will and purpose. God can "speak" through dreams and visions, a big fish and Balaam's ass, burning bushes and great floods, surfeit and suffering, the mouths of babes and prophets, the course of nature and the fortunes of Israel's battles. The biblical materials preserved and honored by Jews and Christians hardly hem God in. But it is not arbitrary if we suggest that the Christian faith has traditionally claimed that two means of revelation seem to loom large in the biblical materials: the creation with its wonders and various events in human history. The former of these is associated with what is called "general revelation" (or "natural revelation") while the latter is referred to as "special revelation" (or "historical revelation").

Actually, human beings are a part of both the natural and the historical realms. We ourselves are natural, biological creatures; but we belong to the arena of human action as well. Likewise, believers can discern God at work in the natural order of things—in the rhythm of sunrise and sunset, in the mysteries of birth and death, in the microcosm of the cell and the macrocosm of the universe; in the absolute terror of the storm and the beauty of the rainbow; in the majesty of the mountains and the mysterious depths of the sea; in the movement of the planets and the captivating beauty of a blossom. The stories of creation in the Bible and the prologue to John's Gospel, along with any number of stirring Psalms, bear witness to God's nature in the handiwork of creation. These natural phenomena "speak" volumes, far more than tongue can ever tell, about God's absolute majesty and God's creative power.

But human beings are also historical creatures. They are not merely passively subjected to the waxing and waning of the natural order; they are themselves actors engaged in making history. Fittingly, then, Jews and Christians from the start have confessed that their God is one who "speaks" not just through natural phenomena but also—even with primacy—through events and persons in history. The two most decisive events to which believers point are those that account primarily for the making of the people of Israel and the community of Christian believers respectively. Those events are the Exodus for Jews and the Christ-event for Christians. Of course, God has also made the divine will and purpose known through revealed commands at Sinai, the oracles and actions (sometimes bizarre) of the prophets, the fortunes of the Israelites in battle as victors or vanquished, and much more. But it is their deliverance from Egyptian slavery that has been the great watershed of Israel's faith in the God to whom they are bound by covenant. And it has been the ministry, death, and resurrection of Christ that has been at the center of distinctively Christian faith. Herein, so it is confessed, God decisively has been present and active to those who have the "eyes of faith" to see.

There is considerable debate among serious Christian believers as to the relationship between general (natural) revelation and special (historical) revelation.[3] But it is generally conceded that the divine self-disclosure of God's will and purpose is more definitive as well as more dramatic through God's "acts" in the history of Israel and in the person of Christ than in the natural world. It should be remembered that the Jews were confessing their God, Yahweh, as the one who in their history led them out of Egyptian bondage and into the land of promise long before they made much of God as Creator—this in spite of the fact that the Book of Genesis comes first in the Bible. In turning to Jesus, while he often uses natural phenomena as object lessons in his teaching (birds of the air and flowers of the field, planting and harvesting, and so on), his preoccupation was with the destiny of men and women in their historical relations with others and with God's rule in their lives. Thus for Jews and Christians, history is more crucial as a vehicle of revelation than nature and, within history, Christians maintain that Christ is the apex in the divine revelation of God's will and purpose.

It is also worth pointing out that insofar as nature by itself is a means of revelation, such disclosure of God is more diffuse, undifferentiated than that which is bestowed via the mode of specific historical events and persons. So if an individual's eyes have not been trained already by God's historical revelation, those who see God active in the natural order may conclude any of a wide variety of things about the character of God and God's will. With attention focused exclusively on natural processes, God can turn out to be identical with the world which is then regarded as God's body (pantheism)—or God can be conceived as totally divorced from natural processes after God's creative work is completed in the beginning (deism). There are other alternatives if one recalls the animism of primitives, the creation stories of the Babylonians, the creator god,

---

[3]There is a good general discussion of this thorny issue in Shirley C. Guthrie, Jr., *Christian Doctrine*, rev. ed. (Louisville: Westminster/John Knox Press, 1994) 39-52.

Brahma, of the Hindus, and so on. However majestic and wonderful is God, the Creator of heaven and earth, God is clearly and ultimately defined in God's "acts" in history. It is in that arena that God encounters human beings most dramatically and most personally. Therefore, what we should say in Christian theology is that the God who creates is the one who is accurately and truly and decisively revealed in the man Jesus Christ. Christians go even further than that: they claim that Christ, as the Word of God in the beginning, is himself God's active agent of creation. God's act as Creator is an act performed in and through God's powerful living Word, Christ. So creation itself is to be viewed from a Christocentric point of view (as will be explained further).

We have been speaking of God's revelation of the divine nature, especially via historical persons and events; we have also noted that these historical phenomena must be seen with the eyes of faith in order to be identified as acts of God. More must be said of these twin concepts: revelation and faith. We can say that revelation is the given, the bestowed, side of the relationship between God and human beings while faith is the subjective reception and appropriation of this disclosure of God. Everything in Judaism and Christianity stands or falls, begins and ends, with the claim that God discloses the divine nature to human beings—primarily via history. The emphasis falls here upon the fact that the initiative always belongs to God. This is partly what is meant when we say that Christian faith is theocentric; it is God's doing. It is strictly imperative to preserve this orientation. One way to call attention to this is to distinguish Judaism and Christianity from other forms of religion in the history of the race. One prominent way to define religion in general is to say that it is the human attempt to know or be united to God and thereby achieve salvation. By contrast, Christianity—and before Christianity, Judaism—points in the other direction: this "religion" is the divine self-disclosure to God's creatures. Instead of an upward movement in religion from human beings to God, Christianity is characterized by God's condescension into human history. In this sense, Christianity is not a religion at all; indeed it is the negation of all religion. The Christian faith is rooted in the God who, in freedom, chooses to make known God's being; otherwise God would remain to us the mysterious, the unfathomable one.

It is important to use the phrase "*self*-disclosure" for revelation since it is God's own self—the divine nature and will—that God reveals. The God revealed is a God who, by analogy to human selves, is known through God's purposive acts. By means of God's activity in history the divine personal will and purpose is "uncovered" in revelation, especially in the event of Jesus Christ. Further, in revelation, it becomes clear that the divine purpose is to establish a personal relationship between God's self and human creatures. Indeed, this has been the divine will from the time of creation—that human creatures shall enjoy a relationship of trust in and fellowship with God. In and through God's own activity of disclosure, then, God would seek to restore mutual relationship with those who have become estranged from God, those who have gone their own way. Thus, revelation in its fundamental nature is not some type of static declaration of truths about anything, not even about God. Rather, revelation has the character of a dynamic "encounter" in which God shows what sort of God God is—the divine will and nature.

But that brings us to the other side of the "encounter," namely, the human self and the exercise of faith. If revelation has to do with God's activity, faith has to do with the human reception of and dependence upon the God revealed therein. It has to do with the subject, the self, the creature for whose sake God has chosen to expose the divine nature. The human act of faith is a deep mystery because, strange as it may seem, it is regarded in a real sense as the work of God within the human heart. It is both God's gift and a genuine human act. But here our attention is focused on the human phenomenon of faith which could be said to include two primary facets: heartfelt trust (*fiducia*) and mental affirmation (*assensus*). It is clear that faith is not reducible to intellectual assent to various propositions as true, not even those of the Christian creeds. Nor of course is faith merely a subjective state or a confident feeling in one's breast and a smile on one's face when thinking about God. The Roman Catholic Church has typically emphasized the intellectual side of faith. The element of trust in the God revealed in Christ has been the primary focus of Protestants since the Reformation. In defense of this Protestant theme, it is the clear intent of much in Jesus' teachings and Paul's letters to underline the centrality of dependence upon God rather than the world if one's life is to be shaped properly by God's will.

Perhaps the following account will be helpful in bringing perspective. If God's *self*-disclosure to men and women is framed in terms of an "encounter," a relationship—even specifically as salvation in Christ—then the component of personal trust or dependence clearly takes precedence over that of intellectual belief. Or again, if in revelation God discloses God's *self* in salvific activity and would, in turn, solicit a response from human creatures, the response is to be conceived primarily in terms of a relationship of reliance upon God and loyalty to God. At the same time, however, in the encounter with God, or in discerning God's activity in Christ, one does emerge with something over and above a renewed self and confidence in God. There is a genuine *knowledge of God* which it is possible to announce. There are those things that can now be confessed about God and the divine nature that arise from the encounter, the "experience" of meeting God in the person of Christ. To be sure, one finds one's heart "strangely warmed"—and without that it might be asked whether faith has taken root. But there is also the constraint to tell others about the God who is present and at work in Christ. Put it this way: precisely from the activity of God—as from the activity of other persons—we come to know God and make claims about what kind of God God is, the very nature of God. And here there is plenty to occupy the mind as well as the heart.

Those who witness God at work in the world—in the Exodus or in Jesus Christ for example—must see these phenomena with the "eyes of faith" if revelation can be said to take place in its fullest sense. Otherwise, God's hand is not "seen" and these events simply remain what they are. That is, in the one case, we have a group of escaped slaves finding a way of escape in the nick of time; in the other case, we have a man who died a martyr's death at the hands of the Romans. In short, when God chooses to disclose the inner being of God, it is not evident on the face of things. Not even the natural order need be seen as God's masterpiece; even there faith is required for discernment. Likewise with historical events. No visible arm of God descended to part the waters of the *yam suph* and Jesus did not have a halo around his head as he walked the roads of Galilee. Not even Jesus' miracles were proofs of his oneness with God except for those who exercised faith in him. For them the miracles were unnecessary as evidence; for those without faith, the miracles proved nothing. Thus, what we must say is that history (along with nature) is the vehicle, the means, by which God chooses to reveal the divine nature in decisive ways. Yet the events in which God is revealed also serve to conceal God from view. Indeed, by definition, revelation is both an unveiling and a veiling at one and the same time. God is not immediately and directly given in revelation; nor is the historical and natural to be identified with the divine. But it is the Jewish and Christian confession that certain phenomena, events, persons can become bearers of divine revelation for those with faith.

Faith and Authority

The ultimate object of faith, that in which faith reposes, is—can be—none other than the God revealed in Jesus Christ. This is the theocentric and Christocentric logic of the Christian faith. But we are not contemporaries with Christ who is the vehicle of God's self-disclosure, the one who is said to be very God and very man. Is this distance an advantage or a disadvantage?[4] However one answers, the question remains: How do we who come later have access to the divine revelation in Jesus' life, death, and resurrection? The answer typically is: by means of the Bible. It is through the witness of the biblical authors that God's revelation in history (and nature) is given tongue (or pen) and faith is born in our lives. Of course, it is considerably more complex than that. There are mothers and fathers as well as teachers and priests; there are prayers that are said and rituals observed; there are sermons heard and verses memorized; there is learning from lives that are good and those that have clearly been derailed. Still, even by these persons and exercises, in the final analysis one is returned to the Testaments, Old and New.

So the Bible has been accepted by all Christians alike as authoritative in matters of faith and morals. In Roman Catholicism there is the additional acknowledgement of the church's authority (in the person of the pope or the decision of councils) to pronounce what truth is contained in Scriptures. Thus an immense body of official church tradition has emerged in the form of conciliar decisions, creedal affirmations, liturgical rites, papal encyclicals, and much else. In all this, it is thought that the church is the indispensable interpreter of Scripture and therefore possesses roughly equal authority along with the Bible. Because of the objections of Martin Luther and others in the Reformation, Protestants have rejected this twin authoritative status of Scripture and church tradition in favor of the Bible alone—*sola Scriptura*. But the dominating point here is that in both arms of Christianity the Scripture is authoritative and serves as the norm for judging any other competing claims.

---

[4]Søren Kierkegaard offers a brilliant discussion of this question in his classic work *Philosophical Fragments*, Kierkegaard's Writings vol. 7, trans. Howard V. Hong and Edna H. Hong (Princeton NJ: Princeton University Press, 1987) 55-71 and 89-110.

But here several contentious issues arise even within Protestantism. It is claimed by all that the Bible has authority because it is inspired, that is, "God breathed." What is meant by this is that the authors were inspired—that is, in some sense, compelled by divine prompting—to give witness as they did to God's own activity in various historical occurrences (especially the Christ event) transpiring either in their very midst or in the past. At this point, however, there arises genuine disagreement among true believers. Some believe that God in some sense dictated the words that were written by the authors of each manuscript—that the writers may be conceived as something like stenographers. This view is sometimes called "verbal inspiration" or "plenary inspiration." To those who support this position, it is important to insist that God is actually the "author" of the Bible since allowing genuine human foibles and weaknesses into the writing of the manuscripts wreaks havoc with their assurance about the divine authority of Scripture. So the Word of God—always powerful and dynamic, but not necessarily nor even typically in the form of words—is now transmuted into the *words* of God found in Holy Writ.

There is a sense in which this view is harmless enough, especially when the intent is merely to give innocent acknowledgment that the Bible is the norm for Christian faith. However, in the final analysis, this position is inadequate in its account of the Word of God (even as it is described in the Bible) and potentially dangerous from a religious point of view. As pointed out earlier, the Word of God is identified in John's Gospel as none other than the everlasting Christ himself, the second person of the Godhead, the agent of creation, the means of redemption for the human race and the future Judge of the living and dead. The Bible is indeed a witness to that living Word; but it is derivative and in the form of human speech. To invest one's ultimate trust in the written testimony to the Word when it should be directed toward the living Word—Christ himself—is a form of idolatry, sometimes referred to as "bibliolatry." Thus the potential danger of the view under discussion. Never should the record of revelation be placed above the source of that disclosure. It is not to honor the Bible but to misconstrue its nature when the book itself—even as a holy book—becomes the object of one's faith or dependence.

Another observation is appropriate here. Often those who espouse the "verbal inspiration" view of Scripture find themselves in the awkward position of having to reject the results of honest biblical scholarship—or of having to formulate frequently farfetched theories of their own to account for the facts. Such individuals see themselves as protecting Scripture against scholarship that would threaten to malign and undermine the inspired—again—*words* of the text which are thought to be identical with God's Word. By contrast, two things should be said. First, there is a sense (noted below) in which the Bible does not need the bolstering defense of those who desire to provide it; the Bible possesses its own intrinsic authority. Second, it should be said here that serious biblical scholarship is neither the enemy nor the friend of faith in the God revealed in Jesus Christ. The Bible simply is what it is: a collection of books written by Jewish and Christian human beings in human language for particular occasions. What Christians dare to confess is that this book is sacred because it points beyond itself to the one in whom God is ultimately disclosed, Jesus Christ. Historically speaking, Jesus too is what he is: a Jew who was born and lived out his life as a first-century rabbi and/or prophet and was eventually executed under Roman rule. What Christians make bold to say is that this man is the one through whom God's inner nature and will for human beings is made final and complete. That is what it means for faith to "see" the invisible God at work in human history and it is in God and God *alone* that faith is to find its repose.

How then does this faith in the God revealed in Christ arise and whence this confidence in Scripture? On what foundation? By what authority? The Bible is the means by which those of us who come later are exposed to the work and person of Jesus Christ. But how does this Scripture that gives witness to Jesus as the Savior come to possess such authority as the powerful, life-changing Word of God in written form? Is it that we believe it simply because we were taught to do so? Or because we take it on the church's authority? Or because priests and parsons say so? Well, most of us begin by believing about the Bible in this innocent way at a young age. In the course of time, however, our faith takes a more lively form and the Bible comes to have a different kind of pervasive sway in our lives.

It goes as follows for many people at least. They find that in a clear and dynamic way God seeks to "encounter" them in and through the pages of Scripture; or, to put it another way, on one or another occasion they find that the Bible has "spoken" to them with a penetrating and transforming power that is undeniable. If and when this happens, it is always because their hearts have been prepared for such reading of the Bible—prepared by life itself, one might say. Alternatively, one might say that God has tilled the soil of the heart and prepared it for the seed of the Word. Perhaps grief or temptation or fear of an uncertain future or a deep consciousness of sin—these and other vicissitudes of life can enable a person to read the Bible in the requisite way. Suffice it to say that when Scripture is taken in with a hungry heart, the written Word of Scripture can become the means by which the God revealed in Christ works directly to change, to edify, to chasten, to comfort, and to restore a life. When and if that ever happens to an individual, he or she no longer needs the authority of parent or pastor, church or council; no longer is there any necessity for proofs or theories (not even "verbal inspiration"). No, in such an instance the Bible has spoken with an inherent power that surpasses any human contrivance. Then, one might say, the Bible has *become* the Word of God for that individual so that it moves his or her existence to the core. Indeed, this is said to be the work of the Holy Spirit of God bringing certainty to those whose eyes of faith have been opened by the words of the Bible.[5]

So the Bible has its inviolable authority because, as the written Word, it bears witness to the living Word, Jesus Christ, and because the witness of Scripture has the intrinsic power to bring judgment and transformation to human lives. Still, over and above Scripture, there is a rich and plenteous body of materials that have made their way into the lifestream and worship practices of the Christian church—sermons and prayers, liturgies and confessions, hymns and letters and theological writings, and much more. One could say that these constitute the "tradition" of the church as it has been passed down over the generations. But traditions are not merely time-honored relics of the past. The most important note to make here is that tradition in all these forms provides the manifold ways in which the church has given and continues to bear living testimony to the single message of Christ over the centuries. Therefore, so long as the church persists in giving voice to this message, or *kerygma*, in every clime and place, tradition is always in the making—adapted to the needs of the moment, formed with different nuances in each culture but always forged from Scripture.

---

[5]The same thing may be said with reference to the "spoken" word of preaching that has been said here about the "written" word of Scripture. God's Spirit can work in and through the human words of a sermon to convict, edify, and generally open the human heart to God's will.

Here the specific Protestant emphasis on *sola Scriptura* comes once more into the foreground. Unlike Roman Catholicism, Protestantism has refused to place the emerging traditions of the church on equal footing with the authority of the Bible. Indeed, the Scripture is to be taken as the test for any formulated tradition just as it is the norm for theology itself. Of course, the Protestant churches also refuse to recognize any human authority or tribunal as having vested in it the authority to pronounce what Scripture says or what the Church's true teachings are. Neither pope nor council—nor any other form of church authority—can be permitted to usurp the role of God's Spirit in leading men and women into Scripture's truth. The doctrine of papal infallibility[6] within Roman Catholicism is the most conspicuous example of the presumption of an inflated place of human authority in matters of religious faith. But other instances are not difficult to discern—for example, the leaders of even some Protestant denominations. Scripture, with its center in Christ, is the only "measuring stick" by which to judge the adequacy or truth of any unfolding form of tradition, whether theology or hymnody, sermons or creeds.

In suggesting the derivative and secondary nature of tradition (by comparison to Scripture), its crucial role must not be minimized in the life of the Christian church. Two functions of tradition are to be observed. First, positively, the various forms of tradition provide the vehicles for expressing and interpreting the content of the biblical faith. Indeed tradition can even make explicit some elements of the faith that are only implicit in the Bible's pages. So, for example, if the doctrine of the Trinity is there in embryonic form in the pages of Gospel and Pauline letter, it has been given fuller development in the creedal affirmations, hymnody and liturgy of the church. By the same token, especially creedal affirmations—about the Trinity or incarnation—have provided a shield against alien elements that run against the grain of the Christian faith. Indeed, various creeds of the church were specifically formulated to combat certain heresies, especially Docetism (discussed later). Therefore, in addition to providing a positive outlet for the Gospel message, the traditions of the Christian community have served a negative purpose—to provide a rebuff to that which does not conform to the central motifs of the faith.

In sum, theology is a part of the dynamic and emerging tradition of the church—along with hymnody and sermons, creeds and catechisms.

---

[6]This doctrine was established during Vatican Council I, 1869/1870.

But more like creeds and other instruments used in the more formal teaching of the faith, theology seeks to make clear what can and cannot be said of God and a host of other concepts central in Christianity. Of course, theology does not legislate any more than creeds do. Rather, both alike in their different ways are efforts to sketch out what is already contained in the language of prophets and apostles, God's Law and Gospel—that is, in the witness of Scripture. It is that language—and its accompanying life of faith—that has been reduplicated in the lives of believers over the generations. So it is no stretch to say that theology gathers up and endeavors to give clarity to the themes already contained in Christian thinking and worship through the centuries. Clearly, the concept 'God' has had a governing place in the faith of Jews and Christians; thus the derivation of the word "theology" or the "logic" of "God." It is to the subject of God that we turn explicitly in the next chapter. In fact, however, in widely varying ways, each of the remaining chapters is occupied with how we speak of God—as Father (chapter 14), Son (chapter 15) and Holy Spirit (chapter 16). Indeed, one of the distinctively Christian affirmations about God is that God is one God in three persons—a Trinity.

GOD THE FATHER ALMIGHTY, MAKER OF HEAVEN AND EARTH

THE NATURE OF GOD: GOD'S ATTRIBUTES[1]

Theology is a description of the ruled ways in which the Bible and the Christian community speak about those things that pertain to God. Theology does not provide otherwise inaccessible knowledge about God to which the theologian alone is privileged. What is accessible to one is accessible to all. But one crucial element in the logic of Christian faith is that such knowledge is centered in one historical person—Jesus, the Christ. Whatever else may be known about God—whether from nature or from history (for example, the Exodus)—and whatever else is said about God—in Bible or church teachings—must be consistent with this focal point of revelation. Thus, the faith of the church (and thus theology) is Christocentric even as it is theocentric. The importance of Jesus Christ (as well as Scripture) resides in the affirmation that God has freely chosen to reveal God's very nature on the plane of history in this human being. But, as already pointed out, in revelation God not only discloses or unveils who God is. Paradoxically, in revelation God also remains concealed. Indeed, precisely because God discloses the divine nature in a historical person, in this first-century Jewish rabbi, God necessarily also remains veiled, inaccessible, invisible, hidden—except to those with the eyes of faith. This brings us to the first attribute of God, God's holiness.

I. GOD AS HOLY

When we speak of God as holy, we mean holiness in a religious as over against a moralistic sense. That is, the reference is not to God's righteousness (which will be discussed below). Rather, the reference is to

---

[1]In this and the following chapters, the work of Gustav Aulen has exercised considerable influence, especially his *The Faith of the Christian Church*, trans. Eric H. Wahlstrom (Philadelphia: Fortress Press, 1960). The debt to Aulen (and more generally to the Swedish school) piled up over several years of using *The Faith of the Christian Church* as the required text in a course on Christian beliefs.

God's transcendence—the divine majesty, glory, or "otherness." These terms themselves suggest that there is that in God's nature that will ever be concealed from us in spite of God's activity in revealing the divine nature to us. If God is the one who reveals the divine nature, if God is the *deus revelatus*, God is nonetheless the God who is veiled from our sight, the *deus absconditus*. That is, God is not simply reducible to what is revealed of the divine nature either in the natural order or in the historical arena. Even if God's nature is made known to us decisively and finally in the person of Jesus Christ, even there—just *because* it is on the human plane that the revelation takes place—God remains for us hidden, invisible, transcendent, untamable, and utterly mysterious. Revelation never gives us God directly. If God chooses to bestow knowledge of the divine nature in revelation at all God must use finite means, and this means that the transcendent God is accessible only indirectly.

Another way to underline God's holiness is to say that in revelation, we discern that God is to be distinguished absolutely from that which is merely human or finite. As one theologian has suggested, there is an "absolute qualitative difference" between the transcendent God on the one hand and God's finite creatures (including human beings) on the other.[2] A qualitative difference is a difference in kind as over against a mere difference in quantity. God is not a superhuman being; God is not human nature writ large. So all of our humanly conceived notions of God pale miserably in comparison to the God who is holy, hidden in divine majesty. Some of our limited notions can be explained innocently enough. For instance, in childhood and adolescence we often form very inadequate notions of God. Perhaps because of intellectual immaturity and sometimes because of ill-prepared if well-meaning teachers, God may get conceived as a resident policeman who stalks the lawbreaker or as a grand old man in a long flowing beard or as a managing director of a universal play in which each actor has his or her role.[3] Sooner or later, however, these

---

[2]The theologian is Karl Barth in his famous *Epistle to the Romans*, trans. from the 6th ed. by Edwyn C. Hoskyns (London: Oxford University Press, 1960). In this commentary, Barth speaks of the "unknown God" who is "wholly other" and emphasizes Christ as the central Paradox of faith. But on these points and others Barth learned much from Søren Kierkegaard in his *Philosophical Fragments*, esp. 37-48.

[3]See the popular little book by J. B. Phillips, *Your God Is Too Small* (repr.: New York: Touchstone/Simon & Schuster, 1997; orig., 1953).

inadequate conceptions are to be shed in favor of notions that do justice to God's absolute holiness, God's invisible majesty.

More serious problems arise if our conceptions of God's nature are framed by our own interests and desires as human beings. We are prone to project for ourselves a God who answers to our deepest longings and inclinations, a God who is merely a product of wish fulfillment. If the resultant conception of God derives from our own individual self-interest, this view of God may be said to be egocentric. If the needs of the human race as a whole are the root source of the God concept, then our concept of God may be said to be anthropocentric. To press this general point, it could be noted that some people shape their view of God in terms of their own national interests (so God has America higher on the list than other nations) or by reference to the socioeconomic class to which they belong. In such instances and many others, unfortunately God is conceived in terms of that which serves us human beings best. The point, however, is that we must vigorously resist such ways of conceiving God in spite of our strong temptation to make God conform to what is most tasteful, compatible, helpful, fulfilling for us. Instead, we must simply permit God to be God in all the divine untamed majesty. If we learn to do that, we can recapture something of what Moses felt—the shudder as he took off his shoes and lay prostrate before the living presence of a holy God in the burning bush. Indeed, the appropriate response to the God who is holy is not reflection but worship, not a pensive look but a bowed head and bent knees. To be in the presence of the holy God entails—logically as well as psychologically—a mixture of awe and a sense of utter dependence and powerlessness. It is what is referred to in the Bible as the fear of the Lord—not fear of something in particular but an awareness of being confronted by that which is absolutely mysterious, totally other, the God who will not be domesticated.

Thus in spite of God's self-disclosure—indeed, in the midst of revelation—there is that about the divine inner nature which is always and utterly beyond our ken, something totally unfathomable, that which would burst the bounds of human limitations. It is this to which we refer when we speak of God's holiness. Whether we should call this an attribute is questionable. Perhaps we should regard God's holiness, the divine mystery, as that which is all-pervasive in God's nature. God's holiness could be regarded as the background against which all the other divine attributes must be properly apprehended. God's holiness is what gives depth to everything else that is said about God in much the same way that a painting possesses depth only if there is an unobtrusive background against which the main focus in the foreground is to be viewed—or in much the same way that the bass part, although not dominant in a musical piece, lends profundity to all the other parts. Whatever may be said of God and whenever and wherever God chooses to disclose the divine nature, God remains the God who is holy, the one before whom we quake.

2. GOD AS PERSONAL

There are many elements of the Christian faith that are strangely, but in a fascinating and even compelling way, set over against one another. The faith is marked by paradox in virtually all directions. When we recognize that God is personal in the same moment that we have emphasized God's holiness, this is immediately made plain. These aspects of God's nature must be held in tension with one another, without watering down either. If God is transcendent over the world, God is also immanent in the world—but without compromising the divine majesty. If God is always and invariably the hidden God, God is also the God who is engaged in the world disclosing the divine being—but without the loss of mystery. If God is qualitatively different from God's creatures, God also acts in history and in the hearts of men and women—but without erasing the absolute distinction. God is both the holy One and the God who is personal. Neither of these can be compromised without distorting the very nature of God. Nonetheless, here our attention falls upon God's nature as personal. What does this mean?

When we speak of God as personal we do not mean that God is a person; we mean to suggest that God is person-like. This comes out primarily when we say that God is one who, rather like human persons, has the capacity to act with will and purpose. The God of Jews and Christians is a God who acts and, in doing so, discloses the divine nature to men and women on the human plane. Such an active God is purposive in what God does in history and in the subjective lives of individuals. This is the first and most important point to make. Indeed, it is by way of God's activities that we come to know what kind of God God is; the divine attributes are exhibited in God's work within the world. Furthermore, in God's central act—in Jesus of Nazareth—it becomes clear that God's special and overriding purpose is to bring evil into submission, overcome its devastating effects on human beings and restore the fellowship with them that God intended from the beginning. But fellowship is possible only with a God who is personal in a more specific manner than simply being an active God. Of course such fellowship also assumes that at least God's human creatures, too, have the capacity for personal relationship. For the moment and with reference to God, however, it must be said that a God who can "encounter" human persons, who can enter into communion with them, is a God who must be conceived as personal in nature.

But there is a subtle danger here. We must be careful not to reduce this "encountering" God and this relationship with God to what we might experience on the human level. God is not to be conceived in a trivial manner as a friend or ally we call on now and again. No, that God is personal—that God is present and at work in our lives—means that God is closer to us than we would actually like to imagine much of the time. Indeed, God is closer to us than we are to ourselves; God knows us through and through. This is both comforting and frightening. It is wonderful consolation when we consider that God knows our needs better than we ever can and before we even can give voice to them. On the other hand, it is certainly dreadful when we recollect those dark corners in our heart which harbor distasteful, shameful, and downright despicable thoughts/desires that we would never divulge to other persons in our ordinary commerce with them. Yet we cannot hide them from the God who is deeply personal. It might even be said that God's presence is so profoundly personal that it returns us to the awareness that God is absolutely distinct from human creatures, that God is also the holy God who cannot be reduced to our finite conceptions.

So there are two ways to go wrong in the conception of the God of the Christian (and Jewish) faith. God's "otherness" can be emphasized to the exclusion of God's being present and active in the world. By contrast, God's immanence in the world can be stressed to the point of denying God's transcendence. Deism and pantheism are the views that embody these two dangers.

Deism is the view that God is utterly aloof from the world and its human inhabitants. There was a beginning at which time God brought things into being. But, rather like a watchmaker, once the giant clockwork was complete God could depart from the created universe, permitting it to run its own course governed by the intricate design of springs, cogs, and wheels. God, then, is totally removed from the world and the human lot.

On the other hand, pantheists claim that God is identical to the world around us or at least those forces that permeate and govern it. The divine fills the universe and is not distinguishable from it. The ebb and flow of the world—typically conceived as the natural order—are identical with the movements of the divine heartbeat. Of course, what the Christian faith affirms is that God, the God of Abraham and Moses and the one incarnate in Jesus of Nazareth, is one who reveals God's nature in the world without becoming identical with it. God is personal and active in a dynamic way in history, nature, and individual lives, but in such a way that God remains the God who is neither identical with the world nor can God be contained in it.

3. GOD AS LOVING, RIGHTEOUS, AND POWERFUL

When God discloses the divine nature, notably in the normative Christ event, God manifests what kind of God God is—and, by the way, what kind of God God is *not*. We learn what we may and may *not* say about God. If God's holiness, the divine hiddenness in revelation, reminds us that much of what we are prone to say about God is bound to be inept, then that which is unveiled of God in the divine activity as personal God compels us to make some positive and startling claims about God's nature. We come to know God through God's active self-disclosure as a God who is characterized by love, righteousness, and power. It is the same God who preserves in the divine nature these quite diverse attributes.

But these three attributes present difficulties. The main question is, How can these attributes be said to be compatible with one another, characterizing one and the same God? The traditional way of presenting the difficulties is in the form of various dilemmas. If God is both all-loving and all-powerful, how can the raw and pervasive presence of evil (especially in the form of innocent suffering) in the world be accounted for? If it is confessed that God is love, then God must not possess the power required to extinguish such evil; on the other hand, if there is insistence on God's absolute power, then God must not be sufficiently loving to do away with the heart-rending suffering in the world. In this dilemma it appears that one must choose between two alternatives—compromise God's power to preserve God's love or vice versa—neither of which is finally satisfactory to the confessing Christian. A similar quandary surrounds the relation between God's love and righteousness: How can God be both absolutely righteous in the divine demands and yet forgive a wrongdoer by means of the divine love?

Needless to say, there is no shortage of proposed solutions to these difficult issues. The proposal here is to take seriously the Christocentric character of the divine disclosure of God's nature. If, as has been argued,

God's revelation in Jesus Christ is the norm for all that is said about God, then there can be no doubt what attribute of God becomes the focal point—it is God's love. In light of what is disclosed in Jesus Christ, God's love, while clearly not the only word about God, is the first and last word about God's inner nature. It is the central and unifying character of God in relating these attributes to one another.[4] At the same time, God's righteousness and power must be preserved without compromise. For while the God revealed in Christ is love, God is not an indulgent God who winks at evil; nor is God an emasculated God who is rendered powerless in the face of evil. Rather, God (on account of the divine righteousness) stands in absolute opposition to the stark reality of evil and is engaged in a struggle with those dark forces. Further, the same God (by virtue of divine power) will ultimately gain conquest over evil. This is the Christian faith and the Christian hope in the life, death, and resurrection of Christ Jesus in whom God's love is disclosed. In fact, two things should be said to relate God's righteous wrath and God's power to the loving will of God: first, God's righteous judgment upon evil is God's absolute opposition to anything that stands as a threat to God's own creation and second, God's power which is pitted against the powers of darkness and destruction is, strange as it may sound, the power of God's sovereign love.

God's love. The central claim of the Christian faith about God's nature, then, is that God is a God who loves sacrificially. This knowledge of God is not the product of human reason; reason could not have conjured such a notion. Nor does it arise as the result of a human being's deepest craving, though there is much here for which the human breast might long. When the Christian believer makes the bold and unexpected confession that, despite his or her own sinful corruption, God has chosen to love him or her, that confession is made only and always in light of God's disclosure of the divine nature in Jesus Christ. This and this only is the beginning of knowing God as love within the Christian faith. Had God not so revealed God's nature, this thought—that God might act in self-sacrificing love for us—could never have been more than a despairing cry of the human heart; it could never have taken the form of glad tidings announced to the world. As the Scripture testifies: "In this is love, not that we loved God but that he loved us and sent his Son to be the

---

[4]The treatment of these three divine attributes owes much to the work of Aulen, *Faith of the Christian Church,* esp. 106-30.

atoning sacrifice for our sins" (1 John 4:10). And "while we were still weak, at the right time Christ died for the ungodly" (Romans 5:6). It is the holy God—the God who is unapproachable in glory, the God who is otherwise unfathomable, the unknown—it is this God who condescends to us—to us whose hearts are dominated by greed, envy, lust, covetousness, and hatred. It is this God who, in self-sacrificing love, enters our world in Jesus of Nazareth to restore our broken relationship with the One who is our Maker. The love with which God loves us is given unmistakable and vivid display in Jesus' entire life and ministry which culminate in his Passion in the city of Jerusalem. In a myriad of ways this love of God may be described in its earthly manifestation in Christ. Perhaps the following characteristics will suffice: God's love is personal, unmerited, and sacrificial.

God's love is *personal*. In saying this, however, we should exercise great care. We must not sentimentalize or soften God's love. So by way of clarification, if we say that God's love is personal we simply mean to point to the fact that it is directed toward individual persons, human beings with real life histories, deep inner conflicts, desperate needs. Although God's love has all human beings as its object and is thus universal, this should not blind us to the fact that it is bestowed on each person in turn and is thus personal. Furthermore, while it should not be forgotten that God cares for all of creation, including all of nature, the divine love is specifically focused on those beings who are made in God's image—that is, those who have the unique capacity for a mutual relationship with God, namely, human creatures. And precisely here is another sense in which God's love is personal: the purpose of God's love is to bring men and women back to a personal relationship—fellowship—with God. This kind of communion, characterized by human trust and obedience, is God's purpose for human persons from the very beginning. The love of God in Jesus Christ is intended to overcome human alienation and realize that purpose of God's loving will.

God's love is also *unmerited* by those who are its recipients. That is, it is not the worthiness of human beings, collectively or individually, that stimulates God's love—not their righteous deeds, not their good intentions, not their religious rituals. Nothing outside of God can be said to be the cause of the divine love. God's love is bestowed upon any and all only and always because God freely chooses to do so—by God's own will and purpose, out of God's own nature. Yet there are many persons, including very religious individuals, who believe that they not only can but must make themselves acceptable to God in order to solicit God's favor or love toward them. "Legalism" is the term often used for this attitude which assumes that the amassing of human merit virtually obliges God to love them. The Pharisees of Jesus' day are the paradigm of such strenuous efforts in obedience to God's Law with their resultant sense of pride and smugness. In contrast, the apostle Paul (himself a Pharisee turned Christian), taught that persons are saved only and always by God's grace revealed in Christ. Indeed, the point is that men and women are hopelessly mired in sin and are therefore *un*deserving of God's love. So it is not *because of* what God finds in the heart and life of human creatures that God bestows the divine love; in utter freedom God confers that love *in spite of* the rebellion and pride that are so evident in their lives.

Finally, God's love is *self-sacrificing*. Human love seeks its own good, hankers for that which is beautiful or pleasurable, desires to acquire what is fulfilling. The Greeks had a term for such normal human love, *eros*, from which we derive the term "erotic" which epitomizes such self-seeking love. By contrast, God's love is self-giving, self-sacrificing; it seeks not its own good but the good of the "other", the object of love, the one most in need, those who are plainly sinners. The cross of Christ is of course the paradigmatic expression of such love in which God gave God's only begotten Son for the sake of all who would believe. But in truth Jesus' whole life was a story of self-forgetfulness in service to the little people of the world, the poor, the despised, the demented, the sick. So from beginning to end, we could say that the movement of God is condescension to the world of sinful humanity, humiliation at their hands, exposure to their rejection and ultimately their deathblow. In the world, this is the fate of a love that is genuinely sacrificial: death. So it is said in Scripture that Christ emptied himself for our sakes, sacrificed himself on our behalf. The Greek term for this kind of love is *agape*; it is the kind of love God has even for those who resist and reject God. God's love in Christ is not human love on a large scale; it is an utterly different kind of love. This form of love is too strenuous for human beings; indeed, the divine love remains a mystery since, as noted, there is no reason to call it forth. So it is no surprise that a person should "stand amazed in the presence of Jesus the Nazarene, and wonder how he could love me, a sinner, condemned, unclean."[5]

---

[5]"I Stand Amazed in the Presence," words and tune ("My Savior's Love")

God's righteousness. When we speak of God's righteousness, the reference is to God's capacity for wrath or judgment against evil in all of its forms, but specifically human sin. In God's righteousness, God stands in absolute opposition to the destructive power of evil in the world. In turn, evil may be defined as that which is antithetical to God's loving will and purpose for creation. Thus we must not water down God's wrath which is forever kindled in its white heat against that which would overturn God's positive and loving purpose. If we ever weaken the opposition of God's wrath to evil, if we think that God does not take evil with utter gravity, then we sentimentalize God's love and turn God into an indulgent father figure. On the other hand, if we preserve God's righteous wrath while letting go of the love which defines God's inner nature, then God becomes a hard and perverse God who takes glee in the suffering of sinners. But this means we have to give further attention to the relationship between righteousness and love as divine attributes.

The work of God's righteous wrath is the expression of God's opposition to evil, the divine hostility toward that which would corrupt and deal a death blow to all that God has created, including especially those creatures who belong to the human race. By its very nature, evil is destructive, corrupting, contaminating, infecting. Yet it makes its way into our lives with such subtlety and power. So we say that evil beguiles, seduces, overcomes, captivates, consumes us. It appears in its finery but when it has had its way with us, it leaves us to wallow in our own stench. The point is that evil in general, sin in particular, is inherently negative, degrading, destructive. Thus, as God's wrath roots out the evil which would annihilate God's human creatures, that expression of the divine righteousness is precisely the means by which God achieves the divine loving will which is to preserve and reclaim God's own. God's wrath works to break down utterly that which is evil so that health and wholeness may be restored. In short, the purpose of God's righteous wrath is never merely negative or destructive; it is ultimately constructive, governed by that love which is determinative of God's nature. The great reformer, Martin Luther, spoke of God's judging wrath as God's strange or alien work (*opus alienum*) while God's redeeming love accomplishes God's proper work (*opus proprium*).

---

by Charles H. Gabriel (1905).

One classic illustration of this relationship between righteousness and love is found in the comparison between Law and Gospel. The typical means by which God confronts human beings in righteous judgment is the Law; characteristically, God as love confronts men and women by way of the Gospel.[6] In Christian belief, one primary function of the Law is to lead, even drive, persons to Christ and the Gospel rooted in him. It works this way. By way of the Law as an instrument of God's wrath, a person is made aware of the manifold ways in which his or her life has gone wrong, the ways in which his or her life has been lived in rebellion against God. Paul refers to the Law as a schoolmaster which teaches the individual the gaping difference between what they *are* and what they *ought to be*. Or, the Law is likened to a mirror which permits individuals to see their true reflection, corrupted and gnarled by sin. The Law undercuts all human pretensions—even religious ones—so there is no ground of merit on which to stand. Bereft of any appeal, standing in one's nakedness before God, the individual realizes that he or she is utterly dependent on God's grace disclosed in the cross of Christ. And precisely here is the Gospel—that while men and women were yet sinners, Christ died for the ungodly. Through Christ, God in freedom has decided to deal with sinful human creatures in love rather than wrath. Their lives are plucked from the destruction and infection that otherwise would have annihilated them. They experience the healing balm of the Great Physician, the only one who can truly help. If God's wrath breaks a person down, makes them buckle at the knees, unravels their own self-assurances, then in Christ they are resurrected, restored to true life. The Law destroys, purges of evil so that the Gospel can recreate. God's loving will is always and ultimately served even in the expression of God's wrath. In this manner, God's righteous wrath and God's love are inextricably interwoven, without division or contradiction.

God's power. God's power is likewise interconnected with God's love and cannot be separated from it. Indeed, God's power can only be

---

[6]We need to be careful not to identify Law/wrath with the Old Testament and Gospel/love with the New Testament too closely. The most strenuous set of demands placed upon believers is in Jesus' so-called Sermon on the Mount (Matthew 5–7). Then, too, God's steadfast love for the covenant people is a constant theme in the Old Testament. Still, in a loose sort of way, Law remains associated with Moses and the Old Covenant while the Gospel is clearly linked to Jesus Christ and the New Covenant.

properly conceived in terms of God's sovereign love. It is even more closely linked than that. God's power *is* the power of God's love. The Christian confession is that love, God's love, is the most sovereign power in all creation since it is able to melt the hearts of sinful men and women. By contrast, power abstractly conceived independently of God's love is power that is arbitrary and tyrannical. It is a power in which God takes satisfaction in buffeting men and women about so that they helplessly cower down before God. Just as in the case of righteousness that is divorced from love, so power conceived independently leads to a sub-Christian notion of God. On the other hand, love that is characterized by powerlessness is a love that is fleeting and fickle; by contrast, God's steadfast love endures forever and has the capacity to overcome even the sinister, captivating, and deeply mysterious power of evil.

Here we encounter one of the most paradoxical features of the Christian faith: the form God's love takes in the exercise of its power. God's love has been characterized as self-sacrificing and its most graphic expression is in the cross of Jesus Christ. Is that not a scandal? Just imagine: God's sovereign power—the power of the divine love—is disclosed precisely in what clearly appears to be weakness and defeat at the hands of evil men and women. The Roman cross was a degrading form of death which utterly humiliated its victims, including Jesus of Nazareth. Arms pinned to the crossbar, Jesus helplessly hung naked before the world as jeers were hurled at him. In a sinful world that is blind and unheeding, this is invariably the fate of the divine love that comes in the form of a servant, emptying itself for the sake of others. Paradoxically, the Christian claim is that in the midst of this debacle is the almighty power of God at work overcoming sin and death and Satan. God's power is not an external force God exercises over human creatures, as though God were imposing the divine will arbitrarily from the outside. God's power—God's sovereign love—works in such a way that God transforms the heart of an individual. By that power, God compels men and women inwardly into God's service. This is not the submission of a slave under the fist of a master; it is the submission of a son or daughter in love toward a parent. The power of God's love recreates individuals inside out, redirecting their interests and concerns such that they become new creatures.

In speaking of God's power, it is clear that we must take seriously the sinister power of evil in the world, particularly in the form of sin which threatens the human self. The Christian faith is realistic in confessing that there are foreign elements in the world which stand in direct opposition to God's will and purpose. There is no interest in glossing over that fact. For example, the biblical faith never claims that evil is not so serious as it seems to be; nor does it claim that evil is really good in disguise. As we will find later, there is no way to explain how evil has made its entrance into the world; its origin is as mysterious as evil itself and the mystery testifies to its power. The conflict between God and evil is a real one. Yet Christian believers also confess that evil in all its forms will ultimately succumb to the almighty sovereignty of God's power—the power of the divine sacrificial love displayed in the cross and resurrection. What appears in the form of humiliation will gain final conquest and be exalted over that which, by all ordinary accounts, holds sway in the lives of men and women captivated by sin. In spite of the way things are in the world, Christian faith affirms that God's love revealed in Christ is the power which can render null the devastating and destructive power of evil in individual lives and in the world generally. This aspect of faith accounts for the way in which believers anticipate those "last days" when the ultimate victory of God over evil will be finalized and there will be no more darkness, corruption, sorrow. Then, but only then, when confronted by the sovereignty of divine love will the impotence of evil be made manifest for all to see. In the meantime, we live in a world in which only those with the "eyes of faith" can sense that, however partially, the conquest has already begun through Jesus Christ.

THE NATURE OF GOD: GOD'S ACTIVITIES

In the discussion of God's attributes it became clear that God is personal. That is, God is person-like. The primary implication of saying that God is personal is that God is a God who acts with purposiveness. God is an active God on the scene of human history and in the world of nature. While there is no single way to summarize the manifold workings of God, it is helpful to think of God as active in the roles of Redeemer, Judge, and Creator. These forms of divine action are thematically related to the three attributes of God treated as love, righteousness, and power. As we earlier noted, these three attributes are related to one another in a Christocentric manner such that love is the determinative hub. Likewise, the activities of God are organically related by means of the central revelation in Christ in which God's activity of redemption has central importance.[7] This is not to diminish the importance of God's judging and creative activity; but it does determine the perspective given to them. All the activities of God have their ultimate *telos*, or purpose, in God's loving will. The saving, redeeming activity of God is the most immediate and direct expression of that loving will. In God's activity as Judge God manifests the absolute divine opposition to that which would infect and destroy what God has created. The act of creation reveals the sovereign power of the divine love in a way that will be treated later.

1. GOD AS SAVIOR

In the Christian faith, the final and absolute disclosure of God is in the man who walked the streets of Galilee—Jesus who is called the Christ. God is active as Redeemer elsewhere in history too; thus we should not have the impression that God was not a saving God prior to Jesus Christ. It is simply that the kind of salvation bestowed by God and the nature of the divine love is most clearly revealed in the Christ event. But there is at least one more classic instance of God's activity as Savior, namely, the Exodus in which God, using the hand of Moses, delivered the people of Israel from their slavery in Egypt. If Christians celebrate the redemptive work of God at Easter, Jews to this very day celebrate God as their Redeemer in the observance of the Passover. Do not tell Jews that their God is not a God of redemption! Their God is the very same redeeming God that discloses the divine nature with more decisiveness and clarity in the person and work of Christ. It is Christ in whom God manifests a form of love (and thus a kind of redemption) that heretofore was undisclosed.

Given the centrality of Christ, we should say that redemption is the primary and proper activity of God's will of love. This work of divine love—redemption—is God's *opus proprium*, God's proper work, by comparison to the work of divine judgment which is God's *opus alienum*, God's alien work. In God's salvific acts, specifically in Christ, God would seek to restore fellowship with human creatures—a fellowship that was intended from the beginning of all creation. Those negative and destructive forces that alienate human beings from God are typically identified with sin and its deadly consequences.[8] The power of sin is so per-

---

[7] See again Aulen, *Faith of the Christian Church*, 138-62.

[8] Sin is usually referred to as "moral evil" while another category of evil is called "natural evil" which includes such devastations as earthquake, flood, birth

vasive and compelling that evil has been recognized as a force standing over against God and the divine loving purpose. Indeed, it has sometimes been personified in the evil one, Satan. The point here is that sin is a disintegrative, infectious, destructive reality which separates human beings from their Maker; it is only by means of God's redemptive work undertaken in love that the estrangement can be overcome. Redemption is a restoration of God's relationship with human beings; it is a relationship for which God made men and women. The term salvation itself comes from the Latin term *salvus*, which is associated with healing. Salvation/ redemption is properly conceived as a healing of a broken relationship, a restoring of that which has been gnarled and misshapen by sin. If sin separates, God's redemptive love in Christ overcomes that separation.

The difficulty is that we live in a world in which the torment of sin and its compelling power still are clearly at work. It is a world in which God's victory over sin in the work of Christ is still ambiguous. In their own lives, believers recognize that sin still has a certain sway with them, that the old self must be put to death daily if the new self in Christ is to emerge. To the extent that one does participate in God's saving act, makes it his or her own, salvation is indeed a present reality in the subjective life of the individual. There really is healing, the blind truly begin to see even if through a glass darkly, the lame walk if only haltingly, reconciliation with God is a joyous experience even if only partial. This real, though also fragmentary, experience of redemption is viewed as a foretaste of that which is promised. It feeds the Christian anticipation of God's final victory over the corruption of evil which is assured in Christ's work.

The dominion of God's will and purpose has begun in the arena of history and in the lives of individuals; but it will be perfectly realized only beyond the scope of history. Redemption cannot be reduced to a "futuristic eschatology" which is otherworldly and associates salvation with the "sweet by and by." Such a view leads to utter paralysis and resignation to the fact of evil in the present life. Neither can redemption be identified with a "realized eschatology" in which the claim is made

---

defects, and much besides. The distinction between these two kinds of evil may be indicated by saying that natural evil is that which *befalls us* whereas moral evil is that for which *we ourselves are responsible*. But to give sufficient attention to the very difficult issue of natural evil is beyond the scope of this chapter. See again Guthrie, *Christian Doctrine*, 166-91.

that salvation is experienced in its fullness here and now. Such a perspective leads to unjustifiable optimism that evil can be extinguished by merely human effort. In a word, the Christian faith affirms paradoxically that God's redemptive activity is both a present reality and a future hope. It is already achieved and experienced in the believer's heart and life; but it is not yet experienced in its fullness.

2. GOD AS JUDGE

God's acts of judgment express the radical opposition of the divine will to evil in the world. As Judge, God absolutely stands in wrathful antipathy to anything that would thwart the divine loving purpose for human beings and their proper relationship to God. But we should be careful in sketching the activities of God as Redeemer and Judge just as we were careful in relating the attributes of love and righteousness. It is not two different gods at work here, one a vengeful and jealous god in the Old Testament who gave the Law and the other a saving and merciful god of the New Testament who is revealed in Christ.[9] Nor is God to be characterized has having a split personality, one kind and benevolent, the other violent and malevolent. It is the one god who redeems who also judges and vice versa, though it is God's loving will that is at the foundation of both redemption and judgment. Indeed both activities are disclosed even in the cross of Christ. For there we see both the deadly judgment of God upon human sin and simultaneously, but paradoxically, the depths of God's redemptive love which would forfeit God's only Son for our sakes.

In speaking about judgment, let us begin by saying that the truth about us human creatures is that, as sinners, we stand before God as Judge and face our own condemnation. The deepest tragedy of the situation is that we bring this judgment upon ourselves. That is, we ourselves choose the very evil that is our own undoing. Sin in all its forms is intrinsically destructive no matter how enticing its appearance may be, no matter how much pleasure it brings. For this reason, God confronts it as an archenemy; it contradicts the divine will for harmony and wholeness in creation. Sin brings disintegration of the self, which is one facet of God's judgment. But the relationship with God as God simultaneously

---

[9]There was an early heretic in the church who pictured things in this very way. His name was Marcion (ca. 150). See the earlier discussions of Marcion in this volume.

hangs in the balance. Dominated by perverse attitudes and interests, hate and deceit, lust and covetousness, men and women stand before God as rebels and thus confront God as their Judge. It is a judgment that runs deep because the corruption is so pervasive; and since it is so penetrating a judgment, it leads men and women finally to despair of themselves. The long and short of it is that this judgment either leads a person to take refuge in the healing redemption of Jesus Christ, or it does not. In the former case, judgment leads (as it is intended to do) to restoration, renewal of fellowship, harmony with God; in the latter case, judgment continues as mutual hostility, enmity between the self and God. One might even say that this is the most deeply religious way of regarding heaven and hell. Heaven is the bliss of existing in proper communion with God; it is not so much a "reward" for a life lived righteously as it is a haven for those who have found redemption in Jesus Christ. Hell means to live one's life in utter and hopeless estrangement and isolation from God; it is not so much a "place" of punishment for sinners as it is the torment of one who is separated eternally from God.

As was noted earlier with regard to God's saving activity, so it is also with God's activity as Judge: there is a this-worldly and an otherworldly aspect to it. God as Judge is active even now on the scene of history and in the lives of individual men and women. Estrangement, separation from God, is not a phenomenon that merely awaits us in the hereafter; it is a dreadful experience in this life as is the joy that redemption brings. So men and women are conscious of God's judgment in their lives in a personal way. How? For one thing, there is the way in which their own hearts can convict them—perhaps one might think of an afflicted conscience here which can even lead to troubled sleep. The haunting thing to observe is that there is no more an escape from oneself than there is from God's judging presence—and these two of course are related. But God's judgment can affect us personally in a second way. It is also the case that sin typically brings temporal sufferings of various sort in its wake. This kind of claim should not be surprising, particularly in light of the fact that sin is destructive by its nature. Of course, there is no simple correlation between sin on the one hand and suffering on the other. Obviously, sin is not always followed by suffering—since often the wicked "prosper" in terms of this world's standards. It is equally clear that nowhere near all cases of suffering are attributable to sin in a person's life; Jesus himself makes this clear in his teachings. (See John 9:1-3.) Yet the loose connection remains and God's judgment in this world takes manifold forms. But there is also what is often referred to as a final judgment. God's judgment is made final and complete (as is redemption) beyond this world and our present existence. From all appearances there are many who ultimately harden/contract their hearts against God and thereby also refuse the divine love. God's love is the most potent force in the world; but that love is not coercive. God will not impose redemption on those who simply will not tolerate God's sacrificial love.

3. GOD AS CREATOR

If God's activity as Judge manifests God's righteous wrath and God's activity of redemption discloses God's love, God's power is demonstrated in God's creative work. It is essential, however, to recall that God's power is not to be conceived independently of the central attribute of God's love; indeed, as already pointed out, God's power is the power of the divine love, neither more nor less. The sovereign power of God is not some abstract notion imported from philosophical speculation; such an abstract concept of power necessarily distorts the God of Israel and of the church. The power of the God revealed in Jesus Christ is that sovereign love in which the vanquished Christ on the cross turns out to be the powerful victor, in which power is at work precisely in the midst of weakness. Further, the potency of this love is made evident in the fact that it brings about a new creation within those who would but open their lives to its abundant life-giving stream. But just now let us address the matter of God's work of creation "in the beginning."

The basic nature of creation is determined by the fact that it is an act of God. There are certain implications in the claim that God is the source of all that is. First, it is clear that there is an absolute distinction to be drawn between the Creator, the Maker of heaven and earth, on the one hand, and that which derives from God's "hand," on the other—heavens, earth, beasts of the field and birds of the air, and, finally, human beings. The difference between God and the natural/temporal order, including the human race, is a qualitative difference—the difference precisely between the infinite and finite, Maker and made. In fact, a central point of the creation stories in Genesis is this: that human beings and all else are utterly dependent upon their Creator for life and breath and everything. That is why believers confess that life itself and the abundance of the world's provisions are good gifts of God. This belief characterizes the way Christians see the world. But this brings us to the second implication of the belief that God is Creator—namely, all that God created is good, very good. This too is made clear in the biblical stories of creation. If

God is the origin, then it cannot be otherwise than a good creation. This is sometimes expressed in the saying "God don't make no junk." One of the classic ways in which the Christian faith has made this point clear is in the teaching that God created the world out of nothing, which is the way to translate the Latin phrase *creation ex nihilo*. Everything that is has been called forth by God's sovereign will and Word; that which is beautiful and good has been derived from a void, nothingness, darkness, vacuum. This means the universe and everything in it, including its material substance—including human flesh—has God's stamp of approval on it. This stands in contrast to a dualism which claims that spirit is good and body is evil—a dualism, by the way, that often insinuates itself into the church. The Christian teaching is that nothing God made is inherently tainted or evil.

One final and important point deserves attention—the relationship between Christ and creation. If the Christocentric orientation could be preserved in redemption and judgment, we can preserve it by reference to creation as well. Here is the crux of the matter: the Bible is pretty clear in confessing that though God is the ultimate source of creation, Christ is the actual agent in the creative act. The Gospel of John declares that the Word of God (which later became flesh) was in the beginning with God and nothing was made without the powerful operation of that singular Word. God's free and gracious creative act simply bestows life upon men and women and surrounds them with the richness of God's manifold other good gifts. The striking thing here is that there is a mirror image shared between what God does (via Christ) "in the beginning" and what God does (again, via Christ) in redemption, re-creation. As noted already, redemption creates persons over again, restoring them to their intended relationship with God—that which was intended in the beginning. Or, think of it this way. A created humanity that was corrupted by Adam's Fall is now fashioned over again in Christ, the new Adam. We become new creatures in Christ. So says Paul in his letters. God accomplishes this redemption, this *re*-creation, with the same absolute freedom and grace that was at work in the original creative act. The culminating point is this: the same power of God—the sovereignty of God's love— that accounts for the redemption of things in Jesus Christ also is at work in the initial will of God in calling things into being at the start. One could argue, in fact, that no adequate view of God as Creator can be formulated except in light of the Christ event—certainly no genuinely Christian view of God's power in divine creative activity. It further makes sense to view the activity of God as Redeemer as a continuation of God's activity as Creator. After all, God does not cease to create after "the beginning"; God's creative activity is to be viewed as continuous creativity. God preserves God's handiwork over the course of time, sustaining, ordering, nurturing, and recreating. In these multiple ways, God continues to exercise divine power—the creative power of God's love—in the world that God calls into being.

We have been speaking of God's various activities in a thematic way as redemption, judgment, and creation. These are the activities of the one God. In Christian teachings, God is at once Father, Son, and Holy Spirit. But it is not as if the Father is linked exclusively to creation or, say, the Son is limited to the activity of redemption. Indeed, we say that God the Father is the one who saves in and through the agency of the Living Word, Jesus Christ. Likewise, we have noted that the Son, the Word, is the means by which God the Father creatively brings things into being in the beginning. Still, we confess that God is Father Almighty, Maker of heaven and earth, while we also say that redemption comes only through Jesus Christ, the only begotten Son of God. So now our focus shifts to the salvific activity of God in Christ.

Chapter 15

JESUS CHRIST,
ONLY BEGOTTEN SON OF GOD

THE HUMAN CONDITION

Creation and redemption (re-creation) are linked. The one God is at work in both activities, exercising the power of the divine creative love that is always bringing something out of nothing. But God's activity as Redeemer is occasioned by the utterly tragic fall of the human race into the darkness and corruption of sin. The question is: How can evil make entrance into God's good creation? How can that which is from God's "hand" be contaminated by sin? The best answer to such questions is that the origin of evil is absolutely *mysterious*. Evil is that which God does not create, does not will, absolutely opposes. It is not a part of God's created order; nonetheless, it is a stark, if also alien, intrusion into that creative work of God. No speculation is ever quite to the point here. Not even the story of the Fall in the Bible is intended to explain the appearance of sin in a good creation, the emergence of darkness, disharmony, and chaos in what was perfectly glorious, symphonic, and orderly.[1] To explain something typically means to be able to maintain control over it; but that is precisely what we are unable to do in the case of evil. Instead of offering an explanation for evil's emergence, that story is more like a sober acknowledgement of the mysterious and pervasive reality of that which is alien, corruptive, and antagonistic to God's will and purpose. To confess evil as mystery is precisely to recognize its deep,

---

[1]Some might argue that the story of the Fall does obviously explain the origin of evil. It is explained—so it is said—by the presence of the serpent who brought temptation. However, this is no explanation; it simply postpones the question. For the question remains: How did the serpent (the embodiment of evil) make its entrance into the perfect "garden" of the world? That is easy, so it might be replied: The serpent is none other than a disguised Lucifer, the angel who in heaven rebelled against God. But this does not provide any explanation; again the question is postponed. Now the question is: How did evil gain entrance into—of all places—heaven?

dark, sinister, and devastating power in our world and in our lives. So Christians are *not* called upon to *explain* but to *overcome* sin in the power of the crucified and resurrected Christ. Still, if we cannot explain the origin of evil, what we can do is describe something of the human condition prior to and after sin's emergence.

I. THE APPEARANCE AND NATURE OF SIN[2]

The biblical account of creation speaks of human beings as having been created in the image of God, the *imago dei*. Just what that phrase means is not made clear in the biblical materials nor in Christian tradition. There is one thing it does not mean. It does *not* mean that God is made in *our* image, namely, that God has hands and feet and face and ears. Rather, to be made in the image of God means that human beings are the kinds of creatures that have certain capacities the other animals do not possess. Primary among these is the capacity to stand in a relationship of trust in and obedience to God, that is, in fellowship with God— or, alternatively, in a relationship of hostility. The image of God in human beings means that persons can deliberately respond to God and the divine will in such a way that they are responsible for their reaction. In this way, men and women possess a different quality of being from the beasts of the field who cannot enter such a relationship. Furthermore, in entering that God-relationship or in making response to God, human beings are typically self-conscious, that is, conscious of themselves in ways animals are not able to think about themselves. Men and women have the unique capacity to stand outside themselves and consider the meaning of their lives, their past, their future, in ways inaccessible to dogs and cats, snakes and fish. All of this is part of the glory—and the tragedy—of human existence.

Let us take this one step further in order to get a clue about sin's appearance and its nature. If every individual has the ability to think about his/her own existence, this also means that such persons can, and typically do, become aware of their own finitude, their own insecurity and vulnerability in the face of the various vicissitudes of life. Hunger, nakedness, illness, accident, flood, fire, desertion, death—these are among

---

[2]Like many others who have learned from him, I owe a considerable debt to Reinhold Niebuhr whose treatment of the topic of sin and its consequences may be found in his *The Nature and Destiny of Man*, vol. 1 (New York: Charles Scribner's Sons, 1949) esp. 178-207.

the threats that haunt a human being. When all is said and done, there is
much that reminds us—even those who are fairly young—of the limited
character of our lives, our lack of control over what befalls us and the
finite number of our days. The point is that we are the kinds of creatures
who can exercise such self-reflection about our own finitude; animals
cannot. For this reason, men and women (unlike animals) are characterized by anxiety, a general sense of insecurity, about their lives. In
becoming anxious we typically place our trust in what is immediate to us,
more or less directly within our grasp or control. Thus, for instance, we
seek to amass to ourselves wealth and the things wealth can purchase, to
gain power over others, to multiply and variegate the pleasures available
to us. The list goes on. When we are not in possession of these things,
we are in hot pursuit of them. These are the things upon which we come
to depend, in which we actually place our trust. In short, in our anxiety
we willfully choose to become reliant upon what the world holds dear
instead of the God who is invisible, not palpable, to us. This is the nature
of the Fall, whatever else we wish to make of it; this is the nature of sin
itself; indeed, this is what Paul means when he speaks of living according
to the flesh versus living according to the spirit. But it needs to be made
clear that by itself anxiety is not sin; instead it is a part of our natural
state as human beings. Anxiety is not sin and it is not the *cause* of sin.
It becomes the *occasion* for sin only when a person refuses to trust God
and places that reliance instead upon finite things.

Let us define sin more specifically in two ways.[3] From a religious
point of view, sin may be defined as unbelief, a refusal to place our
dependence upon God. If faith in God means to live our lives in heartfelt
reliance upon God and submission to the divine will, sin as unbelief is
unwillingness to do so. Unbelief means to repose one's trust in something
other than God, something finite, that which is less than absolute, less
than God. It means to depend on that which is of this world. In the final
analysis, unbelief means to have other false, finite gods—notably in the
form of those things that are transitory, fleeting—before the Lord God.
Such misplaced trust/faith may be characterized as idolatry even when
there is no "graven image" before one's eyes.

---

[3]On this illuminating way of discussing the nature of sin, see Aulen, *Faith
of the Christian Church*, 231-40.

On the other hand, from a psychological point of view, sin is egocentricity (self-centeredness) or pride. This is simply the flip side of what has just been described. For to refuse to trust in God means that one thrusts the self, the ego, into the position of determining one's own destiny. To dethrone God means to place the ego on the throne of one's heart, to take control for oneself, to make the self the ultimate center of concern. Here human beings become willful, self-assertive, sufficient unto themselves. The individual seeks to determine his/her own existence apart from God, by and for oneself. Instead of a life of faith centered in God, there emerges an egocentric life that seeks to manage without God.

2. THE CONSEQUENCES OF SIN

In what has been said it is clear that sin is not so much evil deeds that are committed nor the omission of good works as it is a fundamental condition of a person—namely, a state of unbelief/self-centeredness. It has to do in the last analysis with one's God-relationship, a relationship of unbelief, rebellion—or even perhaps indifference—rather than trust/ fellowship; it has to do with self-assertiveness—or even perhaps lack of a self—rather than submission of the self to God. These ways of speaking clearly do not refer to singular acts which one commits now and then, here and there. They rather refer to a state of being of a person, how that person stands in relationship with God. When sin is defined in this way, it is clear that it is a religious concept and not finally a moral concept. This might be underlined by pointing out that the opposite of sin is not virtue; rather the opposite of sin is faith! Sin has strictly to do with the relationship to God and not with whether one obeys a moral code, not even the Ten Commandments. For after all, one can obey even God's laws grudgingly (and thus in secret resistance to God) or for the sake of the praise their obedient acts generate (and thus in self-seeking).

This brings us to the recognition of the results of sin's entrance into the world. The basic result is that sin is all-pervasive and widely ramified in its corruptive power. In at least two ways sin is devastating in its per-meating consequences in human life: it corrupts the whole self and the entire race. The corruption of the entire self is accentuated when we say that sin has its seat in the innermost being of human creatures—in what the Bible insightfully refers to as the "heart" of a person. So the biblical materials, especially Paul's letters, often speak of sin as a form of slavery; later Christian thinkers would speak of a bondage of the will to sin. The thought is that the dark power of sin insinuates itself, captivates us, holds us in its sway in all our imaginings and our motives, our speech and our deeds. Every way we twist and turn, our reliance on the world and our self-centeredness hold us in a vice grip. Sin corrupts us to the core and affects every aspect of our being. It is certainly not merely our physical passions that are affected. Even our reasoning is skewed by the corruption of our heart's misguided orientation. Indeed, even our most religious/righteous deeds are tainted by the infection that is rooted in sin. We are like apples rotten to the core. This is what has traditionally been referred to by the phrase "total depravity." Despite our being quite "civilized," there is good reason to speak about being under the spell of the demonic—or captive to the law of sin and death—which we harbor in our breasts. The typical conclusion to draw from these observations about the pervasive effects of sin is that no person can be the source of his/her own salvation from sin's plight.

Sin also pervades the whole of humankind. The fact of the devastating and far-reaching effects of sin through the entire species is the main point of the biblical story of the Fall. So Paul says that sin entered the world through one man, Adam, and, subsequently, it has infected the whole species. Just how that infection is transmitted has been the topic of considerable discussion. While many regard it as a biological inheritance, this reading is not required by the biblical account. A rather different view makes considerable sense and simultaneously does more justice to the nature of sin. Instead of a biological model, we may use a sociohistorical model. With this in mind, it is worth pointing out that human beings as created are social creatures who live within the context of a larger community or race. No man or woman is an island. Indeed, all of us are born into a humanity that is already dominated by sin. We are caught up in a massive web of human relations with countless others who themselves are already held in sin's sway. It has become their accustomed way to refuse God and repose their trust in the world. Surrounded by such corruption from the start, it is all any of us ever know. And we are caught up in that entangling web that comes to determine our lives also. So in the history of the race, sin proliferates itself, bearing ever more sin—with a snowball effect. It is as if sin had a life of its own, as if it were some kind of independent demonic force exerted upon the self from the outside in an utterly overpowering manner.

The story of the Fall (that is, "original sin") brings into prominence the overwhelming power of sin's dominance as it is transmitted through humankind. But if sin's power is so absolutely compelling, then can human beings really be held blameworthy for succumbing to this predator?

If the notion of original sin suggests that sin is inevitable, is there no way to maintain human accountability for each person's own fall into sin? This brings us to another paradoxical feature of Christian reflection. As believers, we wish to say both that sin is inevitable, but also, in a genuine sense, voluntary. Even though human beings are bound to sin (given the condition of the species), each individual willfully embraces sin as his or her own in his or her own existence. Thus, in addition to the light that "original sin" sheds upon our plight, we can also posit "actual sin" as the self actually affirms sin as his or her own. Put it this way: there is nothing that makes the entrance of sin into the world a *causal necessity* as the biological model of sin's transmission might suggest. It is not a strange genetic phenomenon that causally accounts for sin's widespread sway among humans; it is the overpowering confluence of the human swarm on an individual human life. In this way, the inevitability of sin is preserved but without forfeiting genuine human responsibility for it.

It turns out, then, that the individual, by willful sin, further contributes to the sinfulness of the race with which he or she is united and by whom the self was infected in the first place. In this light, the tragic and inescapable cycle of sin in the race becomes apparent. If the cycle is to be broken, help must come from beyond the human swarm.

CHRIST, THE MEANS OF REDEMPTION

The Christian confession is that redemption from sin's shackles is made accessible through Jesus Christ who, as the only begotten of the Father, is the enfleshment of God. God becomes a human being in order to bridge the gap between God as Creator and the human lot and to disclose the redemptive love that characterizes the very heart of God's nature. By means of this revelation, reconciliation and a right relationship with God now become possible. This is what salvation consists in: being properly related to the God who in divine love created us for fellowship in the beginning. The translation of God into human flesh is referred to as "incarnation." It is the profound miracle and mystery at the center of the Christian faith—that God's inner being is crystallized in human form so as to be known at least to those who possess the eyes of faith. Apart from such disclosure, God remains incomprehensible to those who stand in absolute need of divine redemption. But there are two facets to the doctrine—referred to as "Christology"—that pertains to this central manifestation of God in Christ.

First, there is a focus on the "person" of Christ in which attention is given to Christ's divinity and humanity. Second, there is the "work" of Christ which is usually summarized under three headings: prophet, priest, and king.

I. THE PERSON OF CHRIST

The daring claim that Christians make about the man Jesus of Nazareth is that in him God was incarnate. He is, so it is confessed, both man and God, one person with two natures. The creeds of Nicea and Chalcedon make this affirmation by asserting that Jesus Christ is "of the same substance" with God the Father. Of course, this has as much to do with what Christians say about the Trinity as it does with what they say about the incarnation. But it is the latter that claims our attention here.[4] To say that Christ is of the same substance with the Father means he possesses within himself God's very essence, God's inner being. Although "substance" is a philosophical concept and not a religious one, this need not distract us from the religious meaning of the creedal affirmation. What we should say is, God's inner nature is not some abstract entity: the inner being, or heart, of God is love. If, as Christians confess, the divine being of God is exposed with final clarity in Christ and if the Gospel narratives and apostolic letters in Scripture are any indication, then there is every reason to claim that the all-determining character of God's inner being—God's substance—is love. So determinative is this attribute that the Johannine author says without equivocation that God is love. (See 1 John 4:8, 16.) Indeed, as was suggested earlier, because of our Christocentric stance, God's other attributes of righteousness and power are properly defined only in light of the love disclosed in Christ. It is the divine inner being/substance of love that is incarnate in the man Jesus Christ. In this sense, we say that God as such is incarnate and at work with the power of redemption. In no other human being before or since has this appearance of God in history occurred. Such is the utter uniqueness of this unrepeatable event. Therefore, in knowing Christ one knows God's own being; God's nature is revealed— if also simultaneously veiled—in human flesh. In affirming this, the primary claim is not so much about Christ as it is a claim about God, specifically a claim about what kind of reality God is. In the person of

---

[4]Again, in this general approach, the reader is referred to Aulen, *Faith of the Christian Church*, esp. 184-89.

Jesus Christ, God reveals the divine nature and realizes God's redemptive will and purpose in the history of the human race.

There are any number of ways to misconceive the manner in which the divine and the human are fully present in Jesus Christ. Two kinds of erroneous or heretical views at either extreme can at least set the parameters for the appropriate Christian confession of the incarnation of God in human flesh. In the one case, the emphasis is upon the humanity of Christ to the exclusion of the divine; at the other end of the spectrum is a view that seeks to give prominence to the divinity but fails to do justice to the humanity of Christ.

Ebionism is the view that Jesus of Nazareth was essentially a human being—the son of Joseph and Mary—who was divinely inspired in the life he led and the teachings he offered. He was especially equipped by God and elected—possibly at his baptism—for his divine mission. His relationship with God was one of intimacy and his life one of obedience. But the Ebionites steered clear of claiming that Christ was himself divine, united with (of same substance as) God in any truly unique sense.

By contrast, those who affirm a *docetic* (derived from a Greek root meaning "to seem") view of Christ make the claim that Christ was so fully God that he could not really be human, could not be composed of flesh, could not really hunger, or even actually die. He only "seemed" to be human; in reality he was a spiritualistic appearance of God, a divine phantom. Docetists believe that since flesh was inherently tainted with evil, God must remain unmixed with that which is inferior to the divine. Thus Christ only had the semblance or appearance of a human body.

These two tendencies have always been present in the history of the Christian Church and they survive to this day in various forms. There are those who erroneously believe that they lift Jesus up by feverishly insisting on his divine status while letting the chips fall where they may regarding his human nature. At the same time, there are those who are reluctant to affirm anything about Jesus that is extraordinary for fear of overreaching their human bounds of knowledge. The truth is that the Christian faith affirms that Jesus Christ is fully God and fully human, two natures in one person. This is the definitive Paradox at the heart of the logic of Christian belief. In contrast to Ebionism, Christ is said to be the incarnation of God's inner being/substance of love. As such he is the Word of God who serves as agent in creation. He is the second person of the Trinity, coeternal with the Father and the only begotten Son of God. Like all these preceding affirmations, so too the belief in the virgin birth is the result of belief already reposed in Christ as God's revelation; it is not a cause or a condition for such belief. In contrast to Docetism, however, the Christian faith also avers that Christ was really human, in all ways like us. He was subject to our limitations of time, space, and knowledge, being a man of his own Jewish culture. He shared in all types of suffering, physical and spiritual—including anxiety, distress, grief, and so on. Death itself was endured by him. He further shared in all of the temptations common to the human lot, though without sin.

If these equally important sets of confessions seem to run counter to one another that is no accident: that is the nature of Paradox; that is the logical shape of the faith. In the final analysis, the Christian believer can only confess that his or her faith is foolishness to all except those saved by it. The confessor humbly acknowledges that the man Jesus of Nazareth who appeared on the scene of human history is precisely the only begotten of God by whom salvation from sin is achieved for those who will open their hearts to it.

2. THE WORK OF CHRIST

The incarnation of God in the *person* of Jesus Christ is the enflesh-ment of the divine love; the *work* of God in Jesus Christ is the achieve-ment of the divine love on the human plane. In this light, there can be no separation between the doctrine of the person of Christ, as God incarnate, and the work of Christ, primarily conceived as redemption. The actual redemptive *work* accomplished in Jesus Christ is precisely the accom-plishment of the divine essence/will of love as embodied in the *person* of Christ. If one leaves to the side any consideration of the work of Christ and treats the doctrine of the incarnation (person) in isolation from it, the result is typically a return to a dry philosophical treatment of the two natures and loss of the dynamic character of God's work in the world. On the other hand, to ignore the doctrine of the incarnation (person) as one assays the work of Christ on earth inevitably means forgetting that the historical work of Jesus of Nazareth is the work of God's own divine loving will. The truth confessed by believers is: the incarnate divine will of love actualizes itself in the dynamic work of Jesus Christ.

In Christian theological reflection, it is traditional to discuss the work of Christ under three main headings: prophet, priest, and king.[5] The

---

[5]See, e.g., the classic work by John Calvin, *Institutes of the Christian Religion*, Library of Christian Classics vol. 20, ed. John T. McNeill, trans. Ford

thought is that Jesus fulfills each of these roles, which are already pre-figured in Old Testament literature. Typically, Christ's role as priestly mediator in atonement and as royal ruler in believers' lives have dominated theological treatments, but let us not neglect his prophetic office.

Christ as Prophet. In discussing Christ's office or role as prophet, primary focus falls upon Jesus' preaching and teaching ministry while on earth. Jesus is thought of as proclaiming the definitive will and purpose of God for humankind. He gives the final and authoritative interpretation of God's will. His teachings are the standard criterion by which all other claims to religious truth are tested. No other message can displace, correct, or surpass that declared by Christ. His message is dominated by the urgency of preparing for the influx of the Kingdom of God—preparation that includes repentance, or a turning away from a life lived in disobedience and a turning toward a life characterized by love for God and for others which places the neighbors' needs above one's own interests.

In short, Jesus is viewed here as standing in a long line of prophets beginning in the Old Testament with Moses and extending through the other prophets of Yahweh. But Jesus is not merely the last of the prophets; he is also the culmination and fulfillment of that prophetic line. So Jesus himself could say that he came not to destroy but to fulfill the Law and the Prophets.

Christ as Priest. As important as Jesus' prophetic office was, his priestly function is often given center stage for it is as priest that he brings atonement for the sin of individuals and the race. Atonement involves primarily a reconciliation between God on the one hand and human beings on the other—the restoration of a right relationship. If sin is what alienates us from God, it is God's work of redemption that achieves reconciliation, or *at-one-ment*, between God and human creatures. It is natural to associate the work of atonement with the Cross of Christ since that is the quintessence of the self-sacrificing love of God. But atonement/redemption is not merely the work of that climactic moment at Calvary; it is the work in which Christ is engaged his whole life through as he submitted himself to the divine loving will and the manifold needs of those around him. God's loving will and purpose of redemption is at work in Christ from start to finish with the aim of overcoming estrangement and reestablishing fellowship. The Cross is the final,

---

Lewis Battles (Philadelphia: Westminster Press, 1960) 494-503.

dramatic, and summary act of self-sacrifice that brings to culmination that single historically protracted act of atonement between God and human creatures. In sum, salvation has the character of reconciliation; as God's act it is intended to replace a broken relationship with fellowship between God and human creatures.

Of course, when the Scriptures speak of redemption, reconciliation, atonement, and related matters, various images are utilized. There are those who imagine that there is but one legitimate picture of atonement—the picture of Christ as a sacrificial lamb, for instance. But this attitude does disservice to the variety in the testimony of Scripture itself and diminishes the richness of those other images. Let us briefly explore three classical images—sometimes regarded as theories—of atonement. Even these are far from exhaustive, but they will suffice as major samples.

Christus Victor View.[6] This view of the atonement has a prominent place in the witness of Scripture. The central theme here is the struggle—often regarded as cosmic in scope—between God on the one hand and evil forces that stand over against God on the other. Sin, death, hell, and Satan (who is the personification of evil itself)—these stand as threats over against God and the divine purposes in creating human beings. Worse than that, human creatures are regarded as enslaved to these demonic powers. Men and women are pictured as being slaves to sin, captives of Satan. Sin is at the root of humankind's alienation from God, the cause of the breach in that relationship. Thus, Christ is pictured as a warrior who—in a life of warfare which culminates in his death—ultimately gains conquest over those alien forces tht would otherwise destroy God's creatures. Christ is the Victor in the pivotal battle on the Cross. As the old hymn confesses, there is "victory in Jesus."

But is that not strangely paradoxical?—that the cross where Jesus hangs limp and dying turns out to be the symbol of victory for Christian believers? Christ gains the victory in what, by ordinary standards, is judged as defeat and humiliation. The cross is confessed to be the culmination of the powerful work of God's sacrificial love in the world bringing defeat to the cosmic sinister power of sin, hell and death itself. But is that not scandalous?—that in Jesus Christ the victorious power of love manifests itself most clearly in what, by all accounts, has the unmis-

---

[6]See Aulen, *Faith of the Christian Church*, 196-213; see also his *Christus Victor*, trans. A. G. Hebert (New York: Macmillan Press, 1958).

takable appearance of weakness? No doubt, that is why the apostle Paul refers to the message he preaches as "foolishness" and "weakness" to those who are perishing, but to those who being saved it is the wisdom and power of God. Through God's powerful victory at Calvary, evil and its enslaving power is vanquished and thereby men and women are freed to live in right relationship with God.

Satisfaction/Latin/Scholastic View. This view finds its classic expression in the work of St. Anselm of Canterbury in his famous treatise on the Atonement, entitled *Cur Deus Homo? (Why [Did] God [Become] Man?*, 1097–1098). The primary focus of this theory is the righteousness of God. Indeed, this is made evident even in the definition of sin: to sin is to fail to render to God what is due, namely, a righteous life. Whoever fails to obey God robs God of honor, dishonors God. The question at the forefront then is: Can God remit/forgive sin by divine mercy without requiring satisfaction for God's offended honor, a payment of some sort? The answer is clearly "No, not if God's righteousness is to be preserved intact." Not to require satisfaction would mean abstaining from punishing evil, which is unthinkable: God cannot permit sin to go unpunished in God's own Kingdom. But then difficulties ensue: if God were to punish sinful men and women in the measure due them, it would mean death for them. Death is, after all, the penalty for sin against God. But this would frustrate God's purpose in creating humankind. The sum and substance of the matter is: only God *can* meaningfully pay the price but since the human creature is the responsible party, only the guilty creature *ought* to pay the price. That, argues Anselm, is why God became a human being: the satisfaction must be made by one who is *both* God *and* human, a God-man. Of course, Christ owed his own perfect obedience to God simply as any human creature would; thus his *sinlessness* does not have merit that can be shared with others. But as a perfect man, Christ was not required to die. By his voluntary death on the cross offered as a sacrifice to God, Christ provides the satisfaction for the sin of all in the race. The superabundant merit won by Christ in this sacrificial act was sufficient to purchase righteousness for countless others. By his perfect sacrifice as a man to righteous God, the infinite debt—which others owed—is paid.

Moral Influence View. The Moral Influence view can be found in St. Augustine of Hippo (354–430), although it is most closely identified with Peter Abelard (or Abailard, 1079–1142/3) in the Middle Ages. Accordingly, Christ's death (as well as his life) is regarded as a manifestation—an exemplar—of God's sacrificial love for sinful men and women. But we must set the stage as follows.

In their pride, men and women have elevated themselves, made themselves the center and master of their own destiny; in a word, they have become egocentric. Sufficient unto themselves, they are preoccupied only with what serves their own interests, that which is of their own choosing and doing. Augustine used the term *cupiditas* to refer to this kind of self-love or pride. But, he argued, when confronted with the love of God dramatically displayed in the crucified Christ—the one who at the hands of sinful men willingly submitted to a sacrificial and humiliating death—something happens in the human heart. When the stark picture of the voluntary victim, the suffering Jesus Christ in all his humility, is placed before the haughty and self-assertive—it strikes deeply and decisively, cutting through the erstwhile preoccupation with self. It is as if an axe is laid at the root of human pride and the heart is melted, won over, wooed by nothing less than the love of God there enacted in Christ's suffering. The inner being is transformed such that *cupiditas* is replaced by a newly inflamed *caritas*, a white-hot love for God prompted by the disclosure of God's prior love in the Cross of Christ. Here the emphasis falls upon the subjective change in the heart of the believer, the "influence" that makes itself felt in the moral and passional life. It is as if one's heart is truly overwhelmed, captivated by the God whose love was illustrated in Jesus Christ the suffering Savior.

Christ as King. The kingly work of Christ is many-faceted. For starters, it could be said that Christ is King from the beginning of all creation to the final culmination of history. He is indeed the Alpha and Omega. So, for example, the Christian Church confesses that Christ is the Word, the agent, the seminal source, through which God created the universe in the *beginning*. He is the King of all creation. Likewise, the church hopes in Christ as King of a Kingdom that is yet to be established at the *close* of time. The ultimate realization of that reign of Christ over all things is from the outset the purpose intended for the created order, and humankind within it. But our primary interest here is in the kingship or lordship of Christ in yet a different sense—that is, as ruler in the believer's life in the present, in the here and now. An early Christian confession was simply "Christ is Lord." Those who made such a confession intended to acknowledge that the crucified Christ who redeems their lives is, at the same time, the exalted kingly Christ who establishes direct and personal dominion over their daily lives.

Precisely at this point a crucial observation claims our attention, one which ties together the priestly and kingly roles of Christ. It becomes apparent that Christ's work can be viewed from two perspectives—as a completed work and as a continuing work.[7] The *completed* work of Christ is his atoning work as *priest* accomplished once and for all by his sacrificial death on the *cross*. In that event, the final outcome of the battle between God and the hostile forces of evil is guaranteed. The priestly work of Christ is a finished work; it neither needs to be repeated nor can it be. In that sense at least it might be described as an *objective* event in the *past*. By the same token there is the continuing work of Christ in the *present*, in the *subjective* lives of individual believers, indeed within the community of the faithful. This is the ceaseless work of the resurrected Christ, which is very much in progress. Yet the risen Christ's continuing work is not a new and different work from the completed work of the crucified Christ on the cross. Rather, the former should be viewed as a consequence of the latter. The victorious work of Christ at Golgotha gives rise to the *continuing* work which is linked to the *resurrection* of Christ who is *King*. It could even be said that Christ's objective conquest over evil at Calvary is realized anew each time an individual is subjectively transformed and given new life by the power of the resurrection. But more must be said about the relationship between cross and resurrection (and by implication the priestly and kingly offices of Christ).

The resurrection of Jesus Christ is testimony to the victory achieved in the cross. That is, the empty tomb reveals the cross as a sign of conquest over evil in spite of all the direct and indisputable evidence of defeat—specifically, the helpless victim pinned to the middle cross. Here we encounter that defining Paradox in the odd logic of the Christian faith—at least for those able to see via faith. The humiliated victim turns out to be the exalted victor over sin and its debilitating force. Let there be no mistake: the actual significance of the cross is incomprehensible when taken in the absence of resurrection. Indeed for many people lacking faith, the life and death of Jesus is merely that of a martyr whose execution, while without justification, is also without redeeming effect. Without Easter faith, the meaning of Good Friday would be impossible to apprehend. But given Easter morn, the resurrection unveils the cross as a battle already

---

[7]See Aulen's extended discussion of the finished and completed work of Christ in *Faith of the Christian Church*, 196-221.

won by means of the sacrificial death of Christ. The cross requires the resurrection in the sense that the victory of God in the crucified Christ is made unambiguous to the eyes of those possessing resurrection faith. The work of the suffering servant/priest is identified as and gives foundation for the work of the resurrected and exalted King/Lord.

The resurrected Christ, then, is Christ the Victor or King. As King, he is active in the present as the central, controlling power in the lives of Christian believers. By the power of resurrection faith they have new life; they are new creatures in Christ Jesus. Their lives are made whole, abundant, victorious because of a certain participation in the power of Christ's resurrection. So one might say with Paul, "It is no longer I who live, but Christ who lives in me" (Galatians 2:20). Christ—now regarded as the *indwelling* Christ—is a powerful presence by which the believer's life takes on an altogether different quality than before. The presence of the resurrected Christ as King is the foundation of the continuing life of the Christian man or woman. Of course, this is not to deny the persistence of struggle in the Christian life. Christian faith does not "zap" a person perfect and impervious to sin. The "old self of sin" continues to do battle with the "new self in Christ." Yet the victory of the risen Christ can be and is made real—existential—in a person's life in the midst of such conflict. When that happens—whether at work or play, in the living room or among the teeming masses—Christ is genuinely acknowledged as King.

It is of utmost importance to recognize the kingly work of the resurrected Christ in the heart of the believer; indeed this is the manner in which the continuing power of the cross is made conspicuous. The indwelling presence of the risen Christ is integrally connected with the spiritual life of the believer. But this does not mean that the resurrection is reducible to a purely spiritual phenomenon. To be sure, the resurrection is not an empirically verifiable fact; indeed it is not an ordinary fact alongside other facts at all. We call a fact only that which is capable of being fitted into our larger understanding of how things operate in the world. And one thing is certain: the resurrection does not fit; it is without precedent; it is unique in its own right; it is what we might call an occurrence only for faith. In the affirmation of belief in the resurrection, the Christian church is confessing a religious belief, not an ordinary belief that is supported or disconfirmed by empirical evidence. But Christian faith has rejected a purely spiritual view of the resurrection—namely, that it was Christ's spirit (as distinct from his body) that was raised from the dead.

This dichotomy of body and spirit/soul is rooted in Greek thought and is strange to the biblical understanding of the human person. No, the Christian church believes in "the resurrection of the flesh," as is affirmed, for example, in the Apostles' Creed. There was a certain corporeal form to Christ after the resurrection. Still, resurrection faith is not merely belief in the resuscitation of a corpse, for then the resurrection would be reduced to an empirical fact, albeit an extraordinary one. No, Jesus' body was of a different sort, far from ordinary as can be discerned even in the testimony of those who saw him. It seems apparent from those witnesses that Christ's body was of a transfigured, imperishable sort. If such an account as this raises as many questions as it answers—and it does!—that is quite frankly because the resurrection is finally a mystery. Why should that surprise anyone acquainted with the logical fabric of the Christian faith?

REDEMPTION OF THE HUMAN SELF

The continuing work of Christ as King is not an utterly new and different work from his completed work as Priest on the Cross. The meaning and content of the present and continuous work is anchored in the Cross which is the locus of the powerful victory of God's love over evil. Still, Cross and Resurrection are distinguishable moments. Not merely temporally but also logically, the Cross is prior to the Resurrection; for the work of the exalted Christ presupposes the finished work of the One who was brought low in humiliation. In a strikingly parallel manner, there are two distinguishable moments in the human experience of redemption. At least among Protestants, they are typically referred to as *justification* and *sanctification.*

Justification is associated with the crucified Christ who takes away the sin of the world, the one who makes accessible God's forgiveness. The Latin phrase *Christus pro nobis*—"Christ for us"—is often used in reference to this facet of salvation. Sanctification is linked with the exalted Christ, the one who empowers the believer with new life and who rules in his or her existence. The Latin phrase *Christus in nobis*—"Christ in us"—is used in reference to this phase of salvation in which Christ's sovereign lordship is established in the heart of the believer. Furthermore, justification precedes sanctification just as the Cross precedes Resurrection. Let us simply say that Christ's twofold work—Priest and King—is mirrored in the two-sided experience of redemption—Christ *for* us and *in* us.

1. JUSTIFICATION—*CHRISTUS PRO NOBIS* AND THE CROSS

Justification is a term used especially by Paul and the Reformers. The phrase "justification by faith" or "justification by God's grace through faith" is frequently used to reflect the means by which a person is saved. In any of these instances, the reference is to the believer's initial entry into the Christian life, sometimes called "conversion," especially in evangelical circles. The "good news" of the Gospel of Christ is this: that a person is justified by the grace of God revealed in Jesus Christ. In embracing God's powerful love manifest on the cross a person is pronounced in right standing before God in spite of the fact that he or she is deeply enmeshed in sin even to the point of being enslaved by it. This is the meaning of the word "justification": "to be declared righteous." A legal context is presupposed in which a person clearly guilty is—lo and behold—set free.

Forgiveness of Sin. Justification is a rough logical equivalent to the concept "forgiveness of sin." In using the phrase "forgiveness of sin," however, it not legal proceedings but personal reunion or reconciliation that is being imagined. The legal imagery conjured up with the term "justification" is harmonious with the satisfaction view of the atonement discussed earlier. By contrast, the emphasis chosen here falls on the fact that fellowship between God and a human being is restored via God's gracious act in Jesus Christ. In that spirit, it could be said with St. Augustine that the human heart is always in a state of unrest until rest and peace is found in proper relationship to and love for God. Or, if we take the case of the prodigal returning home to the Father, the focus is on joyous reconciliation followed by the appropriate festivities. We could say that in receiving God's forgiveness, a person is making his or her homecoming to the God from whom he or she has been estranged. But let us give attention to some features of the forgiveness of sin.

First, we should say that forgiveness is made possible by God's love which is personal in character. It is a sustained theme of Scripture and church teaching that the divine initiative is at the heart of any redemption wrought for men and women in their predicament of sin and its bondage. Indeed, it is by means of God's suffering love revealed on the cross that the victory over evil is achieved and deliverance accomplished. Only because God seeks can we be found; only because God loves sacrificially can we be received back into fellowship with God. But—note well!—it is the same God who utterly opposes evil who nevertheless comes to the side of the sinful to woo them back.

Second, and corollary to the first point, is the observation that it is sinful men and women who are the subjects of God's love. It is men and women who are justly condemned, people who are empty-handed, individuals who are without excuse—these are the sort who are—again, *nevertheless*—embraced by divine love. There is absolutely no basis for forgiveness; there is no worth in the beloved that calls forth God's love. Quite the contrary: there is sin and degradation. The source of forgiveness can only be found in the mysterious, unmotivated, free, and spontaneous love of God. Clearly here God's unsolicited and undeserved love bursts the bounds of Law. The Law—and any strictly ethical deliberation— would require righteousness in those to whom it would extend acceptance. By contrast, God's love rises above ethical considerations. This is precisely what forgiveness entails.

Third, we should note that forgiveness is unconditional, full, or it is not forgiveness at all. When God's forgiveness has been received, a person's sin is, as it were, utterly erased. So we say that the guilt is removed from the sinful one as far as the east is from the west. The guilt is not counted against them. They are free of it. They are given a new beginning, a clean slate. Though sinful, they are received back as righteous. Forgiveness is such that a person is justified while yet a sinner. Or, as Luther proposed, the Christian believer is *simul justus et peccator*, at the same time justified and sinful. This is the miracle of God's grace— and yet another of the paradoxes of Christian faith.

Nothing said here is intended to weaken or dilute God's opposition to evil. That is clearly *not* what forgiveness means. It is not that God winks at evil or takes it lightly. Just remember the cross of Christ and such a thought quickly will be dismissed. The Cross reveals the lengths to which God's sacrificial love will extend itself in order to make redemption possible. Nor should we forget that repentance—sorrow for sin and turning from it—is always closely linked to the forgiveness of sin. Finally, it should be noted that God's forgiving love is a regenerative power in the Christian believer; it has such power that the redeemed self is capable of actual *victory over* evil insofar as the risen Christ rules in his or her life. No, God's grace cannot possibly stretch so far as to take sin lightly; for then grace, logically speaking, could no longer be grace.

The Response of Faith. Faith is the human receptivity of the divine love revealed in the Cross. This is really the "subjective" side of the divine revelation which is rooted in God's "objective" self-disclosure. Revelation must find reception by faith if there is to be real transformation in human hearts. So something should be said about the nature of faith. Whatever else may be said about faith, it is of central importance to claim that faith involves absolute dependence upon God or trust in God. In this fashion, it becomes clear that faith, and not virtue, is the opposite of sin. If, as noted earlier, sin has the nature of unbelief, refusal to trust in God, the emergence of faith in the human heart means that such unbelief, distrust, is shattered and one utterly relies on God for deliverance from sin's shackles. If sin is the dominion of self-will, egocentricity, a life of faith entails submission to the divine will, a life spent with God as the central and consuming loyalty. The individual is liberated from bondage to the self in order to become a servant of God— which, paradoxically, is what it means to be truly free!

Nor is this the only paradox that surfaces here in what we have called the "logic" of faith. Still another paradox has to do with the question whether faith is a *work of God* in the human breast or a genuinely free *human response*. The Christian faith affirms both of these and if one is emphasized to the exclusion of the other, then the truth has been obscured or distorted. So we should say both that faith is created, bestowed by God, but it is a truly human response belonging squarely on the human plane. Alternatively, we might say that God overwhelms a person by the power of the divine love, but that the individual freely turns in trust toward God. So faith is both a divine gift and a human act. Or finally, with Gustav Aulen, we might suggest that "what we call our seeking is nothing else than the *Father drawing* us unto . . . himself."[8] In underlining this paradox, two corollaries follow. First, human beings are saved from first to last only by God's grace—*sola gratia*: everything finally depends upon the power of God's love. But, second, the divine love, while powerful, is not coercive; so faith must be acknowledged as a free human response to God's sovereign love.

2. SANCTIFICATION—*CHRISTUS IN NOBIS* AND THE RESURRECTION

If the term *justification* means "to be declared righteous," the term *sanctification* means "to actually become righteous." Forgiveness does bring in its train renewal, joy, restored life. There occurs an actual deliverance from the bondage to evil; the captive is set free. Renewed fellowship with God (via forgiveness) produces a new life, more abundant life as over against the former life lived in darkness, blindness, and death.

---

[8] Aulen, *Faith of the Christian Church*, 284.

All of this takes place in the actual, concrete life of the believer. We are not speaking here of magic mumbo jumbo or getting snapped perfect or having all your problems solved. We are speaking here about a genuine miracle that takes place in real human lives—often in church or when reading the Bible, at times when one is alone meditating, sometimes in the kitchen or living room, but always in real life. It occurs when the Gospel is received and new life courses through a person as the risen Christ—the Spirit of Christ, the Holy Spirit—begins to live and rule in one's heart. Then a gradual process begins that lasts months and years—a lifetime. It is a process of actually becoming what one is already declared to be—namely, righteous. The righteousness we are declared to have in justification has been referred to as "alien righteousness" because it is bestowed upon, or imputed to, us; the righteousness that in fact begins to make its appearance in our lives is referred to as "actual righteousness" because we actually own up to it and possess it in the power of God's grace. The changes that ensue in a person's life are multifaceted and cannot be treated here in full. But there are two aspects of the life now being sanctified that deserve note.

Conflict. Since the *Christus Victor* view of atonement—which has been an undercurrent in most of our remarks—is dominated by the element of struggle it should not be surprising to find that this is a mark of the Christian life as well. On the other hand, this claim may seem strange in light of our insistence upon the radical changes said to take place in the existence of a redeemed person. Yet it is true that the believer's life is marked by a lifelong struggle with sin. Despite being re-created, in the actual Christian life sin continues to be a menace, as any but a totally deluded believer will confess. The *old* man or woman of sin—rooted in Adam—continues to rear an ugly head; the *new* man or woman—with an origin in Jesus Christ, the second Adam—is never able to rest on his or her laurels. As the Christian life progresses, the aim is that the old self should die daily and permit the newly created person in Christ to come into prominence. In short, there is such a thing as progress—and, unfortunately, regress—in the existence of the believer. The new life in Christ is not an object a person owns once and for all, like money in one's pocket. Like any relationship—with one's spouse or with God—it must be renewed daily. The Christian life is as much a matter of becoming as it is a matter of being. It is both a having and a not having at one and the same time.

To put it in another way, we might say—again paradoxically—the Christian life is both a present reality and a future hope. To say the one thing without saying the other is to undercut the truth. In the lives of believers, it is clear that the conquest over evil is real in the here and now, in this world, in this life. It is not merely "pie in the sky by and by;" it is not merely "payday someday"; it is not just a "heavenly reward." No, the power of the resurrection is denied if the victory is not realized in the present life. Yet it must be admitted that the salvation—the new, abundant life—experienced now and here is only fragmentary. As Paul suggests, it is a foretaste of what awaits us. For, in addition to being a present possession, redemption is also a future hope. The victory over sin and its restrictive bonds is to be finally consummated, brought to its climactic and full realization, only after the curtains of history are drawn. Christ in his death has assured the victory, but the final culmination awaits that last day. So, in an undeniable sense, the Christian believer remains a pilgrim in this world, living life in the mode of hope for the day when every tear shall be dry and every wound healed. But it should be noted that whether fragmentarily in the present or fully in what lies beyond history, the power by which evil is overcome is the power of divine love rooted in the risen Christ who comes to rule in the heart of an existing individual.

Love. Many "fruits" emerge in the life of a believer once he or she has been made whole in the power of God's love. But one such fruit, or gift, of the Spirit that stands out above all others is that of love. The divine love transforms a person into an instrument in God's service, that is, an agent of God's own self-sacrificing love. Divine love always uses human hands, as of course in the case of the incarnate Christ himself. The man or woman who has been saved by God's love is now called upon to express, exhibit such love. As already implied by what has been said, it is not just toward God that the believer's love is directed; the individual also is to show forth God's loving will toward the neighbor. Indeed, if a person does not love the neighbor who is perfectly visible, there is considerable doubt whether he or she can love God who cannot be seen. The redeemed life in the process of being sanctified—in being restored to health—is to produce fruitful loving deeds and demeanor just as a good tree brings forth good fruits. But let it be made clear: it is *not* works of love that save; rather, the good will and works *issue forth from* the new birth that has its origin in Jesus Christ.

Love, then, is the central feature of the Christian life, just as is so markedly evident in the disclosure of God's own nature in Jesus of Nazareth. If God so loved us—so Scripture would have it—we ought also to love God in turn and love one another in unfailing ways. Love turns out to be a natural fruit of the Spirit, of the new life in Christ. It emerges spontaneously and creatively from the heart of one renewed by the power of divine love. There is a transforming, moral influence here. Indeed, one can say that the Christian life, properly matured, is lived beyond the requirements of the Law and its guidance. Love in its sacrificial form of *agape* operates like an inner compass and constantly informs the believer what is required in response just *now* to one's spouse, or that stranger, or regarding this or that policy decision, and so on. The believer is free *and* obliged to serve the neighbor—whoever it may be, singular or plural—in whatever way love may require.[9]

In such decisions, one is guided by the Spirit—the Spirit of Christ, the Spirit of God's love. But this leads us to the topic of the next chapter in which we give attention to the work of the Holy Spirit in the life and witness of the church.

---

[9]As Luther puts it: "A Christian is a perfectly free lord of all, subject to none. A Christian is a perfectly dutiful servant of all, subject to all." See his treatise "The Freedom of a Christian," in *Martin Luther: Selections from His Writings*, ed. John Dillenberger (Garden City NY: Doubleday and Co., 1961) 52ff.

Chapter 16

THE HOLY SPIRIT
AND THE COMMUNION OF THE SAINTS

THE CHURCH, CHRIST, AND THE HOLY SPIRIT

The church's nobility is rooted in the fact that it is where the Word of God is preached and the sacraments are administered. Simultaneously, however, as a human institution, the church is a source of embarrassment, often dominated by prejudice and religious pride. The church is the Bride of Christ but also, frequently, the harlot who sells herself in the marketplace. Like Christian believers individually, the church is to be distinct from the world, but much of the time it is difficult to tell any difference between the two. The Gospel announced in the church is the message of forgiveness and new life; much of the time, it is painfully apparent to all that the church is itself most in need of its own message. In short, the church is a sinful institution in which Christian believers nonetheless participate, albeit ofttimes with heads bowed in shame. While acknowledging this seamy side of the church, our attention now must be riveted on the theological relationship of the church to Jesus Christ and his work on the one hand, and to the presence of the Holy Spirit on the other.

At the outset it should be noted that the church is essentially and not accidentally related to Jesus Christ—in much the way that intertwining branches are related to the main vine. Indeed, the foundation or cornerstone of the church is the finished work of Jesus Christ on the cross. The church's very existence depends upon that root source; without that source the fellowship of believers withers and dies. At the same time, it may also be claimed that the church is identifiable with the continuing work of the exalted Christ as Lord. Christ's resurrection and exaltation form the beginning point of Christ's continuing work in and through the church. The church can be viewed as the beginning of Christ's reign in victory although, it is important to note, under the conditions of the present life. Therefore, Christ's rule as King in the Christian community is only fragmentary—as in the case of the individual believer. But, again like the individual believer, the community longs for the final culmination when every knee shall bow and every tongue confess that Jesus Christ is Lord. The new age of Christ's Kingdom has entered history and it is now spearheaded by the church. The church is the agent by which the victory of God's love on the cross is extended into the world. But with the "last days" the partial conquest over evil will be transcended by total victory, redemption, and fellowship. In the meantime, the Christian community lives in hope; it is an eschatological community. Like its individual members, it exists squarely in this present world; but it has its heart ultimately directed toward the future reign of God's powerful love.

Think of the relationship between Christ and the church in this way: the Church is at one and the same time the *means* and the *goal* of Christ's Kingdom, his rule as King. On the one hand, the Christian community is the means by which the victory of God's love is established in the hearts of men and women in the world. It is by way of the church that the power of evil is broken—via the church's witness to the glad tidings and its ministry of love to those who are in need. The church is the instrument, the vehicle, the army for establishing a beachhead of Christ's rule in the world. On the other hand, the church is that community in which the Kingdom has already become actual, already been made a present reality. In the lives of believers, Satan and his wiles are truly conquered even if in an admittedly tentative and unfinished manner. Here in the context of the church is where a new humanity is being formed—one not rooted in Adam but in Jesus Christ and his victory on the cross. In that sense, the church is an actual embodiment, however fledgling, of that Kingdom that is yet to come.

In light of these remarks, it becomes apparent that the church also stands in an essential, not merely accidental, relationship with the Holy Spirit, the third person of the Trinity. It is clear from the biblical materials, especially Paul's letters, that the Holy Spirit is identical with the Spirit of Christ. These terms are largely interchangeable. For our immediate purposes, we can say that the work of the Spirit is identical with the continuing work of the risen and exalted Christ who is King. They are not two different works.

Another parallel may also be noted. If, as has been said, the finished work of Christ on the cross is the requisite for his continuing work in the world, then in parallel fashion, the completed work of Christ is the condition for the coming of the Holy Spirit in fullness and power. This is suggested by the fact that the Holy Spirit descends upon those gathered at Pentecost only after Christ has been resurrected and glorified as King. The presence of Christ becomes direct and personal, actual and effectual in a person's life through the work of the Holy Spirit. One might say that the work of the Spirit is the power-filled continuing work of Christ as Lord/King in and through the church prior to the final culmination of history.

One related note concerning the Trinity since the topic of the Holy Spirit has been broached. In an earlier chapter, the inner nature of God was defined as self-sacrificing love or *agape*. Shunning metaphysical categories in treating the incarnation, the claim was made that God's essential nature—that is, the divine love—became embodied in Jesus Christ and was lived out in his life history which culminated in his death on the cross. If, then, we should say that God is love (not Love is God!) and if we claim that Christ is the incarnation of that love in human history, then it would make sense to go one step further and maintain the Holy Spirit is indeed the Spirit of that love which is at the heart of God's nature. In proposing these reflections, we remain faithful to the church's Trinitarian teachings, namely, that God possesses one nature/substance (which is love) in three persons (Father, Son, and Holy Spirit). Each person of the Trinity shares the same substance; yet they remain distinct *personae*. It is not being claimed that this handling of the Trinitarian nature of God now makes it perfectly comprehensible. The mystery remains inscrutable. Nonetheless, there is one significant advantage in such a treatment of the Trinity. It is this: the impersonal, philosophical jargon that is employed typically in Trinitarian formulas is here construed in a religious light, thus reflecting more truly the spirit of the biblical understanding of God.

CHARACTERISTIC FEATURES OF THE CHURCH

In general, it would be helpful to notice that the term *koinonia* is often used in the New Testament to refer to the church. *Koinonia* is the Greek term for "fellowship." The church is conceived of as a communion of believers whose fellowship exists *in Christ* and *among the individual members*. Again, as in the case of a vine and the branches, the unity of the members depends on their being united in Christ. To underline this is a way of saying that the church is first and foremost a corporate body, indeed the Body of Christ. Even if men and women become Christians one by one—and they do—they do so only because there already exists a witnessing and ministering church, a fellowship of believers. Christian existence is life in fellowship with others. Just as individual human beings belong to a species that is united in a sinful Adam, so also there is solidarity among the individuals who are bound together by a new humanity rooted in Jesus Christ. It might even be said that if there is no individual human existence separated from the rest of humanity, so there is no Christian existence isolated from the church as a corporate fellowship. That fellowship is knit together by the common head of the Body, the crucified and risen Lord. But in speaking of being united in *koinonia* we introduce the first of four characteristic features of the church of Christ—oneness. As present-day versions of the Nicene Creed declare, the church is "one, holy, catholic, and apostolic."

I. THE CHURCH IS ONE[1]

Oneness here means unity, being bound together. The unity of the church ultimately rests upon the oneness of Jesus Christ. The church is one because Christ is one. There is one Lord, one Spirit, one baptism, one faith, one God—and likewise one Body of Christ. This is not to deny the disharmony, the disunity that is often so evident in churches. There is division between Roman Catholic, Greek Orthodox, and Protestant; there is separation between the multitude of denominations within Protestantism; there is alienation even among believers within the same denomination. And this is only part of the story. But the point here is that the unity of the church transcends the dissonance that is so obvious among the different churches. Paul the apostle understood this final oneness of the church at the same time that he was keenly aware of schisms or partisanship within even the same local church. So his exhortation is that churches—within and among themselves—ought to manifest the unity that belongs to them in Christ, the one Lord. That oneness must be realized in the present, even if only in a fragmentary way and despite all the forces that would dictate otherwise.

It is clear that the oneness of the church resides in the singularity of the one vine with its branches, the one head uniting the members of his body, the single Lord of those who would follow him. The unity is not found elsewhere—not, for example, as some would propose, in uniformity of doctrine. There are certainly basic parameters of what constitutes the central elements of the Christian faith to which one gives assent—that which is to be believed. The content of faith is neither random nor unlimited. For this reason, creedal affirmations are used regularly in worship—and worship is the context for such confession. The unifying

---

[1]In this treatment of the features of the church I am indebted to Aulen's discussion in *Faith of the Christian Church*, 298-308.

factor, however, is the disarmingly simple Gospel message itself as expressed in the Word and sacraments (to be discussed later). The saving grace of God manifest in Jesus Christ and made effectual in the heart of a believer via the Holy Spirit—that is the foundation of the one church. No specific statement of beliefs among Baptists or Methodists or Lutherans or Roman Catholics can supercede or improve upon or make any truer the one Word found in Jesus Christ himself.

In the history of the Christian church there have also been those who have imagined that the unity of the church is to be found in some kind of monolithic structure. But organizational uniformity is not the unity upon which the church is founded. In fact, it can be argued that the church must maintain flexibility in its institutional structures, remaining open to new sets of circumstances to which the church must adapt itself. The primary grounds upon which to determine what organization to employ would be pragmatic considerations. The question to be asked is: What form of organization will enable the church to be the most effective instrument of the Gospel? Some Christian churches have adopted what we might call the Episcopal pattern in which a bishop, usually elected, serves as the head of the church. Others favor a Presbyterian structure, in which there is governance by a board composed of select leaders from laity and clergy. Still others, for various reasons, have preferred a "congregational" form of governance at the local church level wherein all members in good standing determine policy and make decisions. Once more, the point is that the unity of the Church does not depend on uniformity in structure but upon the oneness shared in Jesus Christ as Savior and Lord.

2. THE CHURCH IS HOLY

To say that the church is holy invites all kinds of misunderstandings—most of them deriving from the notion that a "holy" person is one who has achieved an extraordinary amount of righteousness in his or her life. In the Roman Catholic Church, this conception has some basis in fact. Indeed, on just these grounds some persons are recognized and "canonized" as "saints" of the Roman Catholic Church. But this is not the meaning intended here. Rather, for starters, to say that the church is holy is to say that its members—individually and collectively—share in the righteousness of Christ. The holiness of the church's members is founded on the completed work of Christ on the cross. In Christ, their sin has been "covered," forgiven; they are justified, counted as righteous. But just as one is declared righteous in justification, so also one actually becomes righteous through the process of sanctification. So believers participate in the continuing work of the risen Christ and, in doing so, they are empowered to really overcome sin—to actually become what they are declared to be. The crucial observation, however, is that such achievement is not regarded as having its origin in the individual as such. Instead, when such righteousness begins to fructify the actual life of a Christian, it is acknowledged as deriving—start to finish—from the indwelling spiritual power of the resurrected Christ. Thus, even here where in one sense the holiness is a matter of the believer's own willing and doing, the confession is, "It is not I, but Christ living within me." Always the holiness of the church and its members is utterly dependent on Christ's saving work in justification and sanctification, his finished and continuing work in human hearts.

Perhaps these remarks shed some light on that Latin phrase sometimes used in referring to the church—*sanctorum communio*, or "communion of saints." The phrase is used to refer not to an exceptional group of righteous ones who stand head and shoulders above the more "ordinary" Christians. In the New Testament it is used to refer to believers, each and all, who have joined themselves to Christ's church. Thus, the phrase signifies that the church is a communion of sinners saved—justified and sanctified—by God's grace in Christ. What distinguishes them is something different from superabundant merit arising from works performed. Instead, the "saints" within the communion are separated from other men and women by their ready reception of God's grace and by the way their lives progressively are being made new in the power of Christ's resurrection. These movements in the life of a believer—namely, a faith that is active in love—constitute warrant for claiming that these men and women are peculiar people, separate from the world. That, after all, is what the term "holy" means—to be separated. The members of the communion of saints are those who clearly live in the world; they are not recluses. With equal clarity, however, they are not of the world; they hold it at arm's length.

3. The Church Is Catholic

When the Nicene Creed declares that the church is "catholic" it does not mean "*Roman* Catholic." Of course, for more than one thousand years the church was more or less identical with the Roman Catholic Church. So there is a sense in which all current branches of the church are rooted in this "mother" of all churches. Still, as has already been noted, today the Roman Catholic Church is one of three major divisions of the worldwide Christian church. So the term "catholic" in the Creed means something different: it means that the church is "universal." What does "universal" mean? It does not mean that the church is found literally all over the globe—though that is increasingly true. Rather, it means that the church includes all kinds and conditions of men and women. This universal character of the church is rooted—as are all the other features—in Christ's finished and continuing work. Because the victory of God's powerful love over evil in Christ is a victory for all persons, so also the church is open to all who will but become receptive to that love. As Paul has declared, within the *ekklesia* all barriers are shattered; there is neither male nor female, neither bond nor free, neither rich nor poor, neither red nor yellow nor black nor white, neither educated nor untutored, and finally neither Methodist nor Baptist nor Greek Orthodox nor Roman Catholic. Of course, the churches in the South or in suburbia or on the town square do not always reflect this universality of the church. But to the degree that they are the church of Jesus Christ, their doors must be open to all who embrace the love of God in Christ Jesus.

The Reformers acknowledged this universal character of the church by affirming that the church exists wherever and whenever and among whomever the Word is preached and the sacraments are administered. These are the typical means by which God's grace in Christ is made effectual in the hearts of individuals. So, no matter who they are or where they gather or however many there may be, the *koinonia* exists among those who would gather to hear the Gospel and see it enacted before them. Perhaps the definition by the Reformers could be fine tuned slightly. It could be argued that the church exists always and only where the power of God's sacrificial love gains victory over sin in the lives of human selves. That work of God's grace *is* clearly associated with the open and willing reception of the Word, spoken and enacted. Here, however, the emphasis falls not so much upon the outward human acts of preaching and sacraments as upon the inner transformation of human hearts by way of the dynamic operation of the Spirit of God which is the divine love.

4. The Church Is Apostolic

The Church is apostolic in the sense that it is based on the preaching and teaching of the apostles of Jesus Christ. Christ himself commissioned them as the first messengers of the Gospel. So whatever the church teaches must be consistent with the apostolic proclamation; what they declared is the basis for all other messengers who preach in Christ's name. It is the content of that preaching which is essential, namely the

Gospel, the "good news." Another Greek term has its application here. The term *kerygma* is use to refer to the substance, the *content*, of the apostolic preaching; it is also sometimes used to denote the *act* of that proclamation. The relevant point, however, is that the church cannot be separated from the content of that message of the apostles as it is presented in Word and sacraments. Indeed, even the various writings that competed for inclusion in the New Testament portion of the written Scripture were assessed by this criterion. No writing was to be acknowledged as authoritative unless it conformed to the already accepted—*apostolic*—faith of the early church.

So the apostolicity of the church is not rooted in the genealogical succession of bishops, as the Roman Catholic Church has traditionally maintained. No automatic authority is conveyed merely because a person's ordination falls in a successive line of bishops which can be traced back to the apostle John or even Peter. As great an honor as it might have been to receive ordination from one who walked and talked with the Lord, such a distinction is no test for authority. Once more, the test lies in the *kerygma*, the content of the proclamation. Aside from this message proclaimed by the church there is no salvation. Indeed in that sense it can be argued that outside the church there is no salvation. For it is precisely within this community and this community alone that the Word—ultimately the living Word, Christ himself—is given witness. By means of such witness—via preaching and sacraments—the church extends the light of God's love into a world that otherwise remains shrouded in the darkness of its own self-destructive evil.

THE WORD AND THE SACRAMENTS

It has been an abiding theme here that the church is established on the foundation of God's grace revealed in Christ. Not the long and distinguished history of the church, not the manifold literary and artistic treasures of the church over the centuries, not the legacy left by saints and martyrs—none of these forms the indispensable cornerstone of the communion of the saints. That cornerstone is found in Jesus the Nazarene who, in his life, death, and resurrection, came to be acknowledged by some as the Christ, the Son of God who takes upon himself the sins of the world. In him God's grace is made manifest. At the same time, there are typical avenues within the church by which that divine love is made accessible to men and women. These are the Word and the sacraments. Sometimes these are referred to as "means of grace" just because God's grace finds outlet thereby. These are the modes by which God deals with individuals through the agency of the church. Both Word and sacraments have their basis in the person and work of Jesus Christ; apart from that, they are meaningless sounds and empty ceremonies. Perhaps the same thing might be suggested by saying that human beings, by themselves, cannot bestow God's grace—not even those most "saintly" ones, not even those ordained by the church. It is neither the person performing the act of preaching or sacrament nor the act itself nor both together that makes God's grace effectual. This happens in human hearts only as the risen Christ works in and through these means via the power of the Holy Spirit. But this calls for further elaboration.

1. THE WORD

When we speak of the Word of God, the reference is first and foremost to the Living Word of God, none other than Jesus himself, the foundation of the church. All else that is claimed to have authority as God's Word is subsidiary and derivative. Specific reference is made here to two "means" by which God's grace is made available, through which the living Word is transmitted. Those are the written form of the Word of God—Scripture—and the spoken Word—preaching. The Scripture and sermon can become and are the Word of God to the extent that they bear witness to the central revelation—the living Word—of God in Christ. If there is a question about which has priority, it could be noted that the Gospel message—the *kerygma*—was being preached by apostles and other witnesses before Paul's letters or the Gospels were written. So there is a sense in which preaching precedes the written Word found in the Bible. As will be noted below, however, the relationship of dependence is now reversed: that is, the preacher's sermon must now be rooted in Scripture since therein the apostolic message is preserved for us. These things being noted, it is also appropriate to say that in both Scripture and preaching the message necessarily takes the form of human speech. To say that the Word of God is a means of God's grace is to say that the divine love finds outlet in the form of a message—the *kerygma*—the Gospel tidings. It should strike us as more remarkable than in fact it does—that by way of human utterance God's forgiving and creative love can find its target in the hearts of men and women.

The Christian church, therefore, is a witnessing community. It is by the apostolic message the church bears that Christ's reign is extended and evil is vanquished in the world. But of course the church is itself dependent for its own existence on the *kerygma* it announces to the world. The church is a fellowship with a message to proclaim; simultaneously it is that very message that creates the *koinonia*. The proclamation today is—or ought to be—the same as the witness of the apostles. The one difference is that now we have a written text of apostolic authority—the New Testament in addition to the Old Testament—which gives shape to the sermons preached in inner-city churches and in "the little church in the vale."

The issue to be addressed now is: What is the relationship between Scripture and preaching? Of course, the first thing to say is that the Bible is normative in determining the content of Christian preaching. It is the same here as with theology, which also finds its measure and guide in the Christian Scriptures. The proclamation of pastors young and old, in churches large and small, is built around the selfsame witness of the apostles contained in Holy Writ. At the same time, those who preach are responsible for exposing and explaining the content of Scripture. The primary function of preaching is to declare that same *kerygma*, recounting God's marvelous acts—notably in Christ—on behalf of sinful men and women. It is the responsibility of those who mount pulpits to make those tidings, ancient as they are, not only glad but also relevant and lively for contemporary hearers. By way of the preached Word, the Christ-centered message that remains the same is to be made applicable in each new generation. If that task is taken seriously and fulfilled faithfully by preachers in Asia and Africa and America and elsewhere, then men and women of all kinds will find their lives regenerated and straightened by the Gospel. In light of these remarks, it becomes clear both that and why in Protestantism the Scripture and sermon have such central place. These modes involving plain human speech can and do become the means by which God's grace is spread abroad in the lives of grocers and tinkers, the well born and fatherless, the healthy and the dying.

At this juncture, yet another paradoxical feature of the Christian faith emerges. Perhaps we could put it in a striking way if we said that both Scripture and preaching are simultaneously the Word of God and words of human beings. After all, the words are written or spoken by particular men or women in particular contexts and for a variety of purposes. These persons—whether biblical authors or preachers in the pulpit—are marked by specific skills or perhaps the lack thereof. The message, the *kerygma*, is written/spoken by . . . human beings. As we noted in detail in an earlier chapter, however, it is through these human words that the Word of God finds lodgment in this life or that one. Reading the Bible and/or preaching can become the occasion when the Word of God becomes effective in a person's life via the work of the Holy Spirit of God. In ways totally unpredictable and beyond human control, the message can convict and comfort, illumine and edify, bring judgment and bestow mercy. One can only say that the message, written and/or spoken, works by its own intrinsic power or, perhaps better, by the power of the Sprit. In ways sometimes subtle, sometimes dramatic, human hearts are made receptive and faith emerges in the reading or hearing of these human words. In such cases, the words of human beings *become* the powerful and dynamic Word of God for an individual. And it seems that neither the learning nor the eloquence nor the status of the writer or speaker guarantees results; nor of course does the lack of any of these serve as a predictor. Such kneading of the human heart can only be attributed to the free and gracious activity of God in and through the faltering speech of human witnesses.

Once more, and from a different angle, the theory of "verbal inspiration" of the Bible warrants attention. This view, which is said to justify the authority of the Scriptures, is suspect because it does not do justice to the human element in the written materials contained therein. If the Bible is in some sense "dictated" to the authors and they become little more than stenographers, then their human responsiveness and creativity—as well as their foibles—are ignored. The genuinely human element in their testimony to God's self-disclosure is bypassed. In that case, we have a view of the Bible that matches the heretical "docetic" view of Christ's person. In the docetic view, Christ's humanity is denied in favor of an exclusively spiritualistic divine theophany. Likewise here, with reference to Scripture, the human element is given a blind eye while its divine "authorship" is affirmed. Surely, such kinship with an early Christian heresy should be reason enough for a person to balk.

Another set of difficulties also threatens. The authority of the Scriptures cannot be guaranteed in such an external and stilted manner as is maintained in this theory of inspiration. For one thing, we have already become aware that God's own self-disclosure is always indirect and only for the eyes of faith. This points to the fact that the measure of God's "speaking" through Scripture, or through preaching for that matter, has more to do with the internal testimony of the Holy Spirit than with any external guarantee. The kinds of certainty are also quite different in the two cases. In the one instance, the reliance is on a kind of rationalistic argument: "God said it; whatever God says is true; therefore. . . . " In the other, the grounds are not objective or directly given at all: they have to do with the inward transformation of the heart and the Word's reception by faith. Put another way, the authority the Bible possesses is rooted in the fact that God, in utter freedom, chooses to use these pages, or the words of a sermon, as the means of making the divine grace effective in a human breast. When miraculously this does occur, then one should say that the dynamic working of God's love comes to have compelling inward power. Then, but only by means of the divine work of the Spirit, a man or woman is brought into inner submission to God's authoritative presence and Word. The more mechanical view of the Bible's authority hardly accounts for the dynamic and utterly free way in which God can and does use altogether human witness to the *kerygma* as the vehicle of God's powerful grace.

2. THE SACRAMENTS

Protestants on the one hand and Greek Orthodox and Roman Catholics on the other differ in the number of sacraments they acknowledge. There are seven sacraments in the Roman Catholic and Greek Orthodox churches: Baptism, Confirmation (or Chrismation), the Holy Eucharist (Lord's Supper), Penance (or Confession or Reconciliation), Anointing of the Sick (or Healing or [Extreme] Unction), Marriage, and Holy Orders (or Ordination). Protestants generally agree that there are only two: Baptism and the Lord's Supper (or Communion). The major criterion appealed to in justifying a limitation of the number is that these two observances were instituted by Christ himself who issued a direct command to his apostles to practice them. At the last supper with his apostles in the upper room, the Lord's Supper was instituted. Jesus commanded those present to eat the bread and drink the cup in remembrance of him. More specifically, the bread was representative of his broken body and the wine was linked to his spilled blood on the impending cross. Somewhat later, just prior to his ascension, Jesus commanded his apostles to be his witnesses and to baptize those who would follow him. (See Matthew 28:19-20.) As we are presuming a Protestant orientation here, we will take a closer look at Baptism and the Lord's Supper. But one more general note about the sacraments before proceeding.

We have spoken of the living Word—Jesus Christ; we have also spoken of the written Word of God in Scripture and the oral Word in preaching. The sacraments have sometimes been referred to as the "visible Word." That is to say, Baptism and Communion present the Gospel tidings to human sight by means of enactment of that message in their respective ways. If the Word of God can be transmitted by the agency of human speech, it is also the case within the Christian church that God's Word of grace can be conveyed by way of human enactment. It is important to note, however, that it is the selfsame Word of God that is conveyed by means of these very diverse vehicles—speech and enactment. The sacraments, like Scripture and preaching, are rooted in and derive their content from the revelation of God's love in Jesus Christ. Both are means or avenues by which God's grace finds expression. So, as is the case with the Bible and preaching, the observance of the sacraments can become the occasion when Christ himself (via the Spirit) can powerfully and effectually make his presence felt inwardly. Here, the enactment of the Gospel, when appropriated by a lively faith, can become the power-filled Word of God penetrating the heart and life of a person with transforming effects.

When noting the dynamic and free way of God's activity in human hearts with reference to Bible and preaching, we had questions about the mechanical view of Scripture's inspiration endorsed by some. Now, similarly, we call into question a mechanical view of the operation of the sacraments, a view generally associated with Roman Catholic doctrine. The traditional Roman Catholic view is that the sacraments are effective in conveying God's grace through their mere performance. That is, God's grace is said to be issued independently of the receptivity of faith in the heart of the believer. The sacraments are regarded as working *ex opere operato*, that is to say, in their outward performance in and of itself. Grace is thought of as being issued in a quasimagical way, as a "substance" that is transmitted from the hand of the priest. Protestants unanimously reject this view, which relies on an outward action as effective in itself.

The reasons for refusing such a view of the sacraments are strikingly similar to those invoked regarding the mechanical view of verbal inspiration of Scripture.[2] First, such a view is subpersonal. That is, it does not give adequate place to the personhood of the believer who partakes. If a "dictation" view of the Bible fails to acknowledge the genuine humanity

---

[2]These objections directed toward misunderstandings of both sacraments and Scripture are addressed by Aulen in *Faith of the Christian Church*, 312-13 and 334-35.

of the authors, this mechanistic view of the sacraments neglects the importance of the real human responsiveness of the participant in the sacrament. The Roman Catholic position is that, given the priest's blessing, God's grace is transmitted through the mere performance of the rite, no matter what the participant's state of mind and heart. A second weakness is that this wooden approach diminishes the dynamic way in which the power of God's Spirit works in and through these means of grace. God's grace is not under human control, not even that of an ordained priest; nor can its effectual working be predicted. Rather, it must be said that via these visual rites, God's work in Christ may—or may not—take firm root in a human being with compelling inward force. If it does happen, then one can certainly make a genuine claim about Christ's real presence via these means, even though the elements themselves remain unchanged.

Baptism. Baptism is the sacrament that is linked to the believer's initial entry into the Christian life and therewith into the body of Christ. It betokens the individual's reception of God's grace and that his or her life has begun and will continue to undergo a conversion to the new life in Christ. As such, it is one's initiation rite into membership in the *koinonia*, the fellowship of believers. By this sacrament, one is incorporated into the larger body, adopted into the family of God. Of course, baptism—especially immersion—graphically pictures the drama of Christ's death and resurrection. Equally important and in like manner, however, it portrays the continuing dynamic of the Christian life which is a sustained transition from one dead in sin to one who is alive in Christ. The risen Christ—the Spirit of Christ—can be and is really present in this visual enactment of resurrected life by way of the active faith of the participant. In this case, any distinction between baptism with water and a baptism with the Spirit is artificial at best and misguided at worst. At the same time, one should say that the rite is empty in the absence of Christ's active presence in the participant's life.

There are differing views even among Protestants regarding this sacrament. Primary among them is the question of whether infants should be baptized. Protestants have rejected the Roman Catholic view that, with baptism, God's grace is "infused" into the infant and that it has salvific effect in and of itself. Yet many denominations have adopted the practice of baptizing infants. In fact, while it is not the most primitive practice of the church, it did gain prominence early in the history of the church. Protestants who endorse infant baptism often justify it by claiming that it is an enactment of God's *prevenient* grace. That is, they would admit that an infant cannot responsibly claim the faith for himself or herself. They nonetheless insist that in any number of ways God's grace can be and is present and at work even in the very young, preparing their hearts for later reception of salvation by faith. In the celebration of infant baptism, therefore, the emphasis falls necessarily on expectation—that in the future that prevenient grace of God will become actual grace.

On the other hand, there are those who insist on "believer's baptism," sometimes called "adult baptism." Those who favor this position argue that being united to the Christian Church presumes a conscious commitment of faith. The initial appropriation and confession of the divine love disclosed in Christ is the singular condition that binds its members together. Thus, baptism is reserved for those mature enough to be capable of and demonstrating such a response to the Gospel.[3]

Lord's Supper. The Lord's Supper, like baptism—and, for that matter, like the Word written and preached—depends on the presence and activity of Christ (or the Spirit) for its effectual operation. This observance, like the others, is empty in the absence of the dynamic work of the Spirit of the risen Christ. But with his presence, the Lord's Supper provides the occasion for the working of God's sovereign love in the lives of those whose hearts are made ready. Just as with Christ's presence in baptism the believer is empowered to new life, so also in Communion there is occasion for Christ's real presence to revivify the forgiving love of God upon the cross. His presence is not magically controlled by human creatures; there is no guarantee that God's love will work here or there, now or then. Rather, the power of the divine love works unpredictably wherever and whenever God pleases. Yet the Supper is a means of grace within the life of the Church. This means that the sacrificial character of God's love is vividly reenacted in its observance and the divine forgiveness can be renewed any time the cup and bread are taken. In visual form, the finished sacrifice on the cross can and does become effectual and Christ's presence real.

As with baptism, there are differences among those in the Christian fellowship as to how this sacrament is to be understood. Indeed, it has become a hotbed of controversy over the centuries, particularly during the Protestant Reformation. Aside from the view just described which is not

---

[3]Of course, it is important to note that favor toward believer's baptism is perfectly compatible with affirming the role of God's prevenient grace prior to conversion.

really identifiable with any of the following, there are three classical positions. The Roman Catholic view is referred to as *transubstantiation*. Here the thought is that after the priest has consecrated the elements, the substance of the bread and wine are actually changed into the body and blood of Christ. The appearance, taste and aroma—that is, the "accidents"—of the elements remain, but the inner nature or substance is miraculously transformed. As a result, it may be said that the miracle of the incarnation is repeated herewith and that the grace of Christ is literally dispensed to the participants.

In the midst of his other conflicts with the Roman Catholic Church, Martin Luther rejected transubstantiation in favor of *consubstantiation*. While he could not release the notion of Christ's bodily presence, he preferred to think of that presence as being "in, with, and under" the wine and bread, which remain substantially unchanged.

The third view, taken by the Swiss reformer, Ulrich Zwingli, was that the Lord's Supper serves as a mere *memorial* of what Christ did 2,000 years ago on the cross. There is no change in the elements; there is no claim that Christ is especially present—except insofar as the elements elicit thoughts of Christ's death.

ESCHATOLOGY AND THE CHURCH

The Word and the sacraments are the means of grace—the means by which the power of God's love in Christ is given outlet in the world. They are the typical channels by which the rule or Kingdom of God is extended in the lives of men and women. That concept—Kingdom of God—is the central notion in the area of theological reflection referred to as "eschatology." Eschatology specifically has to do with "the last things" or "last days" and, thus, has a certain fascination for lots of people for many of the wrong reasons. Many persons, even preachers, probe the pages of the Book of Revelation to discern what information can be gleaned regarding the "signs" that the end is near. Some become so inebriated with the idea that there is some predictive power in these pages that they sell their goods and move to—well, wherever—and look for the Lord's return. From time to time, some even proffer a date for Christ's Second Coming, called the *Parousia*, and the culmination of history. Furthermore, any number of individuals make considerable money by writing books and making movies about such matters. But mostly these efforts, while captivating to many, are misplaced—certainly with regard to the meaning of the last book in the Bible and with regard to the major lineaments of the Christian faith.

Surely, eschatology treats matters of grave importance in the faith, which generally have to do with the ultimate destiny of human creatures and all things. More specifically, it deals with death, resurrection, life after death, God's judgment, final redemption, and other related topics. As noted, the governing notion is the Kingdom of God—the sovereign rule of God and God's powerful love. The establishment of that rule is actually the goal of all creation from the outset. When God created the heavens and the earth and humankind within it, the divine purpose was that men and women, indeed all things, should exist in harmony with God's loving will. Through Christ, God's final purpose for all creatures has been restored; a new creation has been initiated; the sovereignty of God's loving will has been guaranteed via the cross and resurrection. In light of that event, Christian believers live in faith and hope. Indeed, as noted earlier, the Christian community is an eschatological community for this very reason. Believers look forward, longingly but not perversely, to the day when Christ's victory will be made complete. They eagerly await that last day when evil in all its forms will be vanquished by God's sovereign power (which is God's love) and uninterrupted fellowship with God realized. In light of these remarks, we should view the church from two points of view: as the militant church in the present and as the "Church Triumphant" in that "final day."

I. THE CHURCH IN CONFLICT

It is the church's faith that the church's own ultimate destiny is closely linked with the final culmination of all things and the establishment of the Kingdom of God. But the church and those who comprise it exist in this world where the scars of sin and suffering of all varieties persist. Evil, both individual and collective, is clearly rampant in the present order of things. Indeed we have to confess that God's conquest over wickedness finished on the Cross is still concealed to our eyes by the harsh realities of our individual existence and the larger sweep of history.

At the same time, another note must be struck. In its present state, the church already belongs, however partially, to the new age of Christ's Kingdom; although in fragmentary fashion, that Kingdom is even now present in the life of the church. The church is the locus where God's conquest over evil has already begun and it is the agent in extending that victory into the world. As such, the church is and must be a militant church, an army, a fighting force. In its militancy, the church is empowered by the risen Christ—that is, the Spirit of Christ—to engage in the battle against evil. In fact, the battle in which the church engages is the very same one in which Christ was pitched as a warrior on the Cross. This army of God is the means by which God's loving will remains in constant conflict with demonic, evil forces in the world. Furthermore, the church must always remain militant, and cannot be the church at rest, as long as there is injustice, hatred, hunger, or oppression in the world. As one might imagine, the conflict is highly ramified, but we describe it as taking place on two levels: within the individual life of the believer and in the corporate life of the church.

At the individual level, the Christian believer experiences continuing internal struggle against the destructive forces of sin. There is the old man or woman of sin that continues to threaten the emergence of the new man or woman in Christ. In a person's existence, the victory of the sanctified life is to work itself out. In battle with evil, the individual is to produce good works, works of loving service. The believer is to actually become righteous and, in doing so, actually reflect the victory over evil accomplished in Christ's work. Of course, the individual believer undergoes this lifelong process in the context of the community of other faithful disciples. The Christian life is not a life of a "loner"; it is lived within the body and is nourished and strengthened within that fellowship. Especially important are the Word and sacraments. Likewise essential are the mutual support, discipline, and edification provided by other believers.

At the same time, the conflict is joined at a further level—at the level in which the corporate body of the church is involved. The church, as a potent agent in the world, is to engage in the fray with evil forces with the intent of extending Christ's rule. In general, two kinds of activity are envisioned here. First, there is evangelism. Evangelism is conceived here as the church's organized proclamation of the Gospel, typically to those who have never been exposed to it. Through the announcement of the apostolic message, Christ's victory on the cross is achieved in other lives which are then joined to the church. Second, the church engages in social missions—loving service to the homeless, the hungry, the stranger, the victims of injustice. Frequently, in order to be effective genuinely in this struggle, the church must organize itself for group action—perhaps joining hands with other Christian and even non-Christian agencies. The aim might be to effect legislation, improve race relations, transport food to the hungry around the world. Yet at both of these levels and in all the forms the struggle takes, the point is that the church is a fighting force which has its eye pointed toward a final cataclysmic entry of Christ's Kingdom into the world.

2. THE CHURCH AT REST

If the church is necessarily locked in struggle so long as this world remains, it is nonetheless an eschatological community characterized by a future hope for the Kingdom of God. Although the conflict wages on in the present, the pulse of the church beats in expectation of that final day when the rule of God's divine love will be without challenge. The victory achieved on the cross will finally be established over the powers of destruction and ill. When that conquest arrives, there will be no obstacle to full fellowship with God, Creator and Redeemer—as was intended from the beginning. This is, after all, what we mean by "heaven," unbroken fellowship with God; by comparison, "hell" means utter and hopeless separation from God's presence. But Christian believers too often have imposed an overly individualistic interpretation on these concepts—as though heaven, for instance, has only to do with personal bliss. Such a notion must be held in tension with the more fundamental character of the church as a corporate body, as a *koinonia* among the members as well as in and with Christ. So we should view the Kingdom of God itself as communal in nature. It is composed of those saints who now rest from their labors—all believers who have been joined to Christ and his church. This fellowship extends beyond temporal as well as spatial boundaries and unites believers from all generations. So the Kingdom, like the church, is primarily communal though it is comprised of individual believers.

Still one more paradox is to be noted here with regard to the Kingdom of God/Christ. On the one hand, the ultimate victory of God involves the utter and absolute transformation of all things, including the church. A total upheaval of things is envisioned; a new creation shall be brought into being. Here the biblical witnesses speak with a loosed tongue that is captivated by a vision—often in allegory, metaphor, poetry. There will be a new heaven and a new earth; old things shall pass away and all things shall become new. There will be a final resurrection of the dead whose bodies will be transformed. The redemption which was seen and experienced in only fragmentary ways will now be made complete. All of this will occur at Christ's Second Coming—the *Parousia*. What is implied here is quite simple: when the Kingdom is finally ushered in, it will have no resemblance to a human utopia. The Kingdom of God will totally transcend all human expectations and doings. Therefore there is no room here for any notion of the Kingdom of God being ushered in within the merely human domain.

Yet, the final Kingdom of God has a certain kind of continuity with that battle which is being fought by the present church in the world. God's Kingdom surpasses the church's achievements and even includes the church in those things that are redeemed! Nevertheless, that final Kingdom is the ultimate consummation of the same struggle in which the earthly church is engaged currently through the power of the Holy Spirit/ Christ himself. Therefore, there is no room for utter pessimism in the church's present warfare. In the power of the risen Christ, progress (if also regress) is made possible. Even if the Kingdom of God supercedes all human possibilities, it is not utterly alien to those human efforts now exerted by the church and its members. If the Kingdom is indeed other-worldly, it is also inextricably linked to the combat now raging in this world. One could say that what takes place within the church itself is a macrocosm of what takes place in microcosm as the believer is progres-sively sanctified. The victory is assured; there is progress in struggle against the foe; yet the church and its individual members still see through a glass darkly until that last day when God's Kingdom comes. Then, but then only, the church militant can be the triumphant church at rest.

Eschatology includes topics that range far and wide. The doctrine includes issues that have been bitterly disputed. Unfortunately, many such disputes have been needless and divisive and without much profit theologically or religiously. The focus of the above remarks has been upon general and relatively noncontroversial themes which also place other subordinate (if also popularized) topics in the shadows. No mention here is made of pre- or postmillenialism, a debate which for most has lost importance. Nothing has been said about the issue of the "intermediate state" of a person between the time of death and the final resurrection— whether they go immediately to be with God or await the final resurrec-tion. The "signs" that precede the last days have been given no space; in the most important sense, we always live in the last times. Nor is there any word on the "rapture." If anyone is disappointed in this, it can only be said that these concepts have importance in fairly limited contexts.

Meanwhile, the topics that have claimed attention—Kingdom of God, the Church militant and triumphant—have broad relevance for the religious life and develop out of the materials in earlier chapters. It is hoped that these themes, as well as those treated in previous pages, will cast light on the cohesive logic of the Christian faith. The contents of that faith constitute the subject matter of Christian theology which has been our focus in this concluding unit.

SUGGESTIONS FOR FURTHER READING

OLD TESTAMENT/HEBREW BIBLE

Anderson, Bernhard W. *Out of the Depths: The Psalms Speak for Us Today.* Philadelphia: Westminster Press, 1983.

_____. *Understanding the Old Testament.* Second edition. Englewood Cliffs NJ: Prentice-Hall, 1966.

Ballard, H. Wayne, and W. Dennis Tucker, editors. *An Introduction to Wisdom Literature and the Psalms.* Macon GA: Mercer University Press, 2000.

Blenkinsopp, Joseph. *A History of Prophecy In Israel.* Louisville: Westminster/John Knox Press, 1996.

_____. *The Pentateuch: An Introduction to the First Five Books of the Bible.* New York: Doubleday, 1992.

Bright, John. *A History of Israel.* Third edition. Philadelphia: Westminster Press, 1981.

Clements, Ronald E., editor. *The World of Ancient Israel: Sociological, Anthropological, and Political Perspectives. Essays by Members of the Society for Old Testament Study.* Cambridge: Cambridge University Press, 1989.

Crenshaw, James L. *Old Testament Wisdom: An Introduction.* Atlanta: John Knox Press, 1981.

Fant, Clyde E., Donald W. Musser, and Mitchell G. Reddish. *An Introduction to the Bible.* Revised edition. Nashville: Abingdon, 2001.

Flanders, Henry Jackson, Jr., Robert Wilson Crapps, and David Anthony Smith. *People of the Covenant: An Introduction to the Hebrew Bible.* Fourth edition. New York and Oxford: Oxford University Press, 1988.

Harrington, Daniel. *Interpreting the Old Testament.* Collegeville MN: Liturgical Press, 1981.

Holladay, William L. *Long Ago God Spoke: How Christians May Hear the Old Testament Today.* Minneapolis: Fortress Press, 1995.

_____. *The Psalms through Three Thousand Years: Prayerbook of a Cloud of Witnesses.* Minneapolis: Fortress Press, 1996.

Matthews, Victor H., and James C. Moyer. *The Old Testament: Text and Context.* Peabody MA: Hendrickson Publishers, 1997.

McEvenue, Seán. *Interpreting the Pentateuch.* Collegeville MN: Liturgical Press, 1990.

Miller, John W. *Meet the Prophets: A Beginner's Guide to the Books of the Biblical Prophets.* New York: Paulist Press, 1987.

Murphy, Roland E. *The Tree of Life: An Exploration of Biblical Wisdom Literature*. Grand Rapids: Eerdmans, 1990.

Noth, Martin. *The History of Israel*. Second edition, revised by P. R. Ackroyd. New York: Harper & Brothers, 1960.

Von Rad, Gerhard. *The Message of the Prophets*. New York: Harper Collins Publishers, 1962.

West, James King. *Introduction to the Old Testament*. New York: Macmillan, 1981.

THE NEW TESTAMENT

Barrett, C. K. *The New Testament Background: Selected Documents*. Second edition. New York: Harper & Row, 1989.

_____. *Paul: An Introduction to His Thought*. Louisville: Westminster/John Knox Press, 1994.

Bornkamm, Günther. *Jesus of Nazareth*. Translated by Irene McLusky and Fraser McLuskey with James M. Robinson. New York: Harper & Brothers, 1960.

_____. *Paul*. Translated by D. M. G. Stalker. New York: Harper & Row, 1971.

Bruce, F. F. *New Testament History*. New York: Doubleday, 1969.

Crapps, Robert W., Edgard V. McKnight, and David A. Smith. *Introduction to the New Testament*. New York: John Wiley & Sons, 1969.

Dodd, C. H. *The Parables of the Kingdom*. Revised (fifth) edition. New York: Charles Scribner's Sons, 1961; orig., 1935.

Ehrman, Bart D. *The New Testament: A Historical Introduction to the Early Christian Writings*. Second edition. New York and Oxford: Oxford University Press, 2000.

Fant, Clyde E., Donald W. Musser, and Mitchell G. Reddish. *An Introduction to the Bible*. Revised edition. Nashville: Abingdon, 2001.

Ferguson, Everett. *Backgrounds of Early Christianity*. Second edition. Grand Rapids MI: Eerdmans, 1993.

Freyne, Sean. *The World of the New Testament*. Wilmington DE: Michael Glazier, 1980.

Guthrie, Donald. *New Testament Introduction*. Fourth edition, revised. Downers Grove IL: InterVarsity Press, 1990.

Harrington, Daniel J. *Interpreting the New Testament*. Wilmington, DE: Michael Glazier, 1979.

Harris, Stephen L. *The New Testament: A Student's Introduction*. Fourth edition. Boston: McGraw-Hill, 2002.

Jeremias, Joachim. *The Parables of Jesus*. Translated by S. H. Hooke. Revised edition. New York: Charles Scribner's Sons, 1963.

Kee, Howard Clark. *Understanding the New Testament*. Fifth edition. Englewood Cliffs NJ: Prentice-Hall, 1993.

Mills, Watson E., et al., editors. *Mercer Dictionary of the Bible*. Macon: Mercer University Press, 1990.

Perrin, Norman. *The New Testament: An Introduction*. New York: Harcourt Brace Jovanovich, 1974.

Powell, Mark Allan. *Fortress Introduction to the Gospels*. Minneapolis: Fortress Press, 1998.

_____. *Jesus as a Figure in History: How Modern Historians View the Man from Galilee*. Louisville: Westminster/John Knox Press, 1998.

Roetzel, Calvin J. *The Letters of Paul: Conversations in Context*. Fourth edition. Louisville: Westminster/John Knox Press, 1998.

Sanders, E. P. *The Historical Figure of Jesus*. New York: Penguin Books, 1993.

Stein, Robert H. *An Introduction to the Parables of Jesus*. Philadelphia: Westminster, 1981.

_____. *Jesus the Messiah: A Survey of the Life of Christ*. Downers Grove IL: InterVarsity Press, 1996.

Ziesler, John. *Pauline Christianity*. Oxford: Oxford University Press, 1983.

CHURCH HISTORY

Ahlstrom, Sydney E., *A Religious History of the American People*. New Haven: Yale University Press, 1972.

Bainton, Roland H. *Christendom*. Volumes 1 and 2. New York: Harper & Row, 1964, 1966.

_____. *The Reformation of the Sixteenth Century*. Enlarged edition. Boston: Beacon Press, 1985.

Cannon, William Ragsdale. *History of Christianity in the Middle Ages: From the Fall of Rome to the Fall of Constantinople*. Grand Rapids MI: Baker Book House, 1960.

Dowley, Timothy, editor. *Introduction to the History of Christianity*. Minneapolis: Fortress Press, 1995.

Gonzalez, Justo L. *A History of Christian Thought*. Three volumes. Revised edition. Nashville: Abingdon Press, 1987.

_____. *The Story of Christianity*. Two volumes. San Francisco: HarperSan Francisco, 1984 and 1985.

Latourette, Kenneth Scott, *A History of Christianity*. Two volumes. Revised edition. New York: Harper & Row, 1975.

Noll, Mark A. *A History of Christianity in the United States and Canada*. Grand Rapids MI: Eerdmans, 1993.

_____. *Turning Points: Decisive Moments in the History of Christianity.* Grand Rapids MI: Baker Book House, 1997.

Peterson, R. Dean. *A Concise History of Christianity.* Second edition. New York: Wadsworth Publishing Company, 1999.

Walker, Williston A. *A History of the Christian Church.* Fourth edition, revised by David W. Lotz and Richard A. Norris. New York: Scribner's, 1985.

Ware, Timothy. *The Orthodox Church.* New edition. London: Penguin Books, 1997.

CHRISTIAN THEOLOGY

Augustine. *The City of God.* Translated by Thomas Merton. New York: Random House, 1950.

_____. *The Confessions:* Translated by R. S. Pine-Coffin. New York: Penguin Books. 1961.

Aulen, Gustav. *Christus Victor: A Historical Study of the Three Main Types of the Idea of the Atonement.* Translated by A. G. Hebert. New York: Macmillan, 1958.

_____. *The Faith of the Christian Church.* Translated by Eric H. Wahlstrom. Philadelphia: Fortress Press, 1960.

Barth, Karl. *The Epistle to the Romans.* Translated from the sixth edition by Edwyn C. Hoskyns. London: Oxford University Press, 1960.

_____. *The Word of God and the Word of Man.* Translated by Douglas Horton. Gloucester MA: Peter Smith, 1978.

Calvin, John. *Institues of the Christian Religion.* Edited by John T. McNeill and translated by Ford Lewis Battles. Library of Christian Classics 20 and 21. Philadelphia: Westminster Press, 1960.

Dillenberger, John, editor. *Martin Luther: Selections From His Writings.* Garden City NY: Doubleday, 1961.

Forrell, George W. *The Protestant Faith.* Englewood Cliffs NJ: Prentice-Hall, 1960.

Guthrie, Shirley C., Jr. *Christian Doctrine.* Revised edition. Louisville: Westminster/John Knox Press, 1994.

Holmer, Paul L. *Making Sense of Our Lives.* Minneapolis: MacLaurin Institute, 1984.

_____. *The Grammar of Faith.* San Francisco: Harper & Row, 1978.

Kierkegaard, Søren. *Concluding Unscientific Postscript to the Philosophical Fragments.* Edited and translated by Howard V. Hong and Edna H. Hong. Princeton NJ: Princeton University Press, 1992.

_____. *Philosophical Fragments.* Edited and translated by Howard V. Hong and Edna H. Hong. Princeton NJ: Princeton University Press, 1987.

Moore, Gareth. *Believing in God: A Philosophical Essay.* Edinburgh: T. & T. Clark, 1996.

Niebuhr, Reinhold. *The Nature and Destiny of Man.* Two volumes in one. New York: Charles Scribner's Sons, 1949.

Nygren, Anders. *Agape and Eros.* Translated by Philip S. Watson. Philadelphia: Westminster Press, 1953.

Phillips, D. Z. *Faith and Philosophical Enquiry.* New York: Schocken Books, 1971.

Phillips, J. B. *Your God Is Too Small.* New York: Simon & Schuster, 1997.

Wittgenstein, Ludwig. *Culture and Value.* Edited by G. H. von Wright and translated by Peter Winch. Oxford: Basil Blackwell, 1980.

_____. *Philosophical Investigations.* Translated by G. E. M. Anscombe. New York: Macmillian Company, 1953.

SCRIPTURE INDEX

AUTHOR/SUBJECT INDEX

CREDITS AND ACKNOWELDGMENTS

The maps on pages 8, 27, 73, 114, and 115 and the photo of Gihon Spring on page 52 are from the *Mercer Dictionary of the Bible* (Macon GA: Mercer University Press, 1990ff.).

Page 158. The table detailing the growth of Christianity during the first four centuries is adapted from the table appearing in *Christian History* 17/1, issue 57 (February 1998): 26, from the *Christian History* magazine archives.

Page 162. A sixth-century paten depicting Christ giving communion simultaneously to his disciples in the East and West is also taken from an issue of *Christian History*, courtesy of Dumbarton Oaks, Washington, D.C.

Page 183. The woodcut bust of Balthasar Hubmaier is from the frontispiece to *Balthasar Hubmaier*, trans. and ed. H. Wayne Pipkin and John H. Yoder (Scottdale PA: Herald Press, 1989) courtesy of Herald Press.

Page 191. The likeness of Sussana Wesley, mother of John Wesley (who may have had more impact on his life than anyone else) is also from an issue of *Christian History* magazine and is reprinted by permission of Drew University Library.

Page 193. The painting of George Whitefield preaching in an open field (it was reported his voice was strong enough to preach to 30,000 [!] in an open field without amplification) is also taken from *Christian History* magazine, courtesy of *Christian History* archives.